D0065623

HERODOTOS THE HISTORIAN:
HIS PROBLEMS, METHODS AND ORIGINALITY

Herodotos the Historian

HIS PROBLEMS, METHODS AND ORIGINALITY

K. H. Waters

UNIVERSITY OF OKLAHOMA PRESS:
Norman

Copyright © 1985 by K. H. Waters.
Published in the United States by University of Oklahoma Press,
Norman, Publishing Division of the University of Oklahoma.
Manufactured in Great Britain. First edition, 1985.

Library of Congress Cataloging in Publication Data

Waters, K. H.
  Herodotos, the historian.

  Bibliography: p.177
  Includes index.
  1. Herodotus.   I. Title.
D56.52.H45W37   1985   938′.0072024 [B]   84-19504
ISBN 0-8061-1928-4

CONTENTS

Foreword

Abbreviations

'Life' of Herodotos

1.	Introduction	1
2.	The Intellectual Background	13
3.	The Education of a Historian	23
4.	Selection of Subject-Matter	34
5.	Structure of the History	47
6.	The Herodotean Narrative	61
7.	Sources of Information	76
8.	Religious and Moral Attitudes	96
9.	Herodotean Prejudices	119
10.	The Importance of Individuals: Characterisation	136
11.	Strengths and Weaknesses	152
12.	The Writer and the Historian	167
	Select Bibliography	177
	Index	190

FOREWORD

It may seem presumptuous to assert that no satisfactory book on Herodotos has been published in the last two generations. By satisfactory I do not mean either erudite or brilliant, but one which the general reader can understand, which will aid comprehension and appreciation of the vast achievement represented by the *History* of Herodotos.

One aspect of what is needed by the reader unfamiliar with the ancient classical world has been supplied by A. de Selincourt in *The World of Herodotos*, a companion to his translation of the *History* in the Penguin series. On the other hand quite a number of critical treatises have tended to confuse the layman while failing on the whole to enlighten the scholar. These generally seek to establish some elaborate thesis about the basic ideas underlying the *History* and to demonstrate it by constructing fanciful frameworks of structure or method. The most sensible general books, in English and German respectively, and the most readable, those of Glover and Pohlenz, are fifty years old.

The need for an uncomplicated, straightforward but thorough study of the many ways in which the work of Herodotos differs from that of modern historians, and the reasons for this, became very clear to me during long years of introducing it to Greekless university students.

I hope that I have identified most of the problems that beset such a group, and that in elucidating them I may also arouse interest among and prove useful to more advanced scholars at all levels.

In view of this double aim, I have endeavoured to avoid technicalities in the text, while indicating in the notes major, and especially recent, contributions on problematic aspects. Thus the pages will not be found thickly sprinkled with the names of past giants such as Macan and Jacoby, or of more recent scholars like Legrand or Immerwahr. This is not of course to deny my great indebtedness to them. Instead, where recent studies have brought more light to bear I have given references in the endnotes, which are not essential, I hope, for following my main arguments.

Herodotos should be read carefully before starting on this book; but it is not necessary to read him from cover to cover, for a random dipping will enable people to enjoy the brilliance of his narrative and the flavour of his descriptions of the exotic. Hence I have tried to avoid translating, paraphrasing or summarising the actual words of the historian save where the argument demands it. I have discarded the traditional English title *Histories* for the singular, since Herodotos himself used the singular in his Proem. Despite its diversity of content, the *History* of Herodotos is after all a unity.

K. H. Waters
Hobart 1983

ABBREVIATIONS

The following abbreviations are employed in addition to those used for periodicals by *L'Année Philologique*.

F Gr Hist = F. Jacoby, *Die Fragmente der griechischen Historiker* (3vv Weidmann, Berlin, 1926–58)

ML = R. Meiggs and D. Lewis, *A Selection of Greek Historical Inscriptions* (Clarendon Press, Oxford, 1969)

Powell = J. E. Powell, *A Lexicon to Herodotos* (Cambridge University Press, London, 1939; Olms, Hildesheim, 1960)

'LIFE' OF HERODOTOS

HERODOTOS of Halikarnassos (later of Thurioi), historian.
Date of Birth uncertain but trad. 484 BC.[1]
Son of Lyxes and his wife Rhoio (or Dryo), member of a noted family. (The family may have had partially non-Greek origins, as neither name of father nor of male relative Panyassis (see Chapter 1, Note 1) epic poet, appears Hellenic).
Name of brother Theodoros is recorded.
Early life: no details recoverable.
As young man, reported (the *Suda* sv Herodotos) to have joined in opposition to tyrant Lygdamis[2] and been exiled; spent some years in Samos (this appears confirmed by internal evidence in his *History*) but returned in coup which expelled Lygdamis (but extant inscription shows accommodation between dictator and citizen body, *ML*, no. 32). This would have occurred before 454 BC when Halikarnassos appears in first Athenian tribute list with no name of ruler.
Travels: internal evidence shows considerable journeying in Greek lands, E. Mediterranean and Egypt, perhaps also Mesopotamia and Black Sea where autopsy dubious.
Emigrated at or after 444/3 (date of foundation) and became citizen of Thurioi, S. Italy (Aristotle *Rhet.* 3.9, cf. Plutarch *Mor.* 604). No external evidence for dating the travels, or the first publication of his work, supposedly by 'recitals' at (*inter alia*) Olympia and Athens. Published 'Researches' or 'History', later divided into nine books, covering the E. Mediterranean world as background of events leading up to main subject, the conflict of Greece and Persia which reached its climax in 480/479 BC.
Date of completion unknown; last dateable internal evidence events of 430/429 BC and one passage (6.98) seems to confirm Peloponnesian War in progress. Negative inference from 9.73 shows completed before 413 BC.
No other writings known.
No evidence of marriage or children.
Date and place of death uncertain. Both Thurioi and Pella (Macedonia) claimants for latter.

Notes

1. It is probable that his acme or floruit, conventionally the age of forty, has been attached to the foundation-date of Thurioi (without direct evidence) and his birth-date thus calculated.

2. Lygdamis was a successor to and reportedly grandson of the 'Queen' Artemisia prominent in the *History*; tyrant (*turannos*) was the term used to indicate an unconstitutional ruler.

1 INTRODUCTION

Herodotos wrote the *History of the Persian Wars* (as we may for
the moment label it) with the intentions which he expresses in his
opening sentence: the double aim of preserving the renown or
remarkable deeds of both Greeks and non-Greeks, and of explaining the cause of the fighting between them. The first part of this
statement, incontestably justified by the contents of his work,
reminds us of the epic poems with their heroic tales of Achilles,
Hector, Odysseus — the 'glories of men' (warriors, naturally). But
not, in this case, of gods or demi-gods; human achievements are
specified. We should be aware that since the decline of the epic
genre in the literary activity[1] of an increasingly sophisticated
Hellas, no lengthy narrative had been composed in either verse or
the more recently discovered literary medium of prose.[2] (The
influence of epic poetry on form, narrative method and even
mental attitudes will be discussed later.) We may expect then something approximating to a 'prose epic'; an innovation, perhaps a
revolution, and one certainly revolutionary in its approach to the
past.

Part of the revolutionary approach consists in the rejection of
the whole apparatus of anthropomorphic deities personally and
directly interfering in the action. This is not to say that supernatural control, and evidence of the concern of the divine powers
for human affairs, have been entirely excluded by Herodotos;
oracles and other superhuman manifestations frequently appear,
and on the cosmic level an ill-defined Fate lies in the background.
But no longer do particular spears strike or miss particular targets
at the whim of individual deities, as in the epic, nor are favourite
warriors spirited to safety in a cloud of temporary invisibility. Such
'explanations' of historical events simply will not do for the critical
spirit of this first of historians. Human, rational causes are to be
found whenever possible, though cases will occur where the supernatural is called in to explain the miraculous or 'heaven-sent'. Only
in the next literary generation will the historian deliberately
exclude, almost totally, divine control of the affairs of men
(Thukydides 1.22.4); in this respect Herodotos is found in a
transitional stage. Rationalism is not the most appealing of

1

philosophies to the average person in most societies,[3] and it will be seen from other features of his work that Herodotos aimed at a wide audience; in this he differs from Thukydides, whose work was addressed to the intelligentsia, as is shown by his explicit exclusion of all 'story-book stuff' (*to muthodes*). This important difference does not, however, necessarily indicate a wide chronological or intellectual gap between these two writers, who have constantly been compared and contrasted — inevitably, since despite all disparities, between them they established the art and the science of history.[4]

What then did Herodotos really intend? We cannot fairly say 'history' since that name has only subsequently been used to define the genre of his work, and even now there may be some who would question its aptness. The fact that he used in the proem or title the Greek word *historiē*, of which 'history' is the formal equivalent, shows that he did not intend a work of fiction. The opening words run 'Of Herodotos the Halikarnassian here is the setting forth of inquiry'. Nor did he propose a historical novel, fiction based on fact, though he makes use of devices that have been employed by historical novelists for centuries. Rather, he will give us the results of his researches into the matters announced (rather vaguely perhaps) in the formal 'Proem', as it is usually called by scholars (separate titles were normally missing from such works — even 'Iliad' and 'Odyssey' are not labels offered by Homer himself). That is, his 'getting to know' the facts of historical events, and provision of rational explanation where possible of their causes.[5] (The premises on which such explanation is based belong to later discussions.) A careful rendering of Herodotos' actual words follows:

> Herodotos of Halikarnassos here shows forth his inquiry, aimed both at preventing the history of mankind becoming erased by the passage of time, and at preserving the fame of mighty and marvellous works on the part of both Hellenes and barbarians; and in particular the cause of the warfare between them.

The subject-matter is to include, if not centre upon, the war(s) of the Greeks and Persians, as is made clear by the last two words of the opening sentence, in a subordinate clause but an emphatic position: 'they warred with one another'. That means the so-called Persian Wars, not Greek Wars, since Western society, the claimant heir to the intellectual patrimony of Hellenism, has invariably looked at these events from the Greek standpoint. The reason for this does not however lie entirely in prejudice. For an account of them we now have the Greek account by Herodotos and very little besides, certainly nothing of equal value. Persian kings did not trumpet their military defeats as they did their victories, nor did Persia produce its own Herodotos. The Persian Empire was by far the greatest foreign, and therefore 'barbarian', power encountered by the Greeks, and their escape from subjection to it dominated their patriotic thinking for generations. Only centuries later did they, in decline, pass within the orbit and then the control of the rising Western barbarian power of Rome.

But Herodotos did not work from a purely Hellenic standpoint; indeed he was accused by the patriotic but somewhat imperceptive Plutarch of being *philobarbaros*, a pro-barbarian or pro-foreigner, hence unpatriotic.[6] For the 'great and remarkable' works of the barbarians, Persians, Egyptians and others, are not excluded, and we can be sure from the start that the promised account of Herodotos' research will be multifaceted; kaleidoscopic is not too colourful a term for the diverse subject-matter and the almost encyclopaedic scope of this *History*.

Two very large questions suggest themselves at this point: first, what is to be included and what left out — for after all, it is not an encyclopaedia and there are limits to human endurance. Herodotos provides no definition of content more precise than that of the Proem; at one point he admits that his work does tend to run into digressions, and at another that he feels bound to admit matter of common report even though he distrusts its authenticity. Such intellectual examples do not provide a sound reason for exclusion in Herodotos' eyes, for reasons which will appear in Chapter 4. Second, how will all this disparate material be structured? Since there is surprisingly little agreement amongst recent scholars as to how it is structured, or even as to whether it is deliberately shaped at all, full discussion of this point too will be reserved for a later stage. However, we may note that there were available two obviously basic forms of narrative, requiring a choice, or an adaptation, a marriage between them; namely, following the advice of the King of Hearts, to begin at the beginning, go on until you get to the end, then stop; or to take example from Homer and plunge bravely into the deep end — as the *Iliad* begins in the last year of the siege of Troy, and the opening of the *Odyssey* finds the hero has been trying to make his way home to Ithaca for ten years, and we are to hear his account of his experiences narrated by himself to those he encounters. In fact the latter poem consists almost entirely of 'flashbacks', to borrow a term from modern media; a device that has been popular and at times used to excess in a variety of narrative genres.

A difficulty for Herodotos in making such a choice was the problem of deciding what was the beginning, the starting-point or first 'cause', of the wars between Greeks and Persians. Since he had bound himself to set forth 'the cause' (or *casus belli*, according to one's interpretation of the much disputed *aitia*), he could not merely take up his account at the point when open hostilities began, or even with the planning of the invasion. His choice was to begin, by way of prologue, with the legendary accounts of 'wrongs' perpetrated by Asiatics or Europeans upon one another;[7] for example, Paris's abduction of the Asiatic Helen, or the kidnapping of the king of Argos's daughter by Phoenician traders. But he introduced these ancient tales merely in order to discredit them as history;[8] accounts varied according to the source, European or Asiatic, so no certainty could be reached — and in any case, absconding with young women is no serious crime; the girls would not have gone had they not been willing! Yet it was advisable to include these tales implying long-standing hostility between Europe and Asia because his audience, well aware of them, might argue that he was missing the point of age-long enmity as a cause for recent clashes. But his standpoint becomes clear — and one would love to know the initial reaction of his auditors to this progression — when we read (1.5) that Kroisos of Lydia was 'the first of whom we *know*' that he forcibly subjected Greeks to foreign rule.[9] The old tales then are irrelevant, as well as lacking authenticity; what is important and well authenticated is that an Asian power made war on Greeks (though Greeks living in Asia!) and made them tributary.

In history as in everyday life one thing leads to another, and it was not so many years later that this expansionist monarch met his match in the yet more aggressively imperialist 'King of Kings', Kyros the Persian, who had brought the empire of the Medes under his control, thus acquiring a common frontier with Lydia. Therefore, potentially hostile contact between Ionian Greeks and the Persians was now direct, and the subjection of the former duly followed.

Herodotos records the process, a pendant to the conquest of Lydia, not without lengthy digressions; but then in order to reach a war in which the protagonists were respectively Greek and Persian he takes a most circuitous route. It is circuitous both in space and time, arriving at the actual outbreak of the Ionian revolt against the Persians nearly halfway through the total work in Book 5. How this vast detour is mapped will be examined in Chapter 5. Thereafter he proceeds rather more directly to the several Persian attempts to invade and conquer mainland Greece. We shall here consider only briefly the chronological point at which he chose to end his narrative. (The implications of the fact that the concluding paragraph consists of a moralising anecdote constitute a separate topic.) This chronological term is the end of the campaigning season of the year 479 BC, when the third and last great Persian expeditionary force invading Greece has been driven back after defeat and massive destruction. The victorious Greek fleet has sailed to the Dardanelles to seize the pontoon-bridges by which Xerxes' army had crossed into Europe; and thereafter to remove the grip which Persian strongpoints were still maintaining on this vital avenue of communication with the Black Sea, its Greek settlements and its food supplies. The Spartans, who as the leading military power commanded the allied forces, had suffered heavy losses in two land battles — the defeat at Thermopylai and the victory of Plataia — were anxious to cry 'Hold! Enough' and return home. Accordingly the command, probably later than the initiative, passed to the Athenians, providers of the largest naval contingent. The subsequent anti-Persian activity, which continued somewhat spasmodically for three decades, is not recounted by Herodotos. Perhaps it should have been included in an overall account of 'the war they warred with one another'. However, Herodotos it seems deliberately avoided digressions into later history (see Chapter 4).

But Herodotos was clearly aware (though he does not say so) that a new phase in Greek history had begun. This was the period in which the Athenian Empire was created, controlling many Greek states some of which were members of the original alliance formed to continue hostilities against Persia by liberating those Greeks of Asia and the islands not yet freed from her domination. Others had no choice but to join, as Athens and her allies made them an offer they could not refuse. The unfortunate fact that by accident or design the Athenians inherited or acquired control of the islands, the west coast of what is now Turkey and a good deal besides, led to lengthy internecine warfare as 'the leading states quarrelled about hegemony' (6.98). That is all our author says, explicitly, about the period following his closing date, comparing the reciprocal destruction of those years with the havoc wrought by the Persian invaders. In so far as there ever is a real break between one historical period and another, the end of united Hellenic activity against the Persians proved to be one, and to have perceived this is a credit to Herodotos' historical insight, in choosing to end his narrative at that point. He lived on to see at least the early years of the great struggle, some half a century from the stirring days of the Persian Wars, which eventually brought down the power of Athens.[10]

Within the comparatively brief temporal span of about seventy years, from the fall of Lydia to the repulse of Xerxes — but sometimes extending backwards beyond it for many generations, and just occasionally forward to the time of writing — the narrative is expanded, illustrated and interrupted by innumerable digressions. These contain a great mass of information, much of which cannot on any criterion be considered either historical or relevant to the historical topic. One type however which must be counted as generally relevant to any serious historical investigation is geographical. Modern readers may be surprised by the relative inexactitude of some of Herodotos' information, but four points must be borne in mind. One, the science of geography was in its earliest infancy. The first map had been made by Anaximander a generation or two before Herodotos' birth. Secondly, Herodotos had neither compass nor sextant, nor any adequate measuring instrument for longer distances; when these were not mere guesses, they were based on the highly inconsistent measure of days of travel-time. Nor did he conceive of the earth as a globe; it was to be 200 years before the Alexandrian scholar, Eratosthenes, calculated the circumference of the earth. Lastly, his interest in all sorts of information had been particularly stimulated in the geographical area by the work of Hekataios, whose statements (as no doubt those of others) he sometimes blindly followed. A further stimulus was provided by his own travels (see Chapter 3), which however did not enable him to verify every statement, and may at times, with the written authorities, have been responsible for the inclusion of certain non-essential information.

Anthropology and its daughter-science, ethnology — infant

disciplines at the time — fascinated Herodotos, and his interest here, even when the material was not germane to the main purpose of the *History*, has provided scholars with information useful down to the present day. He was particularly interested in sexual mores, including marriage, and in religious beliefs and funerary rites; this last preoccupation was a national or supranational one, as is shown by prehistoric remains in Greece and historical evidence from Thrace, not to mention the Lycian temple-tombs — or the Pyramids! But diet, habitat, modes of warfare all fall within his scope. Then there is 'natural history' generally; some of it not a little bizarre and tending to give colour to the belief that Herodotos was either amazingly credulous or a bare-faced liar. And this is by no means an exhaustive catalogue, as will be seen; this vast 'rag-bag' (as hostile critics might find it) of miscellaneous information and misinformation amounts to a compilation which today would be far beyond the capabilities of any single scholar. Much of the non-historical subject-matter does not fall into any of the above-mentioned 'useful' categories; myth (not generally as evidence for historical fact), folk tales, apocryphal anecdotes, even 'true' anecdotes about historical characters — which may be admissible as evidence for what the commonalty thought of the eminent — and 'remarkable' facts and figures of every kind. Homer has sometimes been described, not too accurately, as 'the Bible of the Ancient Greeks'; it would be perhaps less flattering but more correct to describe Herodotos (in one of his many aspects) as the *Guinness Book of Records* of the ancient world.

It is clear that the purpose of including much of these types of subject-matter was to entertain an audience. People heard, rather than read, Herodotos at his first 'publication'. A great deal of interest was taken by Ancient Greece in her major sporting contests, and in records of achievement therein (though as times could not be taken, 'records' in the modern sense were not there to be broken). As for mere 'tales', the professional story-teller was not without customers in Hellas, any more than in other semi-literate or pre-literate societies, in the absence of printed books, cinema, radio, television and videotape machines. A persistent school of thought maintains — on the basis of non-contemporary reports, it is true — that Herodotos gave public recitations as a means of publication, and sometimes received pecuniary rewards.[11]

It is clear that his intention in writing the *History* was double-barrelled in another way than that stated at the start. Information, relevant to the course of the narrative or of interest for its own sake, was the first principle, in accordance with the accepted duty of the composer, creative artist — which is the meaning of the Greek word *poiētēs*, our 'poet' — to *teach* his hearers. Many poets other than those explicitly conveying instruction were held to inculcate moral or religious principles. This is true even of Homer, whom Herodotos coupled with the didactic poet Hesiod in the matter of theology. Conversely, writers whose purpose was to convey information, from advice on agriculture (Hesiod) to abstract philosophical theory (Empedokles) chose poetic form. Herodotos, however, very wisely in view of the length of his composition if for no other consideration, abandoned the poetic form, without losing sight of his duty as a 'maker'.

Poets too had a second, perhaps less lofty, but vital function — to entertain their hearers. (One might be excused for reversing this hierarchy, since if they failed to entertain in any sense, their message was in danger of going unheeded.) Some people are entertained, in all societies, by violence and bloodshed, or by romantic adventures, whether within or beyond the everyday world; others, by a different type of romance, as in the earliest Greek prose 'novels', to appear much later. Some again prefer humorous situations; all of these ingredients are present in Herodotos, and he amply fulfilled his second aim.

His new invention, 'the setting forth of research' into historical matters, was still to be a branch of literature. It remains so, in the proper hands; some of its modern exponents have not allowed the gradually preponderating scientific aspect to divorce it utterly from its 'Arts' background. Aristotle did include history, rather grudgingly perhaps, in his *Poetics* and compared it somewhat disparagingly, in the Platonic tradition, with tragedy because the former dealt in particulars, the latter in universals. Nevertheless, history came within the creative arts patronised by the nine muses, and indeed had its own special mistress, Klio.[12]

To recapitulate: Herodotos' *History* stands somewhere between the narrative fiction (or legend) of the Homeric poems and the totally non-poetic productions of certain of his successors. The various influences which conspired to help him advance to such a stance will be considered in the next chapter. History was to decline, in several respects, in the next few centuries, especially in the hands of certain later Greek and Roman writers who made it an exercise in rhetoric. Of course they had a particular public in view, whose task, formed or deformed by the Roman educational system, may be illustrated by the curious fact that the major historical work of the historian Sallust has been lost to posterity — with the exception of a collection of speeches composed by that writer for the leading figures of the period covered. These do little to illuminate the otherwise fairly obscure details of the period, but throw a great deal of light on the author's skill.

But let us not dismiss the non-authentic speech too hastily; the reasons for its adoption by Herodotos will be discussed at length later in the book. One obvious source of this ploy, the speech put in the mouth of a character who is known, or presumed, to have said *something* on such-and-such an occasion, is the epic. The *Iliad* is at least half made up of speeches, and ever since these have been a favourite device of historical novelists. For his great use thereof, together with other features of his work, the unfair accusation that Herodotos was really a writer of fiction has not been unheard. But our author is not the prisoner of such a convention, though he writes speeches in plenty, for various purposes (see Chapter 6). Let us take as an example the critical stage in the Greek defence against the Persians under King Xerxes. The 'immense host' of the barbarians has steamrolled its way into Greece, and a naval battle off the coast near Athens is to be the last throw; defeat of the patriots here will mean the collapse of organised resistance. Now the news reaches the high command on the island of Salamis that the Athenian Acropolis, defended by a small force, has fallen, and panic pervades the fleet; many allied commanders want to withdraw their own squadrons to a last-ditch defence of their respective cities. This is obviously a counsel of despair; but a hitherto unknown character is suddenly on centre stage (if the metaphor may be excused). He makes a speech, urging the Athenian naval commander, the brains of the fleet but not its C-in-C,[13] to insist on holding a fresh meeting of the general staff and obtaining a decision to stay in Salamis and fight. This eloquent gentleman, by name Mnesiphilos, now disappears from the action as suddenly as he came.[14] Thus far, you might say, the historical novel, or a gratuitous piece of dramatisation of what Themistokles 'must' have been thinking. But we do not then get a fine display of oratory from the Athenian admiral to the Spartan commander-in-chief;[15] it is merely reported that he conveyed the arguments of Mnesiphilos, plus additions, to Eurybiades. An epic poet would have repeated more or less word for word the speech originally made by A, now in the mouth of B; and few later ancient historians would have passed up such an opportunity to deploy patriotic rhetoric.

However, when Eurybiades does reconvene the council, we hear Themistokles making a direct personal appeal to the Spartan admiral as the man finally responsible for choosing salvation or disaster. To this effect, in order to be consistent with his popularly accepted character of wily unscrupulousness, he adds a touch of moral blackmail: if the Athenians (who constitute half of the total Greek navy) do not get a favourable decision, they will sail away to a colonial site in the West.

There follow yet further vacillations among the Greek high command, but the die is cast (allegedly by a ruse of Themistokles, who sent an agent with an ostensibly treacherous message to the Persian king). However Themistokles, whose reputation as an orator is attested by Thukydides,[16] has still another speech to make; the traditional 'pep-talk' of commanders to their troops before a battle, as of coaches to their football teams before the game. But once again we are not offered well-turned clichés, ringing appeals to love of country and the spirit of self-sacrifice and so on, nor do we hear what purport to be the actual words of the admiral. Herodotos here records baldly, in a couple of lines, that he uttered a number of antitheses, contrasting 'good things' such as freedom with 'bad things' such as slavery. Antithetical arrangement and epigrammatic statement were the very life-blood of contemporary oratory when Herodotos was writing.[17] Why, if he stood in the epic tradition, did he miss this splendid opportunity to display his powers of composition, as his successor Thukydides so often did? Other speeches on various occasions show him adequately equipped for the task. The reasons for this neglect is, I suggest, that the values of patriotic motivation had been adequately set forth in other places, in particular the speech of Miltiades before the battle of Marathon.[18] Hence all that was required here was a statement that it was to Themistokles — as the virtual though not the nominal commander of the fleet — that the duty fell. And Themistokles had already said his piece on the strategical situation.

Herodotos is not concerned to stir up the emotions of his audience by repeating, however skilfully, the commonplaces of patriotic oratory. And as the sequence of speeches and non-speeches here shows, he has progressed far beyond the limits of the epic convention which 'authorised' him to compose for historical characters speeches of which he cannot conceivably have had any reliable record.[19] The epic also had other influences upon Herodotos, but it is now time to consider just where he stands in the development of Greek thought and knowledge, so that we may better comprehend the complex intellectual attitudes of the historian.

Notes

1. But not in the schoolroom nor at such festivals as the Panathenaia; all educated Greeks were familar with the Homeric poems, and could quote them extensively from memory (as, until recently, educated English-speaking people quoted from Shakespeare or the Bible). Further, Herodotos had a relative who was described as an epic poet, one Panyassis. Only the barest fragments of his work are extant.

2. The earliest known continuous *written* prose did not make its appearance in Greek literature much before 500 BC; perhaps a generation before Herodotos' birth. Laws and decrees of legislative and governing bodies are not authentically recorded from much before that date.

3. The widespread rejection of established religion in (Western) society today finds a compensatory movement in addiction to astrology and many other irrational cults; reason does not appear generally triumphant.

4. Lucian, in the second century AD, wrote 'Thukydides, *inspired by* Herodotos, set the canon for historical writing' (my italics). *Quomodo historia conscribenda sit*, 42. Elsewhere he comments on the great charm of Herodotos' writing (n. 14 to Chapter 2 below).

5. Herodotos is not ashamed to admit that he has been unable to ascertain the exact truth, nor that he cannot confidently attribute a precise cause. Sometimes supernatural causes of events are admitted; see below, Chapter 8.

6. Plutarch *de Malignitate Herodoti* 12 (= Moralia 857a). But to save Plutarch's reputation, it must be admitted that not everyone believes this tendentious tract to be by the usually fair-minded author of the *Parallel Lives*.

7. The equation, European is to Greek as Asiatic is to Persian, is implicit, but not logically worked out — it would not stand up! When Herodotos thought about this carefully, he did not insist on its validity; he says that the Persians *claimed* all Asia, and elsewhere implies that the crossing of the 'natural' boundary formed by Bosporus/Marmara/Dardanelles by the Persians was a transgression of their proper limits.

8. The discussion of Helen's visit to Egypt in 2.120 shows in more detail the historian's attitude to poetical sources. See esp. J. W. Neville, 'Herodotos on the Trojan War', *G & R* 24 (1977) 3.

9. See M. E. White, 'Herodotos' Starting-point', *Phoenix* 22 (1969) 39–48. The story of Kroisos was familiar to the Greeks (by oral transmission) and thus Herodotos could work forward and backward from a known datum.

10. The orthodox view that Herodotos ceased to write, and the work as we now have it was 'published' in the early years of the Peloponnesian War which broke out in 431 B.C., has been challenged by C. W. Fornara, 'Evidence for the Date of Herodotos' Publication', *JHS* 91 (1971) 25. Apart from general considerations such as the tolerant view of barbarians also shown by the later plays of Euripides, he adduces as evidence for a date between 420 and 414 the passages in 6.98 and 7.235

which may be thought to depend on strategic moves of the period, and 9.73 which appears to pre-date the Spartan occupation of Dekeleia. A. French, 'Topical Influences on Herodotos' Narrative', *Mnemosyne* s IV, 25 (1972) 9 reaches similar conclusions. But see also J. A. S. Evans, 'Herodotos' Publication Date', *Atheneaum* 57 (1979) 105, who is unwilling to accept a date later than 424, and J. Cobet, *Hermes* 105 (1977) 2. Fornara's rebuttal of Cobet's arguments, in *Hermes* 109 (1981) 149.

11. The whole matter of Herodotos' mode of publication and his intended audience is discussed in Chapter 6.

12. On the general question, the most useful approach in English is still that of A. W. Gomme, expressed in his Sather Lectures. *The Greek Attitude to Poetry and History* (1954). See also F. Walbank, 'History and Tragedy', *Historia* 9 (1960) 28.

13. Thukydides goes out of his way, in a long digression well outside the supposedly strict confines of his chosen subject, to write an encomium on Themistokles (1.138), apparently because he thought him done less than justice in Herodotos' ambivalent account. See also Chapter 10 below.

14. Plutarch and some other later writers speak of Mnesiphilos as a philosopher, and more precisely, if with chronological implausibility, he was said to be a discipline of Solon — thus Solon becomes the political ancestor of Themistokles. See F. J. Frost, 'Themistokles and Mnesiphilus', *Historia* 20 (1971) 20. That he was no mere fiction is proved by *ostraka* bearing his name for the curious reverse-election, ostracism; a political stance at least is indicated.

15. Eurybiades the Spartan was in every sense the man in command. The size of the Athenian contingent and the fact that Themistokles does appear to have been responsible for the strategy adopted (and the fact that the battle was fought in Athens' home waters) led to the popular view that the Athenian was actually in command.

16. Thukydides, whose historical characters make a long series of pre-battle speeches, implicitly criticises Herodotos for 'writing for effect', a most unjust imputation. His not unduly modest claim that his own work was to be 'a possession for ever' certainly has to be shared with that of his predecessor.

17. Exemplified by many of the speeches in Thukydides' *History of the Peloponnesian War*, written during its course (431–404 BC; also by the notorious *tour de force* of Gorgias of Leontinoi on his embassy to Athens in 427 BC.

18. It is interesting to note that the position of Miltiades at Marathon bore some resemblance to that of Themistokles at Salamis, as the deviser of the strategy and tactics but not the commander-in-chief. In both cases tradition gave the junior commander the credit — possibly owing to rivalries between cities or factions.

19. Oral sources of information, in general all that were available to Herodotos, have severe limitations for the scientific historian. Compare the previous note, and see Chapters 3 and 7. Add J. A. S. Evans' 'Oral Tradition in Herodotos', *Canadian Oral History Assoc. Journal* 4 (1980) 8.

2 THE INTELLECTUAL BACKGROUND

In order to understand exactly what Herodotos was trying to do —
in effect, to establish a new art-form, history or historiography, but
on a scientific basis — it is necessary briefly to examine the
development of Greek thought and its manifestations in literature
down to the years in which our subject's intellectual attitudes and
modes of thought were formed, i.e. roughly, the first half of the
fifth century.

The domination of epic poetry, with its dual purpose of instruction (both as to past 'history' and to moral matters) and of
entertainment, was gradually reduced during the seventh and sixth
centuries. This took place despite the omnipresence of the Homeric
poems in schools and festivals, as writers — mainly poets —
together with society as a whole became somewhat more individualistic. They were not only unwilling to follow quite slavishly the
formal conventions of epic, though these continued to exert
considerable influence, nor did they generally aspire to handling
such vast or universal themes. Poems in the epic metre and
language — the latter a rather artificial 'dialect' suited to the
metrical requirements of the traditional hexameter — continued to
be written, but on special subjects. The so-called Homeric Hymns,
of various dates and by unknown hands, were composed for use at
festivals of particular deities; Hesiod had expounded traditional[1]
cosmogony and the relationships of the innumerable gods and
demigods of the Greek pantheon in like form. But religion was only
one of the number of areas of poetical inspiration; Hesiod also set
forth a farmer's calendar in quasi-epic verse, offering information
and advice often of a most prosaic nature. (These examples are
taken from extant literature, which it may be presumed represents
only the tip of the iceberg.)[2] But while leaving the epic in its
honoured place, many distinguished poets of the two centuries
preceding the composition of the *History* wrote, in metres of their
own choice or invention, on much more personal and intimate
subjects; and of these not a few were thought by most of
Herodotos' contemporaries to have continued to serve the true
duty of the poet, to instruct. The ancient ultra-conservatives would
not have agreed with this view of much of the subject-matter,

13

which often concerned the — apparently inseparable — topics of love (including homosexual love) and wine. Yet these lyric poets — so called from the traditional musical accompaniment to recitation, a tradition clearly documented in the Homeric poems[3] — frequently dealt with 'serious' subjects, and some who wrote during that period and even within that category had a fully serious and public purpose. It is of course important to remember that few people then had the chance, and not all the ability, to read a book — that is, a papyrus roll.[4] Consequently the normal mode of publication was by reading aloud, or reciting, in public. There are clear examples of work obviously composed for just such a medium; the political verses of Solon in the early sixth century were to be 'broadcast', as it were, in the Athenian agora, not read either in the quiet of a study or even at a noisy breakfast-table. Tradition indeed tells of such public 'lectures' by Herodotos himself, at Athens and elsewhere, though by the late fifth century written books had become more familiar objects, and the nature of his composition was not so well suited as verse for oral delivery. And verse continued to be employed for the transmission of information (as by Hesiod earlier) as well as of views and propaganda; for example the philosopher Xenophanes' account, in epic hexameters, of the colonisation of Elea.

However one important area in which prose had to be employed, once records began to be kept on stone, wood or papyrus, was that of governmental decisions, laws and treaties. Poetry tends to be imprecise about facts, vague about numbers, and capable of various interpretations. Legal documents supposedly strive to avoid such imprecision; the fact that they by no means always succeed has meant riches to many, but that is no business of ours at present. Monsieur Jourdain was delighted to discover that he could speak in prose, and so no doubt were the movers of motions in the Council, and especially that body's secretary when he had to record and publish the decisions. At the same time the limited horizons of 'Dark Age' Greece had been expanded, rapidly and widely, in both the territorial and socio-political spheres. International trade, and the colonisation that followed or accompanied it, brought Greeks into contact, often continuing contact, with numerous other societies. Some of these were far less civilised than their own; others could well claim comparison with and in some respects superiority over the Hellenic; a few could boast far greater antiquity. Such contacts, like the increasing importance of the individual (though not all scholars would agree on this) led to a great thirst for knowledge. Inquiry, Herodotos' word for what we call research at one end of the scale, at the other perhaps mere inquisitiveness, was a thoroughly Greek characteristic. Egyptian priests might find the Greeks naïve, childlike, in view of the age-long accumulation of knowledge by Egyptian specialists. This 'younger generation', however, would proceed to systematise and develop a theoretical basis for merely factual, empirical learning.

The awareness of differences between cultures (it should be remembered that there is little observable difference in culture between Homer's Greeks and his Trojans) and the discovery of superior knowledge in certain areas, led to a great search for information among these 'inquisitive' people. We need not here go into reasons why the Greek attitude to knowledge was so different from that of other peoples that the emergence of philosophy and the sciences eventually resulted among the Greeks alone.[5] The application of rational thought to the world we live in was first notoriously manifested (in Greece) in the prediction of an eclipse in 585 BC, approximately a century before the birth of Herodotos, by Thales of Miletos. Babylonian observations were clearly the basis of this prediction, the one essential condition for its making, in the absence of any knowledge of the real orbits of the celestial bodies, being a long series of carefully recorded observations. This was not possible in Greece, where alphabetical writing had been introduced only a century or so before Thales; nor did either society possess the mathematical skills necessary to make such a prediction on a theoretical basis. But Thales' reputation as one of the 'Top Seven' wise men does not rest upon this perhaps fortuitous feat; he was the first philosopher, 'lover of understanding', who sought for some principle in the universe on which to base a rational explanation of its existence and behaviour, rather than accepting a supernatural version. There followed a succession of 'Monists', several of them Milesian, who in the absence of any form of scientific equipment but by the light of pure reason were able to make 'educated guesses' about their supposed 'first principle', most of which are not too utterly far-fetched.

This 'Ionian school' as it has become known produced (like Thales) results in fields other than basic philosophy; all knowledge was their province, and some half-century after the eclipse Anaximander drew, or more correctly engraved, the first map. Of its contents we are unfortunately not informed, but Herodotos gives us a clue to the Asiatic portion. In 499 BC Aristagoras — also of Miletos be it noted, but a politician not a philosopher — took a map to Sparta (Bk. 5, 49ff.) in his unsuccessful endeavour to obtain military aid for the Ionian rising against Persian rule — imposed after the fall of the Lydian kingdom of Kroisos. At much about the same time his fellow citizen Hekataios (who also took a lively interest in politics) was compiling his 'Guide to the (Mediterranean) World', referred to in Chapter 1. The map, or its successors (for we can be sure that there were efforts to improve on Anaximander, some of which are no doubt the objects of Herodotos' criticism, Bk. 2.15), provided as it were the illustration to the verbal account given by Hekataios and others, in continuous prose description with narrative sections, perhaps 'historical'. A 'geographer' mentioned by Herodotos is Skylax of Karyanda (Bk. 4.44) who travelled at Dareios' orders to the Punjab and returned, apparently, via the Indian Ocean.

Another direction in which study began to be more scholarly was that of genealogy. Once again, epic tradition has much to do with such a development, and perhaps encouraged thereby, as well as by their universal curiosity, the Greeks were keenly interested in their own ancestry; like many other humans, they tended to inflate the importance of their own forebears. The epic legends, compiled according to Herodotos about 400 years before his own time, frequently reported heroes as the offspring of casual liaisons between some male deity and a mortal female (rather than the other way round, for obvious reasons). Even the studious Hekataios, who did publish the results of his research in the area, claimed a deity as his ancestor at the sixteenth remove. Herodotos reports with ill-concealed glee the contemptuous dismissal of this claim by Egyptian priests;[6] elsewhere, however, he himself gives the line of the Spartan royal house going back twenty-one generations to Herakles, himself the product of such miscegenation — and therefore to Zeus, Father of All (Bk. 7.204)! Such, in fact, was the official version, and the context of the item was not one appropriate to the debunking of Sparta's kings.[7]

A number of other writers, such as Akusilaos and Damastes, are reported to have compiled genealogies, without apparently striving for literary achievement. Pherekydes of Athens was labelled by F. Jacoby as 'the first Athenian prose writer' but we cannot assess his literary merits. More important for our purpose are Dionysios of Miletos and his fellow-townsman Kadmos, who narrated the history of his city; there was also an account of Samos by one Euagon, probably written before Herodotos wrote. If used by him, they are not given the credit. Especially important were Xanthos, whose 'Description of Lydia', at least partly in narrative form, is said by one ancient source to have 'given Herodotos his starting-point' (see 1.5ff.), and the Olympic victor's list compiled, with other quasi-historical works, by the sophist Hippias of Elis. Lastly should be mentioned Charon of Lampsakos, born during Dareios' reign and still writing in 464 — when Herodotos was perhaps twenty; he dealt with both Greek and Persian material, which was possibly utilised by Herodotos; and the rather less mysterious Hellanikos of Lesbos who is mentioned in several ancient sources as an historian, and called 'successor' to Hekataios by a Byzantine encyclopaedia. He appears to have been interested both in mythology and a primitive form of history.[8]

Genealogy is at least a quasi-historical discipline, its source-material in those times however being almost wholly transmitted by oral tradition, whether in a community or an individual family; at times, it had been enshrined, when Herodotos came to use it, in epic poems,[9] the only written documents available to the genealogists. The development of genealogical studies, like that of geographical description, provided a powerful influence on, as well as a source of material for, Herodotos; these works often contained information, genuine or fictional, about the individuals or places appearing in them, and one can often find passages where Herodotos seems to have used such a source (see on digressions in Chapter 5). It is also important that the only method of dating available for the pre-literate period was by generations 'known' from family or public traditions, or by the similarly transmitted lists of religious or political office-bearers — like the Roman consuls. It continued to be used, the Greeks having no conventional era, even down to the scientific Eratosthenes (see above, Chapter 1) in his calculation of the date of the Trojan War, which he put some eight or nine centuries before his own third-century BC lifetime. (Whether the Trojan War actually took place at all may become a relevant question when we consider Herodotos' attitude to legendary sources.) Thus we shall constantly find Herodotos using generations as a measure of time; a rough measure indeed, for his sources did not consistently use the same conventional length of a generation, apparently varying within the limits of twenty-five and forty years. Herodotos did not attempt to standardise or correlate these vague data, but at least they provide some chronological bases for events considerably earlier than his own time. It is true that Eastern records of the past existed, but they tended to become garbled in transmission, often deliberately (see n. 6) or by sheer misunderstanding. Like other Greeks of his time, Herodotos had 'little Egyptian and less Babylonian' (see further, Chapter 7).

It will have been observed that a number of persons mentioned as important in the rise of scientific inquiry were men of Miletos, the leading city-state of Ionia. Ionia was the central portion of the Western Anatolian coast, extending roughly 200 kilometres from Smyrna (Izmir) and the neighbouring offshore island of Chios to the immediate vicinity of Herodotos' home town, Halikarnassos (Bodrum) on its peninsula just south of the island of Kos. The influence of Ionian learning and investigative attitude cannot have failed to reach Halikarnassos, despite political, ethnic and dialectical differences. The Dorian Greek settlers in Karia, to the south of Ionia, seem to have been more ready to mix with the previous inhabitants[10] and it is possible that the names of some members of Herodotos' own family were Karian. It was no doubt because the Ionian dialect was that predominantly used in late sixth-century and early fifth-century prose literature that Herodotos wrote his book in the dialect of his northern neighbours. However inscriptions show Ionian in use in Halikarnassos itself (see e.g. ML 32). Further, as the twelve cities of the Ionian group were amongst the leaders in trade and commerce (a not insignificant factor in their intellectual progress) their dialect had become familiar to many non-Ionian Greeks, and was well understood in Athens, the reputed 'metropolis' or mother city of the Ionian settlers in Asia (Bk. 1.146f.), whose own Attic speech was not widely dissimilar. Undoubtedly Herodotos did not wish the publication of his work to be confined by dialectical boundaries, and many scholars have thought the Athenians an audience he had particularly in mind. On both counts, Ionian seemed a preferable medium to the Dorian of Halikarnassos.

Some further products of Ionian (or related) learning may be mentioned to illustrate the wide variety of their interests, which are often reflected in the *History*. (A notable exception is the lack of any reference to basic philosophy, whether of the Monists or later thinkers.)[11] The agnosticism of Xenophanes, a contemporary of the Persian wars, who was considered by conventional piety as impious because of his criticism of the extreme anthropomorphism of

Greek religion, was not among these (the historian's own view will be discussed in a later chapter), but his obvious interest in comparative religion shows him not blinkered by any orthodoxy. Alkmaion of Kroton, a Western foundation which became one of the great centres of Greek medicine (see, for example, Bk. 3.125), wrote, in Ionic dialect, *On Nature*, in which treatise empirical knowledge was made the basis of theory. Much medical knowledge was no doubt derived from Egypt, a visit to which ancient culture became almost a *sine qua non* for the savants of the period, from Solon to Pythagoras (reputedly), Hekataios and of course Herodotos himself. Similarly Babylonian astronomy, with Egyptian geometry, were to provide the bases for Greek sciences. Perhaps of particular interest not only to Herodotos but to the environmentalists of today is an anonymous treatise entitled *On Airs, Waters, Places*. This work, which became attached to the so-called Hippocratic corpus of medical writings, was the earliest of such contributions, probably antedating Hippokrates, and may have been published during Herodotos' working years. It deals with the effect of various environmental factors on human life and behaviour, or characters; ideas which are reflected in Herodotos, for instance in the notorious closing passage (9.122) and his comment on the favourable climatic situation of Ionia (1.142).

How far the intellectual climate of Halikarnassos itself was affected by the rule of dynastic monarchs is uncertain. Nor indeed need such influences have been restrictive; political life had not been much affected by theorists before the rise of sophists. In Herodotos' pages we find tyrants as patrons of the arts (e.g. 1.24, 3.121) — a fact of which we are of course informed by other evidence — and engineering (3.60) as well as, obviously, medicine! The ruler of the historian's formative years, Queen Artemisia, had obviously won his youthful admiration (Bk. 8 *passim*). However a late authority informs us that along with other young intellectuals(?) he revolted unsuccessfully against the queen's successor Lygdamis and had to go into exile at Samos. Not a shred of information relative to this episode is to be found in the *History*, but the experience was no bad thing: Samos was a lively community, to the forefront in the developing sciences — witness the engineering feats recorded in 3.60 — and a close neighbour both of Miletos (a trade rival) and the smaller Ionian towns to the south, and of Ephesos and the rest of the league to the north. Our later study of Herodotos' sources will show that Samian friends or acquaintances, not to mention personal observation, provided much detailed information, as well as a stimulating intellectual climate.

The most intellectually distinguished son of Samos had been Pythagoras, who fled from or was banished under the despotic rule of Polykrates, c.520 BC (Bk. 3, 39ff.) but one can detect no influence from him in the *History*, though he is incidentally mentioned, being described as 'no mean sophist'. Herodotos however does show interest in Pythagorean religious practices, which he compares with certain Egyptian rites (2.81).

The progress of philosophical thought had since 500 BC taken a somewhat different direction from that of the Ionian Monists. To pass over somewhat transcendental philosophers, particularly Empedokles and Parmenides in the far west, a manner of intellectual inquiry had grown up which dealt rather with the particular than the universal; it often insisted upon the priority of the individual over society — a shocking notion for citizens of a supposedly close-knit Greek polis, but one frequently enough implicit in their actions. All 'laws', according to the New Thinkers, were artificial creations, limiting the 'natural' behaviour of mankind; thus arose the long-standing argument as to the relative importance and proper relationship of *physis*, 'natural growth' and *nomos*, 'law, convention, customs', which finds its echoes in Herodotos; his own view is most explicitly stated in 3.38, but implicit throughout in the supremacy of *nomos* for civilised — and perhaps also for barbarous — mankind. The sophists, as they were somewhat derogatorily labelled (the term seems to imply 'sham philosophers' or 'professors of wisdom') questioned all conventions, and in this respect their heirs were the later Cynics, represented for most of us by Diogenes and his 'alternative lifestyle' in a dog-kennel. They examined all political institutions, of course, and a probable instance of such an influence on Herodotos may be seen in the Debate amongst the Seven Persians on forms of government, which is alleged to have taken place before the succession of Dareios to the throne of Persia (3.80–2).[12] Thus the work of the sophists was more relevant to Herodotos' historical interests than that of the universalist philosophers. A minor example of sophistic technique is perhaps to be seen in 3.119, the argument put forward by the wife of Intaphernes, which is reproduced in Sophokles' *Antigone*.

Gorgias of Leontinoi (in Sicily), a younger contemporary of the

historian, came to Athens with an embassy in 427 BC and proceeded to *épater les bourgeois* in the Ekklesia with his rhetorical
fireworks. But here is the exception that proves the rule; the
convoluted style of Gorgias had no effect whatsoever upon the
simple, straightforward manner of Herodotos' speeches;[13] its
closest congener known to us is to be found in the speeches
composed by the next important historical writer, Thukydides.
Other sophists were interested in grammar and etymology in
addition to style; whereas the 'logographers' ('prosewrights', to use
Macan's rendering) mentioned above were, to judge from their
scanty remains, by no means remarkable for style. But the ancient
and modern worlds agree upon the effectiveness and charm of
Herodotos' style.[14] In this respect too then, as in the application of
rational investigation into the recounting of the past, he made a
'great leap forward'.

The mention of Sophokles will no doubt suggest a question as to
why what is to many the outstanding artistic and intellectual
achievement of fifth-century Greece has been, so far, neglected in
this survey. The answer would have been self-evident to Aristotle;
tragedy deals with universals, what would happen in certain circumstances with certain characters, history with particulars, what
X did or what was done to him. But the two forms are not so
mutually exclusive after all; the one extant 'historical drama', *The
Persians* of Aischylos (written by an eye-witness of the battle of
Salamis, and still treated by some contemporary historians as if it
were a historical document, not a play) depicts one of the high
points of Herodotos' narrative — and may have left a verbal
reminiscence in the *History*. Sophokles and Herodotos are thought
to have been at least acquainted, not perhaps merely on account of
the *Antigone* passage. And Book I contains what many have felt to
be an adaptation of a tragic drama, the story of Gyges; while the
tale of Kroisos' son Atys and the refugee-murderer Adrastos has
many resemblances to an Attic tragedy. Herodotos, it seems, had a
crop for any corn, or to put it rather better, all was grist to his mill,
and we can be sure that he was extremely receptive to all kinds of
artistic and intellectual influence. How fortunate that he could not
have avoided, even had he wished, the ferment of intellectual
development and progress that seethed in his native area in time to
assist his own.

Notes

1. In the absence of other sources apart from Homer, it is not clear how much of Hesiod's Theogony is in fact original, but evidently, in the manner of Greek thought, he has applied a degree of systemisation to a fairly haphazard bundle of myths. Only those transmitted by Homer or in the lost Epic Cycle had become canonical, and local variants found in late writers are legion.

2. A number of authors' names and titles of work certainly or presumably of pre-Herodotean date are known to us, but they survive only in scanty fragments or not at all. Most unfortunately this is true of some of the probably more immediate influences upon Herodotos. See L. Pearson, *Early Ionian Historians* (1939).

3. Notably Demodokos in *Odyssey*, Book 8.

4. F. G. Kenyon, *Books and Readers in Ancient Greece and Rome* (1932) provides good basic information on such matters. See also E. G. Turner, *Athenian Books in the Fifth and Fourth Centuries BC* (inaugural lecture, 1952).

5. This generalisation cries out for qualification, but it must be sought elsewhere. The important fact here is the dedication of the best minds to rational thought.

6. The priests in turn enormously exaggerated the antiquity of their own civilisation; even if they were using a figure considerably less than a generation, say twenty years, for the term of the hereditary officer in question, the sequence of statues shown to Hekataios and Herodotos would stretch back beyond 7000 BC, or at least 3000 years beyond the earliest beginnings of civilisation in Egypt. See also Chapter 7.

7. Herodotos had to make a great deal of use of 'official versions' but does not always accept them as gospel. See Bibliography Bl.

8. See *Fr.G.Hist.* IA, 107–52, for some 200 quotations or references.

9. The date at which the Homeric poems were first written down — and indeed the question as to whether they were orally composed — is an involved one. Alphabetic writing was introduced to Greece about 700 BC, and 150 years later we hear of a 'definitive edition' of Homer being produced under the auspices of Peisistratos, the Athenian dictator.

10. The original Karians, despite a good military reputation, were regarded by most Greeks as somewhat backward. The Karian figured in the Greek proverbial equivalent of 'trying it on the dog'. Their language remains fairly mysterious owing to the small quantity of evidence.

11. On this subject see H. Barth, 'Einwirkungen der vorsokratische Philosophie auf die Herausbildung der historiographischen Methoden Herodots', *NBGAW* 1 (1964) 173; A. Dihle, 'Herodot und die Sophistik', *Philologus* 106 (1962) 207.

12. Much has been written on the subject of this debate, which will reappear in Chapters 4, 7 and 9.

13. A possible exception in the language and style of the speeches in the constitutional debate (3.80–2) — as in their content.

14. Lucian (cf. n. 4 to Chapter 1), one of the most acute critics of the ancient world, had this to say (*Herodotos*, trs. Kilburn in the Loeb series), 'The beauty of his diction, the careful arrangement of his words, the aptness of his native Ionic, his extraordinary power of thought, the countless jewels which he has wrought into a unity beyond hope of imitation . . .'.

3 THE EDUCATION OF A HISTORIAN

In the first half of the fifth century the intellectual resources of the Greek world available to an enquiring mind were, as we have seen, both valuable and extensive in many fields of study. A beginning had been made which could be drawn upon by a potential historian. But they would not be fully utilised until the student had made the decision to develop that branch of inquiry which was to become history. At what precise stage of his intellectual development Herodotos decided on his own particular course, and set out to equip himself for the task, is practically an unanswerable question. It involves numerous other questions; not only the date of 'publication' or completion of the work, which is a matter of dispute (see Chapter 1, n. 10), and on which for the moment we shall accept the hitherto orthodox view which insists upon the seniority of Herodotos to Thukydides, and considers at least the main body of the work to belong to, roughly, the decade 440–430 BC.[1] It would also involve his probable birth-date, for which see the biographical note on p. ix and for which, like nearly all such questions relating to his life, there is no convincing external evidence, while internal evidence from the *History* is inadequate or non-existent. Thirdly, the order of composition of the sections of the work is of some importance to the question. There have been numerous theories on this, of which the most obvious but too simplistic is that he began at the present beginning and wrote straight through to the end of Book 9. A more attractive if not generally accepted view is that Books 7 to 9, comprising the fairly coherent and straightforward account of the invasion of Xerxes,[2] were written first. But on consideration, Herodotos, now a more experienced historian, then decided to write the (now) preceding six books to provide the necessary background for a proper historical understanding of the narrative.[3] These six books present the rise of Persian power, the extent of its domains, its imperialist policy and the events leading to the two Persian attempts to invade Greece which preceded the invasion of Xerxes. This question will be examined later, when we consider the structure of the *History*.

It is perhaps permissible to assume that Herodotos had formed at an early stage the general concept of a great 'universal' history;

what he eventually wrote evidently constituted his life's work, and we proceed to the further assumption that much of his life was devoted to the vast preparatory labour involved.

The most conspicuous events of the period readily accessible to Herodotos' mainly oral researches, whether or not the most historically influential, were those of the mighty Persian forces gathered to conquer Greece, their almost superhuman organisational, engineering and logistical feats, their early victories and their eventual repulse. This large-scale warfare, involving forces 'uncountable' to the Greek man-in-the-street (but carefully if not altogether credibly enumerated by Herodotos) had already become almost legendary when Herodotos began to write. On the assumption made above, only the youngest participants still survived, and their memories of the events of forty years earlier were by no means unembellished by myth.[4] Furthermore the small states of Greece — they had learnt by now of their relative insignificance — had defeated what both legend and fact declared to be a far more populous, extensive and wealthy power; patriotic fervour had engendered myth to a degree that should hardly surprise societies that can make encouraging patriotic myth out of defeats such as Gallipoli and Dunkirk. To write about such a subject was obviously attractive to anyone with a gift for narrative and description,[5] but a reasoned account, incorporating an investigation into the real reasons for the conflict, was a different proposition, calling for an intellectual breadth of vision and freedom from prejudice that were and still are far from common.

How could Herodotos prepare himself for such a task? One obvious method, and one at least partially documented for us in the *History* itself, was by travel. Travel would enable the student to acquaint himself with the nature of the non-Greek societies involved, more closely than had been made possible by some of those descriptive (though not necessarily analytical) compilations mentioned in the preceding chapter. It would familiarise him with the geographical factors involved in the development of societies and their potential for military power. He could personally inspect the scenes of actual naval and military operations, and see for himself all manner of remarkable sights both of natural occurrence and of human production, the latter perhaps to be included in the 'works' referred to in the Proem of the *History*.

Such travels will have reinforced in Herodotos the conviction stated by one of his predecessors, that 'the Greeks tell many foolish tales'.⁶ In the course of his journeys he rapidly (we assume) established for himself a hierarchy of source material, to which much attention will be paid in Chapter 4. At its head stands 'autopsy', the personal visual investigation which of course cannot vouch for past events in itself, but can examine the extant evidence for them; it ranges from the copying of inscriptions to studying skulls on a battlefield. Next in order comes 'knowledge' based on information obtained orally (in most cases) from presumably reliable authorities, and tested in the light of reason. Third, the 'tales' or accounts commonly given by societies, groups or individuals; again reason has a part to play in acceptance or rejection of 'what is said'. And 'reason' is to be brought to bear upon those accepted.

Some examples of his travels may be given. In Greece itself, he visited most major centres and reached as far to the northwest as Dodona (2.52) — though of course many Greek tourists or religious devotees made the journey with no scientific purpose in mind. Of the great Delphic shrine he shows intimate knowledge. On his way to or from the northeastern parts he seems to have visited Thebes (5.59), Thermopylai (7.198ff.), Tempe and Olympus (7.129). The great sanctuaries of Delphi and Olympia will have had a magnetic attraction for the researcher. Not only would he see many dedications of historical interest and even inscriptions, to be carefully copied; but he also knew the reputation of Delphi as a kind of general clearing-house of information about the Greek world, due to its continual stream of visitors from all over Greece and beyond. The particular curiosity of Herodotos about oracular pronouncements could be satisfied here; a majority of all such items in the *History* emanates from Delphi (perhaps indirectly, through some of Apollo's customers). Olympia too was a place where Greeks from the often hostile city-states met in comparative amity, and where both documentary records and priestly tradition could be freely drawn upon. (Some examples will be given in Chapter 7.)

The amount of time Herodotos devoted to Sparta was evidently not inconsiderable; personal or family traditions as well as those of the state were on offer — there seems to have been no obvious reluctance to impart information! Athens presents a more difficult problem; we are far better (though not nearly well enough, before the age of Perikles) informed about Athens and Herodotos seems not to have dealt with official sources — indeed it has been suggested that his Athenian information was gained, in part at least, from Delphic and Olympic sources.[7]

In the Aegaean itself he visited, apart from the offshore islands of Ionia, especially Samos, the far-famed sanctuary of Delos; his detailed observations (4.34), as at Delphi, make it clear he is not merely repeating common knowledge. And he made his way to Thasos in the far north of that sea, apparently solely to check on a point hardly material to his history (2.44, 6.47).[8] He saw the sea of Marmara and its two famous straits, and apparently travelled on the mainland of Thrace (Bulgaria) to where the 'stelae of Sesostris' stood. A more doubtful area[9] is the Black Sea itself, where his measurements are perhaps more than usually inaccurate, and South Russia, where however 'personal knowledge' is claimed of certain matters (e.g. 4.34); beyond a certain geographical limit in this direction he admits that he could not get even a reliable second-hand account, despite many inquiries from Greek traders and others. To the far west he may have travelled in the first place for personal reasons not connected with his research. The connection of the Greeks of Sicily and Italy with the Persian invasions of Greece proper was held to be indirect, their involvement minimal, and the simultaneity of the Carthaginian invasion of Sicily with that of Xerxes purely coincidental. However, in addition to his western colonial home of Thurioi, the historian shows familiarity with Metapontion (4.15) and Kroton (5.45) as well as with Brindisi and the 'heel' of Italy. There seems to be no evidence for any visit to Sicily.

To the south, he visited Kyrene (2.181) but probably not either the offshore island of the original Greek settlement nor as far west as the Syrtes (Gulf of Tripoli). In Egypt he clearly spent a considerable time and travelled about a good deal;[10] that his measurements of distances can be proved inaccurate at times may be explained by various hypotheses without rejection of his claim to have 'been there' (see Chapters 7 and 11). For instance, he states that he travelled from Memphis to both Thebes and Heliopolis to check on a story told him at the former city (2.3). He ascended the Nile as far as 'Elephant Island' (Philae, near Assouan) (2.29) but no further; not surprisingly, not even his theoretical interest in the upper course and sources of the great and extraordinary river led him to face the navigational difficulties lying upstream. (A hundred years before, Greek mercenary soldiers had left the usual military graffiti upon the leg of the colossal statue of Rameses at Abu

Simbel.) Herodotos personally measured the pyramid of Chephren — presumably with the inadequate assistance of local guides (2.127) — spoke with priests at Sais in the Delta (2.130), saw the crocodiles in Lake Moeris in the Fayum, and the remains of the ships of Ionian mercenaries (as he was told) at Tell Defenneh.

Travels further east are indicated, but not so well substantiated. Unless we join those who consider Herodotos as the father of lies, and a deliberate and pointless liar at that, we must accept his statement of a trip to Tyre (2.44) and the enthusiasm and detail of his comments, even if at times erroneous, on Mesopotamia seem to override the view that he was not able to give a first-hand account of the area including Babylon. 1.135 suggests that the visit to Babylon came after he had been to Egypt. On the other hand, comparison of a feat of engineering in Egypt with one at Nineveh occurs in 2.150, where his statement that he 'knew, by the account' seems to preclude autopsy.

In addition to autopsy, travel enabled Herodotos to make inquiry into all sorts of matters; clearly he would have preferred to interview genuine authorities, but equally clearly this was not practicable. The evidence that some of the information thus gained was often vague, positively erroneous, or even fictional will be considered in the chapter on sources. But one of the most striking features to any reader of Herodotos is the continual recurrence of formulae such as 'The Persians say', 'The Egyptian priests told me' or simply 'It is said' or 'There is a story'. Within the Greek world, written evidence was very scanty even for the great events of the years around the historian's birth, and for earlier times practically non-existent; in the long-civilised countries of the Middle East it was of course plentiful, but useless. Not only did Greeks, with their feeling of racial superiority, not bother to learn foreign languages, they certainly had no chance of interpreting the strange non-alphabetic scripts of the monuments. It should be remembered that modern Europeans could not read Egyptian hieroglyphics till the first quarter of the nineteenth century, nor cuneiform till the third quarter. Perhaps the ancient Greeks, like their modern descendants, thought with the Anglo-Saxons that any intelligent foreigner should be able to understand the only sensible language. Therefore talk, and talk in Greek through interpreters of varying competence, was the order of the day; it must have involved many hours, and often a good deal of frustration.

In any case, the determined collection of information and

misinformation went on. The next, and very difficult question is how it was recorded. Not on tape nor even in shorthand, unless Herodotos had invented a system of his own which died with him. (No such method is heard of in Ancient Greece, the earliest recorded system being the obscure Notae Tironianae, invented by Cicero's secretary). How bulky then must have been the travel-diaries which Herodotos (or his slave or slaves) lugged about the Mediterranean. Were they made on rolls of papyrus? How unhandy for reference — indeed the nature of the papyrus roll exercised a very restricting influence on the form of much ancient literature, and particularly perhaps upon an encyclopaedic and scholarly work such as that under discussion. What alternatives exist? Parchment was not in common use till centuries later, and is comparatively bulky; wax tablets have great limitations, as do the occasionally found wooden panels for writing. I have never heard of any constructive suggestion in this respect.

In the absence then of a convenient card index, are we to suppose that Herodotos kept all this vast mass of information in his head? Even to have found among a mass of written records the appropriate matter for the occasion would seem no mean feat; imperfect or delayed recollection from his cerebral storehouse (of how many megabytes?) may well account for some rather odd misplacements of certain information. Certainly he will have made copies of Greek documents such as inscriptions, which were available to the public, and such scraps of corroborative evidence as survive confirm his accuracy.[11]

Herodotos' purposeful preparation for the writing of his inquiry will undoubtedly have included the study of many of the books mentioned in the previous chapter though, as we shall see later, the modern scholarly practice of due attribution of material to its authors was as yet unthought of. But a general education, not at all intentionally vocational, included wide reading in the purely literary output of previous generations.[12] Like all cultured persons, Herodotos was thoroughly familiar with the Homeric poems; precise quotations appear at 2.116 and 4.29, other references are too numerous to mention. He also knew the later additions known under the general label of the Epic Cycle (2.117, 4.32); he referred to Hesiod as a main influence, along with Homer, in standardising Greek theological notions (2.53) and quoted him elsewhere for information on the legendary Hyperboreans, dwelling 'beyond the North Wind'. He displayed the normal familiarity with the other major groups of Greek legendary stories, of the Argonauts, the Theban cycle and so on. Since the manner of his references to this literature makes it clear that Herodotos expected his audience to be *au fait* with the legends, one can hardly ascribe the historian's own knowledge to a deliberate research programme, seeking the basis for 'modern' history in the other literary works. But a glance at the first few paragraphs of the *History* will show how well Herodotos could distinguish between myth and history. The ironical tone in which he discusses, and dismisses, the various legendary stories of abductions as *casus belli* is reinforced by the explicit statement (1.5.3.): 'I am not going to pronounce on whether this or that account might be correct but I shall proceed by indicating the individual whom I *know* [my italics] to have been the first to perpetrate unjustified aggression against the Greeks.' However he did utilise statements of the recorders of legend as a basis for detailed reasoned argument bearing upon historical, genealogical or geographical facts or theories, e.g. at 6.53, 7.197. Modern readers, whose notions of Medea or Iphigenia derive from Euripides (writing certainly no earlier than Herodotos), or even considerably later writers, may find unfamiliar aspects; most myths, having been transmitted orally over generations and even centuries, had acquired more than one form.

These tales (*logoi*) in various versions seem all to have been retained, along with the extensive information gleaned in his travels, in the future historian's stupendous memory. A certainly historical epic poet, Aristeas of Prokonnesos, much later than Hesiod, was known to Herodotos most probably in a written version (4.13), but the lyric poets naturally did not provide much grist for his omnivorous mill. Sappho and Anakreon receive incidental mention, but not as evidence for historical fact. However, Archilochos and Alkaios each produce one item, the former on the fascinating career of Gyges of Lydia (1.12), who 'got lucky' at Sardis and founded the dynasty which ended with the defeat of Kroisos by Kyros of Persia; the latter for an eye-witness account of his own inglorious part in a battle between Mytilenians and Athenians (5.95). Arion's lucky rescue by a dolphin after being made to walk the plank may be apocryphal, it is not reported on the basis of his own compositions, and is only marginally relevant historically as evidence for the tendencies of Greek tyrants.[13]

A contemporary of the lyricists, the reformer and 'first economist' Solon of Athens was also a considerable literary figure, but the lengthy episode of his interview with Kroisos in Book 1, 29ff. makes no mention of his propagandist poetry. However these poems are referred to in connection with affairs in Cyprus, in Book 5, 113.

Other literary references are the slighting one about the 'River of Ocean', called an invention of 'Homer or one of the earlier poets', and that to the consensus of all the poets against the official Spartan version of the arrival in Laconia in 6.52. (Had Herodotos checked them *all*?) Also to Lasos of Hermione for his piece of literary detective work over the 'oracles' forged by Onomakritos — perhaps the earliest known piece of such 'literary criticism' (7.6) — and to Pindar in the celebrated passage Bk. 3.38, for the axiom that 'Custom [*Nomos*] is undisputed lord.' But this last may only be from general knowledge of a much quoted apothegm, rather than direct knowledge of Pindar's poems, a view made more probable by the fact that where the laudatory odes of Pindar to Sicilian tyrants might well have been laid under contribution, that is in the digression on Syracusan history (7.153ff.), they have left no trace.

Two tragic poets, as far as is known, concerned themselves with the history of the period. Phrynichos composed a play, now lost, entitled *The Taking of Miletos*: such a reminder of the disastrous ending in 494 BC of the Ionian revolt against the Persians caused the Athenian audience so much distress, and no doubt feelings of guilt for having quickly withdrawn their initial support of the patriotic front for the liberation of Ionia and their 'cousins' the people of Miletos, that the playwright was fined by the Athenian government.[14] Herodotos reported this (6.21), but gave no details concerning the play nor, wisely, did he adduce its content as evidence for the course of events. The same poet wrote another historical play, the *Phoenician Women*, apparently on much the same theme as the following item. The other tragedian, Aischylos, was himself an eye-witness of some of the events of the Persian invasions, and in writing his own epitaph claimed remembrance for having fought at Marathon,[15] saying nothing of his subsequently famous tragedies. Presumably he was present at the Battle of Salamis ten years later,[16] which he vividly, if not necessarily accurately, depicted in his 'historical tragedy', *The Persians*. Herodotos undoubtedly had read this (it is pretty certain he was not in Athens early enough to see its presentation in 472) but he did not follow Aischylos' account very closely; a verbal echo of a famous line at 8.68 γ may, like the Pindaric aphorism mentioned above, have resulted from common knowledge, perhaps quoted by one of those knowledgeable Athenians Herodotos interviewed in the course of his enquiry into the events of 480. Aischylos, not mentioned in this apparently appropriate context, is however directly referred to for representing Artemis as daughter of Demeter, following the 'Egyptian version' according to Herodotos in contradiction of all his poetical predecessors (2.156). Had Herodotos checked all these unenumerated references?

A word must be added on the subject of oracles. There existed written collections of such pronouncements, genuine (if the term is permissible in such a case!) or false — witness the Onomakritos/ Lasos affair above — and Herodotos seems either to have had access to or perhaps himself made such a collection. The more memorable, or perhaps the more obscure, of these were generally in 'epic' hexameter verse, and a number are quoted with apparently the same exactitude as the verse epitaphs also given verbatim. The importance thereof in the general scheme of Herodotos' work is a subject for later discussion (Chapter 8); that importance is guaranteed by over eighty references to oracular utterance — many, of course, reported from general hearsay — including no less than twenty-seven examples of verse, ranging from two examples of a simple line apiece to the dozen lines of each of the 'alternatives' offered to the Athenians before Salamis, at 7.64f.[17] Delphi, as the pre-eminent but by no means monopolistic oracular shrine, predominates; as well as other established centres, the individual pronouncements of the rather mysterious figure Bakis gain four mentions, while the undoubtedly legendary figure Mousaios appears in three citations.

How was Herodotos, after amassing all this material from literary sources, inscriptions and his own research and observation, able to organise, select and present the considerable proportion (what proportion cannot by any means be estimated) which composes the extant *History*? Once again we are at a loss; the internal evidence will be dealt with later on. One might suggest one main criterion for inclusion would have been the supposed degree of authenticity of material; but that will not stand up to investigation; Herodotos at times includes what he knows to be false — not, however, putting it forward as gospel — and omits material he believes authentic; he presents variant versions, and even tells us that he was bound to include 'what was said', even if he was not convinced of its verity. However, in the main, as we shall see, he worked on the assumption that what he himself saw (*opsis*) was so, that his verbal authorities (*akoē*) were on the whole reliable, and that the numerous 'tales' (*logoi*, including 'they say' and similar formulae) about the past could not be totally discarded, though their authority ranked lower than that of the expert witnesses. But so far we have only criteria of admissibility, no means of judging appropriateness for inclusion, nor for the complex structure of the work.[18]

Notes

1. Although Herodotos may have hinted, in 6.98, at the destruction wrought by the Peloponnesian War, or to be more precise that part of it called the Archidamian or Ten Years' War (431–422 BC), the latest datable event referred to is the Athenian arrest of Spartan envoys to Persian in 430 BC (7.137). However it is also possible that the traditional date of Herodotos' birth, like that of some others, has merely been calculated from his 'floruit' or 'acme' at the supposed age of forty. For the ancient scholars this (a) had to be at a decent interval (not less than ten years) before that of Thukydides, set at the start of the Peloponnesian War, and (b) was naturally associated with the only (apparently) datable event of the historian's life, his migration to Thurioi. This was taken to be at the colony's foundation in 444/3, but there is nothing to show that Herodotos went with the original settlers, and the whole structure is therefore a house of cards.

2. However, most of the similar structural features, including non-historical or extra-historical digressions, do appear in the supposedly 'later' books also.

3. This is, in general, the theory of R. W. Macan, one of the first modern scholars to attempt a serious rational assessment of Herodotos' work (see bibliography).

4. The various tendencies of 'oral history' will be examined in Chapter 7.

5. Of course, in the absence of any other works attributed to our author, there is no way of telling whether Herodotos was aware of his outstanding gifts before he began on the *magnum opus*. It is not, in the present writer's view, possible to distinguish 'early' and 'late' passages in the text on stylistic or other internal grounds: exception may be made of some apparently added 'notes'.

6. Hekataios of Miletos *Genealogies* (?) *ad init.*, quoted by two ancient writers (*F.Gr.Hist.* IA).

7. A. J. Podlecki, 'Herodotos in Athens?' in *Greece and the Eastern Mediterranean in Ancient History and Prehistory* (Stud.Schachermeyr) (1977) 246ff. believes Herodotos spent far more time in the Peloponnese, especially at Olympia and Sparta. Olympia, like Delphi, could have been the source of much Athenian material, while the Athenian colony of Thurioi, Herodotos' later home, must not be left out of calculation.

A different view is found in J. Schwartz, 'Le séjour athènian et les redactions des histoires d'Hérodote', *BFS* 36 (1958) 335–41; 'Hérodote et Périclès', *Historia* 18 (1969) 367. See also J. A. S. Evans, 'Herodotus and Athens; the Evidence of the Encomium', *AC* 48 (1979) 1.

8. But important to his own assessment of the relationship between Greek and Egyptian religion; see further Chapter 8.

9. Criticism of Herodotos' claimed or assumed autopsy in (e.g.) J. M. Bigwood, 'Ctesias' Description of Babylon', *AJAH* 3 (1978) 32; F. Oertel, *Antiquitas* 18

(1969); O. Kimball Armayor, 'Did Herodotos ever go to the Black Sea?' *HSCPh* 82 (1978) 45–62, and 'The Homeric Influence on Herodotos' Story of the Labyrinth', *CB* 54 (1977/78) 68–72. On the other hand a recent book gaily assumes that Herodotos had been to every place he describes; R. P. Lisler, *The Travels of Herodotos* (1980).

10. There is much current endeavour to minimise the duration of Herodotos' stay in Egypt, the extent of his travels, and personal investigation rather than reliance on the work of Hekataios. However, his intense fascination with all things Egyptian which is constantly displayed, together with a considerable favourable balance of correct over incorrect reporting, convince me that most of his evidence is first-hand — not to mention his own statements on the matter.

11. The accurate reporting of insciptions by Herodotos should be compared with his quotation of verse oracles (but see below, and n. 17).

12. It has to be borne in mind that even in the literate communities of Herodotos' time there was no abundance of written texts of poets and other writers, and as yet apparently no public libraries. In his youth he may have acquired much information by listening to oral deliveries; 'reading' in the present context is to be taken very flexibly! See also below on publication, Chapter 4.

13. See my *Herodotos on Tyrants and Despots* (1971).

14. The plays for the Athenian dramatic festivals had to be submitted beforehand to the authorities, as only a stricly limited number could be staged. But this was not the only occasion on which the 'selection committee' appears to have ignored the possible effect on the public — or on individuals, in the case of comedy.

15. Where his brother Kynegiros was killed, as reported by Herodotos at 6.114. The epitaph however makes no mention of Salamis, and as will be seen later, Marathon practically monopolised Athenian patriotic mythology.

16. It has been suggested, on account of the prominence given by the poet to the factually small part of the infantry contingent under Aristeides, that he was a member of it. The supposition is unnecessary, and Herodotos' identification of these troops as 'men of Athenian stock' has been thought to indicate that they were not Athenian residents.

17. J. Fontenrose, *The Delphic Oracle* (1978) suggests that Herodotos may well be responsible for the reputedly 'traditional' verse form of some oracular responses. The untrained and uneducated priestess issued answers in brief if ambiguous prose statements; but Herodotos would feel as free to clothe them in suitable literary garb as he did to compose speeches. One may object that verse appears in only half the reported Delphic responses — but elsewhere I have argued that variation is one of the historian's favourite techniques (see next note).

18. For selection of material and structural arrangements, see Chapters 4, 5 and 7, and Waters, 'The Structure of Herodotos' Narrative', *Antichthon* 8 (1974) 1.

4 SELECTION OF SUBJECT-MATTER

A vast diversity of materials, we have seen, was available to Herodotos in writing down the results of his researches — historical, quasi-historical and pseudo-historical. The problem of selection of the appropriate material in this area is however completely overshadowed by that arising from the historian's decision to include non-historical matter. Now much of this, but by no means all of it, was relevant or even essential to the proper understanding of historical processes and events. A third category comprised all the matter of merely general interest, or pure entertainment of the audience.[1]

It may be argued that Herodotos failed to overcome the difficulties presented by this deliberate policy of what might be called non-selective inclusion. Some individuals tend to be dazzled, or even dazed, on a first reading, by the proliferation of digressions, the constant breaks in the narrative, and the enormous number of unfamiliar proper names: names of individuals, nations, remote and obscure tribes, of geographical features, plants, animals and weapons. However no one who has read Herodotos more than once would be prepared to sacrifice all the skilful story-telling, the picturesque descriptions of the exotic, the anecdotes, that enliven his vast canvas, in favour of a succinct and unadorned account of the actual campaigns which constitute his nominal subject — or part thereof. Each re-reading brings out some piece of information that has failed to register on previous occasions, and the infinite variety of topics ensures Herodotos being 'all things to all men' rather than falling between several different stools. Parables, anecdotes and varia of all kinds are included not because they are factual, or 'true' in any historical sense; the reported test, for instance, by Dareios of the power of *nomos* by challenging the respective views on burial customs of Greeks and Kallatian Indians is extremely unlikely to be authentic. But this item is functional, as are numerous others because they illustrate various aspects of Herodotos' 'philosophy of history'. It is interesting that the historian does not, as a rule, draw the moral; he leaves the inference to the reader. A case in point is the much-discussed observation of Kyros at the end of the work.

To start with the strictly historical material, clearly Herodotos was faced with numerous problems concerning his sources; their authenticity and other limitations, and his own limitations regarding access to non-Greek sources. These problems will be examined in Chapter 7; for the moment, let us recall that Herodotos could not avail himself of any continuous written narrative, as a guide if not a model, from either the Greek or the barbarian side. But on the Greek side, on the other hand, he could have been overwhelmed by the profusion of oral accounts based on legend, tradition, hearsay or (for the latest period covered) personal participation. How was he to deal with these? Every city, and very often also interest groups or clans within the city, had its own official version of particular past events — versions redounding to the credit of X or the discredit of Y. These are often the origin of accusations of bias against the historian, a charge which will be discussed in Chapter 9.

If only one version became available to him the problem was reduced to one of assessing its reliability by *a priori* reasoning, or the bringing in as evidence of some fact known to him. On at least seventy occasions this type of criterion is applied[2] to all kinds of reports, from both Greek and barbarian sources. For example at 1.172 he goes so far as to reject the claim of the partly-Hellenised people of Kaunos, a town in what is now southwest Turkey, to have originated from Crete. He denies it on linguistic grounds — the fact that on other evidence he was no great philologist (another infant science) is immaterial. The Samian exiles at 3.45 could not, he decides, have been victorious over the tyrant Polykrates as claimed, or they would not have needed to appeal to Sparta for assistance in the 'patriotic' struggle. But these rejected versions appear, none the less, in the text.

A similar case is that of variant or contradictory versions. In the matter of Samian exiles just mentioned, there are dual versions of those political opponents sent by the despot to serve with Amasis in Egypt, and two alternative reasons why the Spartans agreed to help the exiles against Polykrates. Herodotos in such cases sometimes makes his choice, with or without explaining his reasons; frequently he leaves it to the reader (an example is 5.44, on the war between Sybaris and Kroton) or admits that he finds himself unable to arrive at the truth. One reason for including the rejected version or versions may be the desire for completeness of record, which no doubt underlies the whole work; another may have been the wish to show up the inaccuracy of non-researched common belief, as in the ironic commentary on myths in the opening section of Book 1. One is reminded of the statement of his (partial!) predecessor Hekataios about Greek popular and erroneous 'tales'. At times Herodotos simply relates 'I cannot believe this', without adducing any grounds; his undeserved reputation for blind credulity ought to have been dispelled by observation of such a practice.

The 'official versions' (indicated generally by such phrases as 'the Spartans say') were of course always to be included. Much the same goes for the Persian accounts of their own history, and their own side in the campaigns. An obvious case of a Persian 'official version' is the long and detailed account of the end of Kambyses (though Egyptian influence is to be seen here), the usurpation by the False Smerdis, and his assassination by the Seven Persians, all leading to the accession of Dareios (Bk. 3, 61–119). It happens that there is some evidence on these events available to moderns — but not, as we have seen, to Herodotos — from Persian documents,[3] and a great deal of scholarly criticism of the Herodotean version has resulted.

But the reason for the inclusion in detail not only of the accession of Dareios, the monarch under whom the Persian *Drang nach Westen*, in particular, gained its greatest momentum, but of much ancillary material as well, is to provide the most complete picture of the re-establishment of the Achaemenid dynasty.[4] The type and manner of this regime are also to be fully illustrated, for the understanding of these matters is important for the study of the Persian imperialist aggression against the Greeks, and thus what may appear to be digressions find their justification.

One of the most conspicuous and frequently discussed sections in this account comprises what has been termed 'The Constitutional Debate' amongst the Seven Persians at Book 3, 80–2.[5] It will concern us again when we examine the credibility of sources used by Herodotos, in Chapter 7. The present question is why these three speeches, most probably quite unhistorical, were put in the mouths of Persian nobles and inserted at this juncture. Hardly anyone doubts the Hellenic origin of their content, despite Herodotos' own repeated assertion of their authenticity. The arguments for and against despotic government, aristocracy or oligarchy, and democracy were very much to the fore in Greece when Herodotos wrote. His use of these allegedly genuine speeches seeks to explain why, after the unfortunate experience of an apparently psychopathic despot, and a usurpation of the throne by a pretender, there was an immediate reversion to despotic government in Persia. Herodotos had considerable admiration for some features of Persian society (see Chapter 9) and felt the need for a plausible explanation of why no more liberal form of administration was achieved; he argues, implicitly, that it was not merely rejected out of hand. He was aware that not all individuals in Persia necessarily approved of absolute monarchy, and cited both the exemptions granted to Otanes, the proponent of democracy in the putative debate, and the later consent of Mardonios to the establishment of democratic government in the reconquered Greek states of Ionia (6.43).

Herodotos went on to recount the regrettably hybristic behaviour of Intaphernes, another of the seven, towards the palace guards. The men on duty at the Great King's private suite, intent on their loyal duty, denied the nobleman entrance on the ground that he was sleeping with a lady. Intaphernes refused to believe this and mutilated the supposed offenders with the scimitar which he normally wore. Not unnaturally, the king determined on condign punishment; after making sure that the outrage heralded no attempted coup, he arrested the entire family of Intaphernes. When taken in conjunction with this episode, the ensuing section makes it clear that the reason, or rather *one* reason, for the inclusion of the affair of *Intaphernes*, like the episode (3.121−8) of Oroites,[6] was to illustrate the firm hand of Dareios, especially on those close to the centre of power and the often unruly satraps who governed his far-flung provinces. To both of these incidents we shall return.

When the accession of Dareios had been achieved (by hook or by crook?) Herodotos next proceeded to inform us of the organisation of his empire, and its fiscal arrangements. Since Dareios had the reputation of being the great financial organiser (3.89) of the subsequently proverbial wealth of the King of Kings, this information too was included as fully relevant to the historical topic of the moment; nothing could be more basic to the design of a successful invasion of Europe than a well-filled treasury.

Oroites, as it happened, had impinged upon the course of history in another way, besides falling victim to Dareios' relentless drive for organisation and good order. He was responsible for the death of Polykrates, the already-mentioned ruler of Samos, the island lying just offshore from Oroites' territory. Now Polykrates was a figure of considerable moment in Aegaean history (not to mention that Herodotos showed great interest in tyrants), and in fact his maritime empire, or perhaps more exactly his sphere of influence and ability to take piratical toll, from about 525 BC formed a buffer state between the power of Persia, established for some time in Western Anatolia, and the central Aegaean and Greece proper. It thus constituted a quite serious obstacle to Persian designs of westward advance, and Oroites, the satrap at Sardis, no doubt felt that he would obtain royal favour as well as increased personal power and influence by the removal of its driving force. His plan to trap Polykrates succeeded, but his come-uppance was not long delayed and the tyrant was — too late — avenged. Thus the tale of Oroites' misdeeds and punishment had to be included in the historical background; there is no question of its direct relevance to the central theme of the advance of Persian imperialism.

Interestingly enough, the section that begins with the hubris and death of Kambyses is preceded by quite a lengthy excursus on Samian history. The relevance of events on Samos in the latter part of the sixth century BC has already been demonstrated; but as a conclusion to this passage, Herodotos informs us, somewhat dis-ingenuously, that he has spent more time on Samian affairs because of the three mighty constructions the island boasts.[7] These were the 1200-metre-long tunnel bringing water through the hill to Polykrates' capital (now called after that other distinguished citizen, Pythagoras); the mole protecting the harbour; and the temple of Hera some kilometres to the west, the largest temple in the Greek world. There is perhaps marginal historical relevance in mentioning these engineering feats if they are to illustrate the magnificence of the tyrant's rule but, unfortunately perhaps in view of the remark quoted above, any inference is left to the reader.

This example brings us to the consideration of a large quantity of information which at times may be totally unconnected with the main narrative. It is not at first sight clear why Herodotos decided to encumber himself with the task of describing, not only the organisation of the Persian empire, but the dress, life-style, religious beliefs and so on of all the diverse peoples living under Persian sway. In some cases, certain of these aspects could conceivably have had a bearing on the value of their contingents to the invading armies, and thus gained marginal relevance; but very rarely is this the case. The argument also falls to the ground when we consider that many peoples who never came under Persian control, even though aimed at by some of the imperialist ventures of Kyros, Dareios and Kambyses, nevertheless come in for full anthropological examination. These include the various inhabitants of South Russia and those of North Africa westwards from Kyrene.

A possible answer lies in the theme which constantly recurs in the *History* — the power of *nomos*. A famous passage (3.38) sees King Dareios conducting an experiment in the force of custom. Herodotos gives his approval to its result, which confirms the Pindaric text quoted and already mentioned. Throughout the work, the law, customs, manners and beliefs — all of which are subsumed under the Greek word *nomos* — of differing communities are set forth, sometimes with approving or disapproving comment, more often without. And when we recall that argument between the supporters of *nomos* as the overriding principle, and the proponents of *physis*, natural endowment and development, was highly topical at the time of writing, it would not be difficult to include another major intention of the historian to those already defined; that of writing a sermon, as it were, on the text 'Custom rules'.

Herodotos indeed is a prime example of those fairly rare individuals in whom travel does actually broaden the mind. Here, in his own case, it is difficult to apportion the credit between natural endowment and experience. However it is hardly a rash assumption that in his travels, rather than from his reading, he had become fascinated, at first hand, with the differences of behaviour between societies. Not only did he record the obvious and superficial features, such as dress and housing, but areas such as religion and social law or custom which demanded a good deal of inquiry. It cannot have happened that a whole series of fortunate coincidences enabled him to be present at the celebrations of births, deaths and marriages amongst many diverse communities. Having become deeply interested himself, he assumed that the information would stimulate the interest of his audience also, and therefore elected to include it. The proper study of mankind is man, and in common with some other intellectual figures of the period, Herodotos advanced it to a considerable extent.

For persons not professionally interested or wishing to become expert in the fields of ethnology or social anthropology, the information of this type supplied by Herodotos still merits inclusion for its intrinsic interest. But some of the more technical matters described have perhaps a more limited appeal. The status and powers of the Spartan kings, who constituted a rather unusual form of dyarchy, were of importance for the conduct of Spartan foreign policy and warfare. Therefore these were of direct concern not only to inter-city relations but to the actual conduct of the war against the Persians. But of what relevance is the fact that they received a double portion at meals? And indeed if we accept the contemporary estimate of the frugal Spartan bill of fare, the consumption of a double helping might well have been regarded as a punishment (6.57).[8] Yet there were undoubtedly individuals to whom this type of specialist information was of interest.

Zoological and botanical data abound. Without here questioning the authenticity of accounts of snakes with wings or gold-mining ants, the interest of exotic flora and fauna is undeniable, if not in every society, at least in those which establish zoological and botanical collections not only for scientific purposes but for public edification — or entertainment. Thus the two underlying 'poetic' purposes of instruction and of providing entertainment, are jointly responsible for the inclusion of at any rate the greater part of such material. True, this type of subject-matter contributes nothing, in a modern view, to the main historical subject. But it must not be forgotten that Herodotos was first in the field of large-scale historical writing, and accordingly entitled to draw up his own terms of reference.

Besides being potentially a distinguished historical novelist, Herodotos would also have made an excellent journalist. Consider several types of material which would never reach the pages of a modern historical work except, perhaps by indulgence, in a footnote. (The compulsory absence of footnotes will be noticed in the next chapter.) One such type is produced by the already-mentioned fondness for 'records' — the very stuff of modern popular journalism. A hundred or so reports of recorded 'firsts', 'greatests', and other superlatives are included in this work. Many of them are qualified by a formula which has acquired some notoriety, and by his dedication to its principles Herodotos' claim to a scientific attitude is supported.[9] 'Of all those we know', says the researcher; the first person plural is not the editorial 'we'; Herodotos uses the singular when speaking of his personal views, knowledge or judgement, so the plural must generally be taken to imply 'within the knowledge of our society', that is, known to Hellenes.[10] Among the 'firsts', inventors constantly receive credit: Arion invented the dithyramb (1.23), the Lydians first used coinage

(1.94) — and also invented the games the Greeks play. The Phokaians were the first Greeks to use 'long ships' (1.163), the Egyptians first 'discovered' the year (2.4). In other areas of endeavour, the Pharaoh Necho was the first ruler to order the circumnavigation of Africa — a feat which will reappear in our discussion of Herodotos' critical faculty — while Polykrates was the first 'after Minos of Knossos and any predecessors he may have had' (an ironic touch) to establish a thalassocracy.

Athletic records are numerous, and any notable historical personage who had achieved eminence in the 'games' receives due credit for it. Eurybates, remarked on for feats of single combat, had, fittingly, been a pentathlon champion (6.92); Demaratos was the only Spartan king to win an Olympic four-horse-chariot race (6.70); the failed Athenian revolutionary Kylon's only other claim to fame, apparently, had been an Olympic victory (5.71).

Personal qualifications other than athletic are not absent. Artachees held the double distinction of being the tallest Persian, at more than 8 ft, and having the loudest voice of all (7.117): Kallikrates, an unlucky early casualty at Plataia, was the most handsome man of his day in Greece (9.72), but his record was equalled perhaps a little earlier by Philippos (5.47), who held two other distinctions, one as an Olympic victor and the other posthumously, when a Sicilian city (with which he had no recorded connection) gave him 'the unparalleled honour of a hero's shrine'.[11] These facts are the sole reason for the inclusion of a paragraph on the fate of Philippos, in a digression within a digression!

Despite Greek prejudice (possibly exaggerated by moderns) in favour of male beauty, women qualify for praise in this respect. Ariston's wife was 'by far the most beautiful of all women in Sparta' — a field which though not very large had a good reputation for standard of looks (6.61). One can imagine that it was not difficult for the lady's claim to be recognised, the more so as she eventually became a king's consort. Her beauty was also a factor in the struggle between rival claimants to one of the two Spartan thrones, and, what is more, was alleged to be the result of favourable intervention by the semi-divine Helen (the female equivalent of a hero, see p. 46 n. 11). Thus her case is not on a par with that of Philippos.

At 6.103 we hear of the feats of a team of mares which achieved the almost incredible, winning the Olympic 'Derby' three times in succession — which means, of course, not in successive years, but at two four-yearly intervals! Nevertheless their record was equalled by the animals of the Spartan Euagoras, evidently a conspicuous spender despite his provenance, just as was the Athenian owner Kimon (6.103).[12] Kimon was the head of the Philaid house, a figure of great influence in Athens, whose son Miltiades was to play a prominent part in the Persian Wars. Euagoras on the other hand only achieved mention because of the jointly-held record.

Moral and intellectual qualities do not go unremarked. The Egyptians are the best educated — or perhaps they tell the most tales! — as well as being the healthiest in Herodotos' experience (2.77); Demokedes of Kroton was 'the best doctor of his day' (3.125). The Persians honour brave warriors most (2.238), while Leonidas, the defeated hero of Thermopylai, was the man 'most heartily admired' in the defending force. That looks like legend, and a corresponding comment shows not only Herodotos' fair-mindedness but perhaps his equal liability to accept tendentious statements from barbarians as well as from Greeks; of all his 'countless' host, 'no one was more worthy than Xerxes, through stature and appearance, to hold such power' (7.187). That comment might well bring down the accusation of 'pro-barbarian' — and admirer of despotism! Curiosities include Arganthonios (1.163) who ruled Tartessos for eighty years and lived to 120, a rival to Nestor and even Old Testament longevity; and the Atarantes of Skythia who are 'the most anonymous' individuals.

Records in inanimate spheres are less prominent, but do occur in the geographical sections, or are mentioned as particular items of note, as in a tourist guide. We have noted the engineering feats on Samos, while those of Egypt were obvious candidates for inclusion. Natural features range from the most fertile soil, in Babylonia, to the largest of rivers, the Danube (apparently outclassing the Nile on account of its more constant volume) — and 'the most bile-forming grass' of Russia. Had our traveller witnessed an autopsy on a bloated cow?

'Marvels', another tourist guide ingredient, are often listed precisely as such — in answer to the presumed question 'What is worth seeing now we're here?' Others turn up, suggested by some historical connection with the area; thus the Ardericca oil well, which also produced both fresh and salt water, is mentioned in the context of the settlement nearby of Ionians transported after the collapse of the revolt (6.119).

A favourite notion of journalists is 'human interest'. We return to the Persian noble, Intaphernes, last seen, with all his male relatives, languishing in gaol. We would expect all to be executed, for 'root and branch' was ever the motto of despots, and the point has been made that Dareios brooked no insubordination even from former close associates. The record of their execution would require only a brief phrase; but there intrudes the pathetic tale of the appeal made by Intaphernes' wife, who surprisingly had not been arrested (Dareios of all people should have been aware of the potent political influence of women). When granted the life of one member of the family she chose not husband or son, but brother, producing (sophistic?) reasoning which appealed so much to Sophokles that he borrowed it for Antigone. Unlike the events that necessitated it, this incident had no historical impact, unless possibly as evidence, in Herodotos' even-handed manner, that even a Persian despot need not be totally deaf to pleas for clemency. Indeed, Dareios doubled his original offer and spared one of the sons as well (3.119).

A good story of any kind appeals to journalists and laymen alike, whatever emotions it may arouse. One extraordinary example of Herodotean addiction to such tales is the very long digression (placed within the longest 'digression' of all, the Egyptian *logoi*) which may be called 'The Tale of the Clever Thief' (2.121ff.). Too long even to summarise here, it is totally fictitious, the Pharaoh concerned unidentifiable (though Rhampsinitos might just be a Hellenic corruption of Rameses[13]) and clearly derives from folklore. Having some features in common with Ali Baba, the hero, despite losing his brother in the course of their depredations of the king's treasury, is finally pardoned and in the best fairy-story manner ends by marrying the king's daughter. Herodotos does not add to the implausibility by stating that 'they lived happily ever after'; and it is to be noted that in more ways than one he emphasises that it was merely 'a tale that is told'.[14] If anyone complains that the inclusion of such a tale is the negation of 'proper' history, Herodotos would argue that light relief is a necessary ingredient of a long discourse (as Shakespeare felt with his tragedies) and that the story was too good to leave out. The Gyges affair already mentioned certainly demanded inclusion on this count, in addition to its claim to historical relevance.

But sometimes Herodotos left things out. If his criteria for inclusion were remarkably elastic, one would not expect a large number of reasons for exclusion. One that is explicit is religious scruple, a feeling that certain matters were 'tabu'. He 'prefers not to say' why the Egyptians represented 'Pan' as goat-faced, not merely goat-footed as in Greece; nor does he find it 'seemly' to state the reason, though he knows it, why pigs are sacrificed only to 'Selene and Dionysos' (2.46f.). Such reticence is particularly common in the Egyptian *logoi*, but appears in a Greek context also, e.g. 7.197 on the rites appertaining to Phrixos and Helle.

Names of individuals may be withheld, as that of the Samian who 'acquired' the goods of a fugitive eunuch (4.43) or the names of commanders of ethnic land force contingents[15] in the Persian army (7.96). This last is excused by their relative unimportance, and the fact that the real commanders were the Persian generals; many of these units in reality never went to Greece. However, Herodotos does go on to name ten national commanders of naval squadrons, plus Artemisia his heroine, whose contribution in the number of ships was minor. Maybe this was a device to introduce the queen's name well before the stage at which she became prominent.

Occasionally, limitations of space can be adduced as reasons for omission. Herodotos the tireless researcher ascertained the names of all the 300 who fell at Thermopylai, but such a list would have been wearisome, despite a certain fondness for catalogues (which seems to have been part of the epic narrative inheritance).[16] He fails to list all the Ionian captains who distinguished themselves on the 'wrong' side at Salamis; his normal procedure after a battle account is to name those on both sides who most distinguished themselves, in accordance with the penchant for 'records'. But possibly the Ionians, constrained to fight under *force majeure*, were excluded on patriotic grounds — though collectively, their adequate performance is recognised. And such a suggestion is notably weakened by the case of Artemisia, whose dubious exploits are retailed.

What else is omitted? There are indeed plenty of gaps where the historical narrative is incomplete or unsatisfactory. These occur more often in the earlier phases of the war history; while the account of Marathon (490 BC) is defective, more so is that of the Ionian revolt, 498–494 BC, but less so that of the invasion of Xerxes, 480–479 BC. From these chronological data it is clear that the lack of reliable information — by Herodotos' fairly liberal criteria! — is to blame, while local rivalries, jealousies and even open hostilities had contributed to the perversion of traditions. Occasionally the author tells us that he was unable to ascertain the truth of such and such an event; the five alternative reasons offered by various sources for the end of Kleomenes (6.84) provide an outstanding example.

If information was to be found in his notes or in his memory, his tendency was to include it. 'The eunuchs and the harems at Susa became as important and interesting to the Athenians as the habitués [*sic*] of the White House after 1945 to contemporaries.'[17] Yet though so much diverse material is included, with one eye always upon the audience, this is no miscellany or anthology. The *logoi* are the continuous literary expression of the results of *historiē*; digressions within digressions, as Herodotos pointed out, occur naturally, in the absence of arbitrary, or indeed logical, conventions as to the limits of interest. Various reasons for gathering the diverse kinds of information have appeared; we must next proceed to consider how he would order and arrange these very different, even miscellaneous[18] areas, gobbets and shreds of information to create a reasoned history of the Persian War.

Notes

1. 'The materials cannot be separated, except *a posteriori* into the now-separate disciplines of history, geography, anthropology and so on; for they are all the result of Herodotos' *historiē*.' A. Roveri, 'La nascita delle forme storiche da Ecataeo ad Erodoto', Bologna Univ. Inst. Fil. Class, *Studi* 13 (1963) 3–52 (p. 23). See also H. Barth, 'Zur Bewertung und Auswahl des Stoffes durch Herodot', *Klio* 50 (1968) 93.

2. The importance of the application of reason or judgement, *gnomē*, to source material cannot be overstresed. The process represents one of the greatest breaks with the tradition of merely repeating uncritically what was handed down by earlier generations. (But note that scepticism had already been expressed by Hekataios.) Herodotos' public, by and large, were not educated to his own level of sophistication, and he explains for them as simply as possible the procedure adopted. See further Chapter 7.

3. Recent studies have advanced understanding in this area; see in particular R. Drews, *The Greek Accounts of Eastern History* (1973).

4. Whether Dareios in reality re-established the original Achaemenid dynasty or set up a new one of his own is a question lying beyond the scope of this book. Herodotos accepted the official version, and it is unlikely that he had much alternative.

5. For discussion of this notorious passage see the chapter on sources and the bibliography there cited.

6. The Oroites material may be classified as a separate logos, as has been done by Laura Boffo, 'Il logos di Orete in Erodoto', *Rend. Acc. Lincei* s.VIII, 34 (1979) 85–104.

7. There is scholarly dispute over the connection of the tyrant with the Heraion; but though Herodotos does not mention the name of Polykrates in the paragraph in question it can hardly be doubted that he implicitly associated all three constructions with the tyrant. (For the historian's 'Samian connection' see Chapter 7).

8. A modern commentator has described the menu at the Spartan common table as, first, a kind of porridge, and second, a kind of porridge. The enemies and rivals of Spartan power no doubt exaggerated.

9. See for example B. Shimron ('The First of Those we Know') [Greek title], *Eranos* 71 (1973) 45–51. J. Wikarjak has pointed out the historian's fondness for the term μοῦνος — 211 occurrences.

10. The Greeks in general notoriously took an exclusionist (or racist) view of their own society — a failing in which unfortunately they are not alone. Herodotos, while taking a more liberal view, could not claim universal knowledge. On a couple of occasions he does use the first person singular in making such a statement; e.g. 2.77 'of those I have visited' and 7.238 'of my personal knowledge'.

11. The Greeks paid quasi-divine or semi-divine honours not only to legendary heroes of the past (as Adrestos in Sikyon, 5.67) but also, *post mortem*, to founders of colonies, i.e. individuals officially commissioned to organise the new community.

12. Another recorded item of similar interest is the easy victory of Persian over Greek horses in a test race held by Xerxes, 7.196.

13. On 'Rhampsinitos' and the story generally see the commentary of How and Wells, *A Commentary on Herodotos* (1928), and for all Egyptian matters A. B. Lloyd, *Herodotos Book II, Introduction* (1975). *Commentary*, 1–98 (1976).

14. Constantly he uses such expressions as 'is said' or 'they say', and the whole tale is reported in *oratio obliqua*, indirect speech, which distances the author somewhat further from the report than the use of *oratio recta*.

15. The forces of Xerxes as catalogued by Herodotos would appear to represent the total army list of the Persian Empire, derived directly or indirectly from an official source. A number of these contingents never reappear in the narrative and most probably did not form part of the invading force. The main squadrons of the fleet, however, were present at various actions and of course were essential to the campaign, though it is not beyond dispute what part some of them actually played.

16. The question has recently been examined by R. Ball, 'Herodotos' List of the Spartans who Died at Thermopylae', *Mus. Afr.* 5 (1976) 1–8.

17. E. J. Bickerman and H. Tadmor, 'Darius I, pseudo-Smerdis and the Magi', *Athenaeum* 66 (1978) 239.

18. Not however constituting a miscellany, nor an anthology; see the sensible discussion by A. Roveri (n.1 above).

5 STRUCTURE OF THE HISTORY

In the preceding chapters we have specified the chronological and geographical scope necessitated by the choice of the Persian imperialist aggression against Greece as Herodotos' main topic. We have also seen that the starting-point of the main narrative lay in the reign of Kroisos of Lydia, perhaps around 560 BC, while the account ends with the capture of Sestos on the Dardanelles from its intransigent Persian defender late in 479. But there is a great deal that falls outside these sixty-odd years; not however *after* the defined *terminus ante quem*, save for two or three passing references.[1] Herodotos appears to have deliberately eschewed many enticing digressions offered by the later events.

There is a strict necessity for this divergence into the past, for one striving to write a reasoned history as Herodotos was. How was it, for instance, that Kroisos, King of Lydia, was in a position to make tributary the coastal Greek towns on Ionia? We are taken back, immediately, to the establishment of his dynasty, the Mermnads, after brief mention of their predecessors in the rule, who clearly belonged to the realm of legend rather than that of scientific history, but are reported none the less because 'that is what the Lydians say'. (Note too that like the Spartan royal houses which will be of direct interest before too long, they claimed descent from Herakles, son of Zeus!) Now this transfer of power was attributed to circumstances of a romantic and intriguing nature, the relating of which gave Herodotos an opportunity to indulge his penchant for such stories as well as to display his narrative and dramatic skill. The story of Gyges, certainly a historical character mentioned in Assyrian records, was also dramatised by an unknown playwright, fragments of whose work turned up some years ago in Egypt.[2] A brief account of his successors and their growing dominance of Ionia down to the fifth, Kroisos, is amplified by digressions small and large (to be considered later), but in particular by historical digressions on Athens and Sparta.

These two states undoubtedly played a leading role in the successful resistance of Greece to the attempted Persian conquest, and it is therefore of vital interest to know how they came to be the leading cities of Greece, in power and in political initiative, during the relevant period. The peg on which these two excursuses hang is the convenient one of an appeal by Kroisos, whose wishful thinking about the meaning of oracular pronouncements had encouraged him to project a preventive war against Kyros the Persian king, to the leading states respectively of the Ionians and the Dorians (1.56).

A tyranny, or dictatorship, had recently been established in Athens (c.556 BC). Dictatorship had been a fashionable political development in Hellas from the seventh century, and few states had not experienced a tyrant or a whole dynasty of tyrants at some time, Sparta being perhaps the most conspicuous exception. The manner in which Peisistratos gained control of Athens, a combination of trickery, political razzmatazz and force, and consolidated his position (temporarily!) by a dynastic marriage, enlightens the reader on an important stage in the progress of Athens to eminence.

From Athens we move to Sparta. The real facts of the emergence of the notorious Spartan socio-political and military system known as *Eunomia*, the 'Good Customs', are fairly obscure even now; what Herodotos offers is a mixture of myth, popular belief and official statement. However it was an indisputable fact that by the time in question the Spartans had military supremacy in Southern Greece. Their consent to Kroisos' request for a military alliance is then explained by further digression into previous relationships and the mention of interstate difficulties arising out of a Spartan present to Kroisos' predecessor Alyattes — a bronze bowl of 10,000 litres or 2,500 gallons capacity![3] So smoothly can a record-making item be introduced.

The connections, and the reasons for the content, of these digressions are evident enough. However Sparta and Athens then disappear from the scene, the latter totally until Book 5 is reached, the former achieving a couple of purely incidental mentions on the way to the same temporal conjuncture — half a century later. Once again a mission from east of the Aegaean visits Sparta and Athens seeking military aid, and in each case a further instalment of their history is introduced. This time the appellant is no barbarian, but a patriotic Greek canvassing support for an effort by the Ionians, under his leadership, to throw off the imperialist yoke. Digressional material of every kind is included, ranging from matters intimately connected with the historical events to purely 'informative' details which, by any standards other than those of Herodotos, could well have been omitted. The peculiar privileges of Spartan kings have already been noticed, and on the Athenian side the ancestry of the 'tyrannicides' perhaps falls into a similar category, though the particular interests in genealogy of both writer and public must not be forgotten. But a further dividend of this latter passage is that it leads to observations on the introduction of Phoenician alphabetic writing to Greece — an indubitable fact, but dated far too early; before the Trojan War in fact, instead of 400 or 500 years after the traditional date of the siege of Troy. One is prepared to forgive the error over this dating, to Herodotos untestable, but 'reasonably' attached to a legendary figure 'known' to have arrived in Greece from Phoenicia; the more so as he offers his personal opinion backed up by autopsy of epigrams, which he quotes. (The fact that modern knowledge makes the authenticity of these as originals more than dubious is hardly material to the present discussion; see below Chapter 7).

Certain aspects of this double introduction of Athens and Sparta at stages fifty years apart might seem to afford grounds for those who seek to persuade us that for Herodotos historical events fall into convenient categories, for each of which he had devised a 'pattern'. Apart from the inherent improbability of such a naïve view of history in so intelligent an individual, the way the two cases are handled presents more differences than similarities.[4] First, the order of appearance is reversed, and this would appear to depend on historical fact rather than the author's fancy. Next, no body of anonymous envoys, but a conspicuous individual, whose *ipsissima verba* are ostensibly recorded, in several interviews with the Spartan king. Thirdly, the outcome of the appeal to Sparta is the reverse of that earlier, while Athens, written off on the previous occasion by the Lydian envoys as insufficiently stable for an alliance, now offers to back the revolt.

The double introduction of individuals or peoples is however a feature of Herodotos' compositional method, as may be observed in a number of cases less vitally important to the main narrative. Kleisthenes of Sikyon, grandfather of the Athenian statesman of the same name, is first introduced in the excursus on Athens just mentioned; the changing of 'tribal' names for the Athenian constituencies by the younger Kleisthenes recalls a similar[5] name-changing by the despot of Sikyon; however unconvincing the statement of Herodotos that the grandson was imitating his grandfather — here *gnomē* appears to have failed the historian unless the comparison is deliberately ironical (see Chapter 9) — the train of thought provoked by the coincidence brings in a number of intriguing items concerning the Peloponnesian city, its ethnic make-up and class system, religious observations for heroes, and even the earliest literary evidence on the still rather obscure origins of tragic drama in Greece.

The next appearance of the elder Kleisthenes is at 6.127 where he is called on to provide one of the reasons for the noted prestige and wealth of the Alkmaionid family. Megakles, a young man of that clan, made wealthy already through their friendship with Kroisos (the subject of a humorous anecdote (6.126)) sued for the hand of Kleisthenes' daughter in competition with a number of highly eligible bachelors from all over the Greek world. The demanding father of the maiden set a number of tests, in which Megakles was running second on aggregate marks until the final, crucial trial — a dinner party with unlimited quantities of wine. The leader at that point unfortunately let it go to his head, proceeding to give an exhibition of solo dancing which failed to please the host. Even less did the concluding item, in which the aspirant stood on his head and gesticulated with his legs. When one considers the dress of Greek youths, it is hardly surprising that he was disqualified, and Megakles won by default.

Here again we have a story, depending on the facts that Megakles of Athens did marry the daughter of the Sikyonian tyrant, a somewhat unusual occurrence,[6] and that no doubt the father was concerned to find a suitable potential ally for a son-in-law; the rest is fairy- or folk-tale, with parallels from other societies,[7] but the opportunity provided by the historical events to tell a good story cannot be passed over, remembering always that pure entertainment was one of Herodotos' aims, or perhaps more correctly, part of his method. 'Tell a joke occasionally so that the audience don't go to sleep.' But does the length of many such insertions into the historical framework prevent the audience from due concentration on the main narrative? This question presents itself more acutely in the cases, by no means uncommon, where the principal excursus involves further digressions within it (some examples have been given in the previous chapter) and yet more appendages seem to lead even further from the main path. Obviously, in the end, the historian brings his public back to the chief issue, but sometimes by devious routes. Individual readers must judge for themselves whether their interest and enjoyment are impaired or enhanced by these procedures. If all the material contained in the *History* had been presented in chronological order no reader or hearer would have been able to make head or tail of it. On the other hand, the snippets of material which would today appear only as footnotes had to be included in the main text because of the physical form of the book.

It is worth noting that the epic narrative, which could not fail to be influential with Herodotos, also indulged in digressions small and large; Homeric similes frequently become digressions by elaborating the picture far beyond the initial point of comparison; the lengthy identifications and genealogical lectures offered by warriors to one another before they join combat, and the vast 'flashbacks' so prominent in the *Odyssey* could be compared in detail with Herodotean practice.

The complex mass of discursive material[8] in Books 5, 52–96, and 6, 51–93, however, raises no more severe a problem than that posed by the preceding four books. In the first two, it is perhaps the length rather than the complicated structure of the digressions that is somewhat daunting. It is clearly impracticable to examine every one of the major digressions, long and short, down to 'one-liners',[9] which overall total at least 200. The first major one for examination is that after the conquest of Lydia by Kyros has been completed, in which the earlier career of Kyros is related. As Herodotos himself put it, his story 'demanded explanation' of how the Persians came to be in contact with Lydia; at the same time, emphasis is implicitly placed on the underlying 'motive', Persian expansionism, exemplified in the military exploits of Kyros. And of course as the Persian rulers had acquired the empire of the Medes to reach that situation, the rise of the Median monarchy too and its relationship to the Persian also suggested themselves as valuable, if not essential topics for discussion (1.96ff). The folk-tale source of much of the narrative of Deiokes (which serves perhaps not only to adorn a tale but to point a political moral), of Astyages, Harpagos and the young Kyros is evident. Yet overall it provides not too irrational an account, though Herodotos has more than one sceptical observation to offer.[10] At 1.141 he takes up the topic of Greco-Persian relations in the aftermath of the fall of Lydia; the annexation, by force where necessary, of the western coasts of Anatolia is of course an essential part of the main narrative. But Kyros did not carry out this supplementary conquest in person; he was busy elsewhere, and in particular with the metropolis of Mesopotamia, Babylon. The account of the reduction of Babylon is both preceded and followed by fairly brief descriptions of the city, the geography of Mesopotamia, and Babylonian customs. But the previous history is reserved, in a statement at 1.184, for separate treatment — a matter to which we shall shortly return. Kyros then ventures upon further aggression to the north, and with much picturesque and doubtless unhistorical detail, meets an appropriate end.

Book 2 begins with the accession of Kambyses, and the next stage in imperialist expansion, the projected invasion of Egypt. Such a move was the most obvious one, the highest priority for the consolidation of empire in the Middle East. Egypt, once great and powerful, constantly in rivalry with the rulers of Mesopotamia, had declined in military strength and presented little difficulty, save the logistic one of the desert crossing. It fell rapidly, and was never to regain its independence in ancient times. But its rich agricultural and technological resources made it a most desirable acquisition. Herodotos of course did not state all this explicitly, but the procedure he followed made very plain his opinion of the importance of Egypt.

Herodotos' account of Egyptian history is partial, chronologically preposterous and of little value, save for the most recent period;[11] however, the study of Egyptian culture is both full and fascinating, and to it he devotes most of the second book and the first thirty-eight sections of Book 3. He presents a great mass of detailed description of buildings, of religious, social and domestic practices, and Egyptian specialities such as embalming, not to mention the exotic fauna.[12]

This is by far the longest 'digression' or semi-independent *logos* in the work, and has both demanded and received special study from modern scholars.[13] The historian's favourable attitude towards the Egyptians and the achievements of their culture is undoubtedly the principal reason for the length of this mighty excursus — itself filled out, as we saw earlier, by at least one totally fictitious story, amongst other curious features — and manifestly he could hardly avoid being impressed, like any modern tourist, by the architectural splendours, but the 'scientific' side is of equal interest to the researcher. The presence, at the point where Persian designs lay claim to Egypt, of a section or chapter of background material needs no justification and is in Herodotos' usual manner; it is the extent of the *logoi* which needs further consideration.

A third factor certain to have led to the amplification of the Egyptian section was the popular interest of fifth-century Greece in

Egypt. This has been compared to eighteenth-century European interest in China, an 'upside-down land', where, as in ancient Egypt, everything seemed to be done the other way about (2.35) in a culture immemorial by comparison with that of its Western observers. In particular also Athens, which was obviously one of Herodotos' intended 'markets', had sent forces to assist the 'Egypt Liberation Army' fighting in the Delta to overthrow the Persian imperialists, on more than one occasion in the middle years of the century. The motive for this intervention was perhaps less strategic or ideological than economic. Trade with Egypt had been most actively carried on earlier by the Greek cities of the Asia Minor coast, as well as Rhodes and Aigina,[14] and important evidence thereon is supplied by Herodotos (2.178); these cities were now included in the Athenian sphere of influence.

The search for 'remarkable things' or 'wonders' that Herodotos maintained throughout his inquiries met its most fruitful field in Egypt, as he himself observes in the passage referred to above (2.35). 'I am spending a deal of time on my account of Egypt because it contains more marvels than all the rest of the world and more remarkable works as well.'[15] We noted above that the presence of three 'remarkable works' was put forward as justification for the length of the Samian *logoi*, and the same verb is used in the statement. The strange customs and the geography demanded no less attention than the Pyramids and the Labyrinth.

The length, detailed nature and partial lack of historical exactitude of Herodotos' account of Egypt suggest that it may have been separately composed. The 'Egyptian Tales' could indeed have stood as an independent publication, with very little editing; and one may then proceed to the assumption that what Herodotos first planned was a series of amplifications — and corrections, to be sure! — of similar works of Hekataios *et al.* A pointer is given in this direction by the casual reference to future 'Assyrian Tales' (1.184), which however fail to appear in the extant text of Herodotos. This incompleteness, evidently unintentional, has been much discussed, including argument as to the probable placing of such a section.[16] The latter question is unimportant, since pegs on which to hang such digressions turned up almost inevitably; the second capture of Babylon, by Dareios after its revolt, is an obvious candidate for the position, but Herodotos' mind went off on another tack, following the Hellenophil or Athenophil descendant of that Zopyros whose self-sacrifice had facilitated Dareios' victory. If one asks why the relatively important historical background material should have been postponed, instead of being given at the first appearance of that great centre of civilisation in historical affairs germane to the wars of Greeks and Persians, an answer has already been provided by the examples of multiple introduction discussed above.

A further case that illustrates the procedure is that of the Korinthian tyrants. Periandros appeared briefly early in the first book, as the interpreter of an oracle for his fellow-tyrant Thrasyboulos of Miletos; the case of Arion versus the pirates is appended. But here there is nothing as to the important part played by Periandros and his father Kypselos, the founder of the dynasty, in the history of Korinth. Korinth, after all, was perhaps the most important power behind Athens and Sparta in the Persian Wars. Periandros however reappears at 3.48 in the context of Korinthian/ Samian relations, and is guilty of a truly tyrannical deed,[17] consigning 300 youths to his ally Alyattes of Lydia for castration. There follows a dramatic account of Periandros' domestic troubles. But it is not until 5.92 that we hear the romantic tale of the escape from plotted murder of the infant Kypselos and his eventual securing of the lordship of Korinth, a story much embroidered from folk-tale sources. The power was subsequently transmitted to his son Periandros, but the occasion for the excursus is long after the death of Periandros and the later extinction of the tyranny, a fact not mentioned by Herodotos. It occurs in a speech by a Korinthian delegate to the meeting of allies called by the Spartans to assist them in restoring the tyranny at Athens; they had been instrumental in its removal but found the subsequent 'democratic' regime not at all complaisant. Soklees of Korinth, otherwise unknown to history, seizes the opportunity to point out the evils of tyranny, using the history of his own state to lend colour to his sermon.

Thus Korinthian 'history' only appears after several mentions of the city and its famous tyrants. There is therefore no substance in the view that Assyrian, or any other, *logoi* should be inserted at what seems to modern scholars the most appropriate place. As it happens, the 'Skythian tales' are incorporated in the account of Dareios' fairly unsuccessful invasion of South Russia; Skythians had received incidental mention on numerous earlier occasions. Similarly, the 'Libyan' anthropology is inserted in the record of an alleged Persian project of overrunning the North African coast — probably with a view to eventually annexing Carthage.

If the great 'digressions' were composed separately — there are, according to a recent publication, no less than twenty-eight of them[18] — then they have been pretty smoothly incorporated into the historical framework. One may criticise the length of some of them; the two passages quoted earlier suggest that Herodotos was not unaware of this possibility. The inclusion of descriptions, as in the last two digressions mentioned, of communities which never formed part of the Persian dominions might also be judged superfluous. But we have seen that Herodotos always intended to cast his net widely[19] and had few scruples as to the propriety of including exotic materials in what is only primarily a history of the Persian Wars.

The case for the unity of the whole work has in recent years been persuasively argued by J. Cobet.[20] Since there was no accepted form, no conventions for writing history, structure and arrangement were entirely at the discretion of the author. And even if originally the major *logoi* were formed independently, that is no reason why they should not form part of a unified design, as with a cycle of novels — or indeed the movements of a symphony.

The question of the order in which the various parts were composed is also immaterial to the unity of the whole. Every major component is skilfully and smoothly keyed into the grand design of the narrative. (The same cannot be said of many minor, incidental gobbets of information, but 'asides' are permitted to a lecturer, without detriment to the form of his offering.) It does not much matter then whether Herodotos began by being 'a Hecataean geographer' in A. B. Lloyd's phrase, and was led by his *historiē* into the question of origins and development of societies, their forms of government and so forth — a course which must lead in turn to consideration of historical processes. Alternatively he may have begun to write an account of the history of Xerxes, as has sometimes been maintained, and then found himself impelled to fill in the background.[21] What concerns us is the ultimate result. Still apparently unfinished at his death, as suggested by the absence of the Assyrian *logoi* and perhaps by some brief notices which suggest themselves as later additions,[22] the work deals substantially with the total subject, and deficiencies of information cannot be used to argue lack of design.

Another factor to be considered in assessing the unity of the composition is the method of publication. There certainly cannot have been anything resembling the process of modern publishing,

with numerous copies of the whole work made available simul-
taneously. If, as suggested earlier, the traditional belief in public
readings is correct, would not the writer of so lengthy a work
organise it so that excerpts could be presented as quasi-independent
offerings? This is the basis of Cagnazzi's theory (n. 18 above). We
should not look for too fine a finish overall, from that point of
view. It is of course known that the existing division into nine
books is not, or not necessarily, one decided or envisaged by
Herodotos himself; Alexandrian librarians were responsible for
plucking the number nine apparently out of the air,[23] for several of
the books are far too long to be comfortably managed on a single
papyrus roll. The Egyptian *logoi* in particular were so massive that
they could not be forced into the confines of a single, even
abnormally long roll. It looks as if Herodotos had other things in
mind than the convenience of booksellers and librarians — even
perhaps of readers.

Doubts concerning the appropriateness of the placing of some
shorter digressions may suggest a lack of care in detailed structuring. A case in point is the notorious passage describing the
Persian royal courier services, which provided a motto for the US
Postmaster-General's Department. That this should occur only in
Book 8, not in the Persian *logoi* of Book 1 or, preferably, in Book 3
with the general reorganisation of the empire of Dareios, has struck
commentators as strange. The item would be of great interest to
Greeks, whose means of communication were notoriously
primitive.[24] But is it not probable that Herodotos, reaching the
historical point of Xerxes' victory-despatch from Athens, was
reminded of the means by which it was conveyed and said to
himself 'Damn! That should have been in Book 3'? But having
already (perhaps!) delivered that portion to an audience, he could
not send out 'correction slips'. Quite a number of such brief
digressions would appear to stand where they do because suggested
to the author's memory by a parallel; this might be the case with the
first Kleisthenes excursus with its fanciful parallel.

Knowledgeable readers will be uneasy at the fact that no discussion has yet been offered of the lengthy and probably unhistorical account of the dealings of Solon with Kroisos. The philosophical aspect must be deferred till later; no problem of
appropriateness of placing arises. Kroisos has for the moment
become central to the action, and the cue for Solon's arrival is the
attractiveness of his court, practically a world capital by

Mediterranean standards. The chronological implausibility may be ignored;[25] both protagonists rapidly became figures of legend to whom tales were attached.

In the previous chapter adequate justification has been provided for the inclusion of both this episode, and the 'tragedy' of Atys and Adrastos which follows it, and bears a philosophical link with it and with the attitude of Kroisos to oracles. But whether Herodotos has selected Solon's wisdom and the follies of Kroisos as a demonstration of his own philosophy of history is doubtful; their positional prominence bears a more prosaic interpretation. Nor can one attach too much importance to the apparent emphasis laid by the length and detailed nature of any excursus on its subject-matter. The 'one-line' reference to Perikles in what is as near to a footnote as possible would in that case appear to suggest that Perikles was less historically important, in the historian's eyes, than the handsome Philippos (see Chapter 4). But he was well aware of the part played by the Athenian politician in the struggle for hegemony which he blamed for the contemporary troubles of Hellas. On the other hand, the tale of 'Rhampsinitos and the thief' is told at great length; one would be hard pressed to find either relevance or a moral lesson therein! And is Egypt more important to the *History* than Persia?

The *History* (as it stands) ends with a moralising observation attributed to Kyros; some commentators accordingly seize on this 'proof' of a predominating moral interest (for which see Chapter 8); others find that it cannot have been written by Herodotos! Let us not approach such matters with unconfirmed prejudice. Another possible reason for ending the *History* with the Kyros anecdote (supposing that to have been the author's intention) was to achieve the 'quiet close' exemplified by the ending of the *Iliad*. Such an epic device also perhaps appears at the end of Book 7, where the 'coda' to the disaster of Thermopylai is the anecdote of Gorgo's unique ability to decipher the secret message.

One final point as to structure. The historian is concerned with variety of method, rather than with 'patterns' of narrative (still less, patterns of events). A good example is the use of both direct and indirect speech in reporting the (supposed) words of characters. A case in point is the affair of Mnesiphilos and Themistokles discussed earlier. Though descriptions of strange lands and the exotic customs of their folk tend to have common programmes there is no barren similarity between the various accounts; 'variety' would seem to deny 'pattern'. Anyone who doubts Herodotos' literary skill in this area would do well to look at *Marco Polo's Account of his Travels*. This displays many of the same natural interests as Herodotos, but in many cases Polo (or his editor or ghost-writer Rustichello) constantly repeats the same formulary phrases.

Notes

1. The most important are 6.98, referring to the Peloponnesian War generally, 7.133 the Theban raid on Plataia which opened hostilities in 431 BC; 6.98 to the earthquake at Delos, and 7.137 to the fate of the sons of Sperthias and Boulis in 430. For the striking omissions, see Fornara (Chapter 1, n. 10 above).

2. Plato, *Rep.*, Book 2, 359d–360, tells a quite different story, a fairy-tale concerning a magic ring. Thus Kroisos' ancestor had also become a figure of legend. Possibly the real Gyges appears in the Old Testament as the troublesome King Gog. No moral lesson, surely, is to be drawn from the Herodotean story? However the repeated statement that Kandaules' behaviour was contrary to *nomos* (but only in the mouths of the other characters) might suggest otherwise.

3. The iron bowl of Exampaios, 4.81, was alleged to hold twice as much again, and accordingly some commentators regard it as mythical. The Spartan product however is rendered more convincing by the famous 'crater' of Vix in central France, part of the grave-goods of a Gallic princess, certainly Greek and generally thought to be of Spartan manufacture and sixth-century date.

4. It might be argued that Herodotos has used the historical basis of the visit by Aristagoras in 499/8 to construct a parallel version, unattested, of a mission under Kroisos. But the king was in regular touch with the Greek world both through his Ionian tributaries and the 'international' shrines; and such a theory would totally deny the conscientiousness of Herodotos as an historian — too drastic, surely.

5. But totally otherwise motivated, despite the political aims of both personages. Obviously in the second case, the change from four 'tribes' to ten necessitated a change of nomenclature.

6. Many Greek states only recognised as legitimate marriages between persons of citizen status; but tyrants could make their own laws and frequently used dynastic marriages to form alliances with their counterparts in other cities. That this marriage was recognised in Athens was really quite surprising, despite the temporary political alliance of Alkmaionids and Peisistratos.

7. W. Aly, *Volksmärchen Sage und Novelle bei Herodot und seinen Zeitgenossen* (1921; 2nd edn, 1969) is the authoritative survey of folk-tale elements in the *History*. See also H. V. Rose, *Handbook of Greek Mythology*, 293.

8. H. R. Breitenbach, in a paper entitled 'Herodotos Pater Historiae', *Schweiz. Zeitsch. für Gesichte* 16 (1966) 465–500 offers the amusing illustration of a cactus (Exkurskaktus) for these multiple digressions. See also my 'The Structure of Herodotos' Narrative', *Antichthon* 8 (1974) 1–10; and C. W. Fornara, *Herodotus; an Interpretative Essay* (1971) *ad init.*

9. The form of the papyrus roll itself prevented relegation of interesting but inessential snippets of information to the end of a book. On the other hand, the lecture-form requires their inclusion at the moment their 'peg' appears.

10. Herodotos was well aware that these versions of the past could not be taken *au pied de la lettre*; he enjoyed the tale, and not without irony offered a political lesson for Greek hearers.

11. It happens that the quantity of Egyptian documentary evidence is less than for many earlier dynasties, and the value of Herodotos' account is thereby enhanced. See A. B. Lloyd (n. 13 to Chapter 4).

12. The humorous attitude of Greeks, or perhaps especially the mercenary soldiers — among the first Greeks to make any prolonged stay in Egypt — to strange fauna such as crocodiles, hippopotami and ostriches appears in the facetious nomenclature given them in Greek: 'yellow cowards', 'river-horses' and 'camel-sparrows'.

13. The first detailed examination was that of Sourdille in 1910, the most recent and sound that of A. B. Lloyd in 1975 (n. 13 to Chapter 4).

14. References to Egypt and to Greek voyages thither occur as early as Homer (Lloyd, *Introd.*, pp. 10ff.); trade, as well as the adventurous mercenaries (cf. Herodotos 2.152) of whom the graffiti on the gigantic leg of Rameses II (ML no. 7) are the most notorious evidence, had brought constant visitors during the sixth century. Naucratis was the principal emporium, as Herodotos notes in the passage cited.

15. See Lloyd (Ch. 4, n. 13).

16. J. G. Macqueen, 'The Assyrian Logoi of Herodotus and their Position in the Histories', *CQ* 38 (1978) 284 and R. Drews, 'Herodotus' Other Logoi', *AJPh* 91 (1970) 181.

17. Periandros is the Machiavellian tyrant in his advice to Thrasyboulos to 'fell the tall poppies'; not so in the Arion story, though he is shrewd enough to catch the pirates out. However his solid achievements in promoting Korinth's economy are perhaps best illustrated by the diolkos or tramway for transporting small ships across the Isthmus, revealed by archaeology.

18. S. Cagnazzi, 'Tavola dei 28 logoi di Erodoto', *Hermes* 103 (1975) 385–432. She would divide the whole work into 'manageable' sections of about 25–30 Teubner pages, which could then be 'recited' in about a couple of hours.

19. The 'barbarians' of the Proem, clearly Persians in the first instance, may easily be extended to include other peoples within the Persian Empire; no great obstacle precludes its further extension to any nations whatsoever.

20. J. Cobet, *Herodots Exkurse und die Frage der Einheit seines Werkes*, Historia Einzelschriften 17 (1971). See also the article by Breitenbach (n. 8 above). Less emphatic is Truesdell S. Brown: 'At times the plot seems mainly a device for tying together a fascinating series of digressions on the peoples of the world', *Historia* 11 (1962) 269. An opposing view, held by E. Howald (*Hermes* 58 (1923) 113) and others, is that Herodotos wrote not history but a collection of stories. More recently Drexler, in partial agreement, denied the title of historian to Herodotos, *Herodot-Studien* (1972) 57.

21. Many critics have felt that the last three books, with the invasion of Xerxes as their subject-matter, are more unified, have fewer digressions, and are closer to the epic in narrative style. Naturally there are fewer long digressions of the anthropological type, but short digressions are especially numerous in the second half of Book 7. Catalogues occur in this part for obvious reasons; while the motive for giving the genealogy of Leonidas, said to be an epic feature, is evident, and no epic genealogy, I fancy, is of such length.

22. Possible examples include 3.160 (the descendants of Zopyros), 7.233 (the son of Leontiades raids Plataia in 431 BC), 9.73 (Spartan respect for Dekeleia). At 7.190 the note on Ameinokles' misfortune has been thought an addition by some other hand, since it is so tantalisingly imprecise, but it stood in the text used by Dionysios of Halikarnassos, around the Christian era.

23. The names of the Nine Muses were at some stage attached to the nine books, a nice compliment to Herodotos' versatility, perhaps because the work had already been divided into nine sections. Conversely, the Nine Sisters may have been selected as patrons, and the history divided appropriately. Diodoros, writing in the time of Augustus, is the first to mention the ninefold division.

24. Not only did the Greeks of Herodotos' day have nothing approaching a road (except possibly the Sacred Way from Athens to Eleusis), they had never thought of relays of messengers. In a dire emergency, the Athenian government sent a single runner to cover the 200+ kilometres to Sparta — with an oral message (6.106)!

25. Since modern scholars are not in agreement over the actual date of Solon's legislation (and consequently, of his travels abroad), Herodotos may perhaps be forgiven this lapse. See, for example Molly Miller, 'The Accepted Date for Solon; Precise, but Wrong', *Arethusa* 2 (1969) 62–86.

6 THE HERODOTEAN NARRATIVE

A number of factors must be considered to have influenced the methods adopted by Herodotos in telling his long and complicated story. Most of these have already come under brief scrutiny; they include the influence of epic poetry on narrative style, the vast variety of topics covered, the audience(s) aimed at, and the method of publication.

Certain features of content, not necessarily always dictated by historiographic needs, reflect the dominance of the Homeric poems over most Greek writers. While deliberately discarding the form, and distancing themselves from the epic, no Greek poets were able to escape it entirely. Tragic writers too were bound to feel it, especially in those cases which were said to have been described as 'slices from Homer's rich banquet'.[1] The presence of catalogues is a prominent feature of epic poetry, the Catalogue of the Ships in *Iliad* Book 2 being only the most familiar example; it is paralleled, if that is not too precise a term, by the great catalogue of Xerxes' invasion forces. Many other, lesser lists can be cited; of Ionian cities, of Greek fleets and so on. In a modern work, should it be thought necessary to include the detailed information, a footnote would be its usual position.

Genealogy, the importance of which to Herodotean historiography has brought it to mention in each of the preceding chapters, is another component with an obviously epic ancestry. In the oral transmission of the legends fixed points were provided by genealogical references, which may or may not have been of much importance to the story (though in certain cases having vital relevance), but were of no small interest to later individuals or groups who claimed, with or without justification, to be descended from such-and-such a hero or part-historical personage. The sort of difficulty into which such a belief might lead an overenthusiastic searcher for ancestors is amusingly displayed, not without a hint of malice, by Herodotos in relating the discomfiture of Hekataios at the hands of Egyptian priests. These gentry could very easily demonstrate that none of their own contemporaries could possibly have been descended from a deity at the distance of a mere sixteen generations; gods were simply not around among men at such a

61

late date (2.143)! Hekataios' family tree was however not at all dissimilar in length to those of the Spartan kings Leonidas (7.204) and Leotychidas (8.131). Their descent was, it seems, guaranteed for Herodotos by the generally accepted official Spartan version.[2] The epic nature of the Leonidas passage, coming at the beginning of the semi-legendary battle of Thermopylai, is reinforced by the statement that he was 'the most admired' or 'impressive' of the entire force.[3] An epic king or chieftain must always be 'the greatest'. And to show that patriotism is not the only motive for such glorification, a similar statement had been made about the Persian king Xerxes a half-dozen pages earlier (7.187).

An episode such as that of Onesilos and his squire, displaying epic chivalry and *philotimía* would fit very neatly into an epic (5.111). So would the preliminary stages of fighting at Plataia (9.21ff.) with the appeal of the hard-pressed Megarians, the prowess of the Athenian cavalry, and above all the death of Masistios and the subsequent scene of mourning, with the 'heroic' Greek admiration of the enemy's corpse, remarkable in its stature. The claim is probably correct that a greater number of epic borrowings or parallels are to be found in the last three books than elsewhere. The fact has been used to support the thesis that these books were the first part composed.[4] But it is in these later books that the events, at least those in which the Greeks are directly involved,[5] move on to a truly Homeric stage. Verbal reminiscences are quite numerous, but it is pointless to list them for Greekless readers; certain phrases such as 'What a word hast thou uttered' (7.103) in the mouth of Xerxes (once more!) are striking; it had occurred in an earlier passage (5.106) where Histiaios so addresses King Dareios — no one would describe Histiaios as an epic character — and other such reminiscences may be detected at 3.14, 5.17, 7.10, 7.159 and 9.60. Particular words found otherwise only in epic occur at 7.10 and 223, 9.50.

'Ring-composition', in the limited sense of a return at the end of a section (digressive or otherwise) to the subject announced at the beginning, in a formulating phrase, is a conspicuous epic mannerism. Most readers will be familiar with the closing line of the *Iliad* 'In this way they celebrated the funeral of Breaker Hector'. Compare an episode in Book 7 of the *History* which is introduced by 'King Xerxes took it very ill . . . So King Xerxes took the death of Artachaes very ill' (7.117). The divisions between the twenty-eight *logoi* enumerated by Cagnazzi (n. 18 to Chapter 5) are all marked in this way.[6] It may of course be objected that this procedure is typical of the ancient Greek language in general rather than of the epic in particular.

More important however than such somewhat superficial reminiscences or resemblances, is the technique of dramatisation. Herodotos viewed the epic not as a reliable historical source — we have noted his disposition to criticise its reliability as evidence for 'historical' fact — but as a *praeparatio historiae*;[7] myth, as non-rational narrative, can develop into *logos*, a *rational* account; *historiē* may confirm a statement of the poet, but equally and in the light of *gnomē* may condemn it. But more central to Herodotos' purpose was the method of presentation (which indeed in itself was in no small degree responsible for the charm of the old tales) and I think we may take it that if any external influence induced the historian to make such extensive use of dramatisation it was the epic.[8] By dramatisation I mean the putting of speech, either as dialogue or as more formal orations, into the mouths of his personages. Any reader of the Homeric poems does not have to be reminded how large a proportion of the whole is speech, purporting to have been uttered in council or at banquet, on the battlefield or in the ships. The dramatic skill of the poet has meant that we remember scenes of public or private dialogue perhaps more sharply than the fearful mêlées before Troy. Similarly, Herodotos never hesitates to make his people talk, and this is one reason why his work makes such a vivid and naturalistic impression upon his readers. The phenomenon is self-explanatory as regards conversation, dramatic scenes not merely narrated but 'staged' as it were; one thinks immediately of Kandaules, Gyges and the former's wife, of Kroisos and Solon, Dareios and Atossa, Xerxes and Artabanos. It is hardly necessary to point out that in by far the majority of cases Herodotos can have had no real evidence for what was actually said. No more of course did his epic predecessors, save by virtue of that 'hot line' to divine inspiration which they claimed — but which in the serious (if not always solemn!) context of history was replaced in Herodotos' claim by *historiē*, research. Of the above examples, the first has all the marks of fiction — though the framework was almost certainly not Herodotean fiction. The conversations were highly confidential, spoken in a non-Greek language, not recorded in writing, and indeed in the circumstances one might suppose they were not intended to be overheard even by trusted members of the royal entourage (1.8ff.). Lastly, nearly three centuries had elapsed between Herodotos' date for the episode and the time of writing. The historian here employs his narrative/dramatic powers for the benefit of his audience; the episode is historically unimportant and it is difficult to extract a serious moral import from it, unless it be that the sins of the fathers are to be expiated by the fifth generation of their children.[9] Herodotos makes no apology for his licence, nor should any be required; various implicit justifications for dramatisation are to be found, but the technique itself is taken for granted. For such a scene, the pleasure of the hearing (and no doubt the telling: Herodotos would seem to be an artist who enjoyed his work) is adequate justification.

The bedroom scene between Dareios and Atossa (3.134) falls perhaps into a similar category of historical implausibility, but it has a purpose directly connected with the second great aim of the historian, rational explanation. The Great King might, it would not be unreasonable to suppose, indulge or not in imperialist adventures at his own discretion. The emphasis upon the role of the individual in the *History* has received much attention and a good deal of unfavourable comment — but that is another story. However, individuals themselves must be motivated to action, and Atossa's remarks to Dareios combine neatly an appeal to personal prestige and the *nomos* of the Persians with a suggestion of the difficulty Persian rulers notoriously experienced in controlling the noblemen. Such considerations could have been advanced by the historian himself; but he preferred to dramatise them, and chose a particularly fitting mouthpiece. It has been alleged that one of Herodotos' principles of causation was 'cherchez la femme' and maybe that operated here; but the Persian royal ladies did possess influence — which is hardly surprising to most of us — and Atossa was in a particularly strong position to exercise such influence, as she herself represented one of Dareios' real bases of power.[10] Now slaves may have manned (if that is the appropriate term for eunuchs) the approaches to the royal bedchamber or the chamber itself; but they are not likely to have overheard, understood or made notes of such a conversation, and it is too fanciful to suggest that the Greek doctor Demokedes, on whom Herodotos certainly had good sources of information, was in Atossa's confidence to the extent implied by the story. But the motives, all credible, for Dareios' decision to invade Greece have been vividly presented in this fictional scene.

As the story moves closer to his own place and time, Herodotos may conceivably have received oral tradition about what was said. When Aristagoras went to Sparta just after 500 BC, he was received by that extraordinary character King Kleomenes. Aristagoras was not, in Herodotos' account, one of the most impressive individuals in that period of history, despite the important part he played in the events leading up to the Persian invasions of the Greek mainland.[11] Kleomenes, on the other hand, appears (though somewhat ambiguously at times) as one of the most striking, political and individualistic men to occupy either of the Spartan 'thrones'. He overreached himself, no doubt, was eventually checkmated by 'the system', and came to a dramatically wretched end, so ambivalent traditions prevailed about him in Sparta, where the accepted orthodoxy held him to have gone mad and committed suicide. A story about the irregularity of his birth was also current (5.40f.). Yet his positive achievements were such that there was undoubtedly a contrary myth, and though Kleomenes shows less than perfect rectitude towards the foreigner's proposition, and has to be prompted by his nine-year-old daughter, his final decision is presented as correct and laudable. An orally transmitted version of these dealings may have come to Herodotos during his stay at Sparta — apparently a quite lengthy stay, to judge by the quantity of detailed information he offers, in Books 1 and 5 particularly. So it is possible that the famous remark attributed to the precocious Gorgo is not an invention of Herodotos, who allows Aristagoras a quite lengthy discourse, evidently composed to suit the occasion. To this the king's reply is reported in indirect speech, to the effect that he would take twenty-four hours to consider the request. Finally, with the true Spartan laconicism, he utters three lines only of dismissal to the ambassador. Clearly, some attempt at characterisation underlies the differences — but the traits disclosed are those of stereotypes rather than individuals; characterisation is not the main purpose of dramatisation, but subsidiary.[12]

Aristagoras' visit is no doubt historical. His speech represents what he considers 'suited to the occasion' (as Thukydides defined his own fictional speeches). Unfortunately he overplayed his hand, and the reason he is made to do so is that, as Herodotos knew, his mission was unsuccessful; the known (or assumed by fifth-century Athenians) reluctance of Sparta to send forces far from home was to him the real reason for its failure, not a mere pretext.

We have already noticed the episode of the speech-making before the battle of Salamis and need not re-examine it here. But these orations supposedly were presented, not only at a major crisis of the greatest of the Persian invasions but also (with one exception) in public or at least within the high command, and only fifty years at most before Herodotos wrote; they differ therefore in circumstances from the purely fictional. It is not improbable that memory survived of the *kind* of things that were said, impressed on the minds of auditors deeply enough for them to remember them many years later. Not likely however that survivors repeated them directly to the historian himself; the high officers of 480 BC were not still around, one imagines, when Herodotos collected the material thirty or forty years on.[13] A younger generation however surely showed sufficient interest in such a famous victory to have preserved *a* version — or versions, differing according to where the research was conducted. What Herodotos has done in such cases is to supply the literary dressing, and dramatise the perhaps bare, perhaps too decoratively embroidered, body of tradition.

An intermediate case between complete fiction and approximation to fact is provided by the interviews between King Xerxes and two of his advisers, Mardonios and Artabanos, and also those between the Great King and the Spartan exile Demaratos. In the case of the Persian grandees — uncles of the king, no less — it must be extremely improbable that Herodotos acquired any genuine information. What went on in the king's throne room was certainly more public than confidences in his bed; but the most likely explanation of the content of these speeches is Herodotos' awareness that there were at least two schools of thought in Persia regarding imperialist adventures. One, as he had been at pains to indicate on more occasions than the remarkable Atossa episode mentioned above, firmly regarded Persia as the destined ruler of the world — a world perhaps originally limited to 'Asia' with a western boundary at the still artificial dividing line of the Bosporus and Dardanelles. (Both sides of the narrow seas had been colonised by the Greeks, and both form part of Turkey today.) Mardonios is selected as the mouthpiece of this view for the simple reason of the obvious inference from his command on two separate occasions of an invasion force. Artabanos, on the other hand, who was (historically, we may believe) sent back to base by Xerxes before the invasion proper began (7.53), is a fitting spokesman for the opposing view. Whether the character with which he is thus invested bears any genuine relation to the facts is indeterminable, but the tradition of the king's dreams that form the opening of Book 7 will have had some influence. (These matters will merit further investigation in the next chapter.) The two speakers then put forward the opposing arguments, as the historian assessed them.

Information about Demaratos is extraordinarily copious in Herodotos' account. His actual importance in the campaign of Xerxes would not appear to have been very great, though obviously if he was trusted by the king, as the Herodotean story is at pains to establish, the value of a knowledgeable Spartan commander to the Persian intelligence service could have been considerable. Some source closely connected with the exiled king has been postulated, in addition of course to the no doubt conflicting versions current in Sparta; but once again, direct knowledge of conversations between Demaratos and Xerxes is not to be credited. Herodotos has used Demaratos, as well as Mardonios and Artabanos amongst others, to put forward certain ideas of his own — or ideas accepted by him — about the strategy of the Persian invasions, as well as reflections of a moral variety. In the epic, the poet, concealing his own personality, would never have adverted *in his own person* to the strategic situation. Herodotos' successors might well have done, but often they preferred to set forth such considerations in speeches attributed to historical personages. The conversations of Artemisia and the king (8.68f., 101f.) also deal with the military situation: knowledgeable as the queen may well have been, the tradition of her intimate (and secret!) interviews is clearly a Halikarnassian version, gladly accepted by Herodotos; Artabanos is no longer around and his views on strategy need a proponent.

It has recently been pointed out that in early Greek historio-graphy the narrative is (with some exceptions) reserved for *events*; explanation and analysis are found in the speeches.[14] Herodotos however, illustrating the intermediate stage of rational narrative, is not always reluctant to speak *in propria persona*. At times indeed his self-revelation has offended critics, for instance in the some-what specious defence of the Alkmaionids against the charge of 'Medism'; it was alleged that they had communicated with the invading enemy after Marathon (6.121). Again, his encomium on Athens as the principal agent of victory against Xerxes is not entrusted to any speaker, but put forward as the historian's own considered view (7.139). To conclude, the technique of dramatisation is principally adapted from the epic, its artistic purpose is to vivify the picture for the benefit of the audience, and its historiographical purpose the propounding of views on strategic, political and other questions in a manner readily acceptable to that audience. 'Actors', usually but as we have seen not invariably principals, expound the thinking and motivation which the historian believed underlay the actions.

The fact that these speakers are not necessarily important historical personages may prove to be significant. It used to be urged that Herodotos, novelist or dramatist *manqué*, placed direct speech in the mouths of individuals to characterise them. Of course character may and does emerge from speeches, but this is not the main object of Herodotos' speeches (with certain exceptions). A simple and evident but sometimes neglected fact should make this clear. A number of important speeches are put in the mouths of otherwise insignificant personages. Soklees of Korinth appears on one occasion only, to make one of the longest orations in the *History*, his tirade against dictatorship (5.92). Mnesiphilos of Athens is momentarily heard of, urging Themistokles to a better strategic course, then vanishes as suddenly as he appeared. What purpose could there be in characterising such persons? They are mere ventriloquists' dummies, dolls brought out to put forward a particular view or recommend for or against a certain course of action. What is more, we also have speeches in the mouths of anonymous persons, or of groups — the latter an example followed by Thukydides, notoriously in the 'Melian Dialogue' (Book 5 fin.). Thus 'the envoys of the Greeks' address Gelon (7.157) and 'the envoy of the Athenians' follows up the tyrant's rejoinder; true, the Spartan envoy Syagros is named as befits the head of the mission, and utters his half-dozen lines — but never appears again thereafter. In such cases, quite manifestly, the purposes of dramatisation are as defined above.

It is of course *prima facie* quite likely that Herodotos was considerably influenced in his tendency to a great deal of dramatisation by the tragic drama of Athens. However, such plays are not primarily narrative, except for the artificial convention of 'messenger's speeches', but consist of exploration of a given situation; and their interest lies mainly in character — what sort of person will act in what way? The character dictates the type of response to the situation. But in writing history, the 'plot', so to speak,[15] is foreordained. Herodotos is not about to pervert the actual course of events, and in fact it is rather misleading to use such a term in connection with history. The motivation (and non-personal causation) of events can be explained by means of speeches put in the mouth of participants; in a sense, the converse of tragic writing.

Of course Herodotos does not invariably use direct speech in reporting what his characters may be supposed to have said. Indirect speech, which in Greek, it should be pointed out, is more strongly differentiated from direct than is the case in English, is used more sparingly in the *History*. Frequently an incident or 'scene' shows a combination of the two; for instance at 1.153 Kyros' 'actual words' to the Spartan envoys are presented, but the reply of the Spartans is a mere reported statement. The same phenomenon occurs between Anaxandridas and the Spartan ephors at 5.39; at 6.1 the reverse order of variation has question and answer between Artaphernes and Histiaios in reported speech, followed by the actual words of the satrap's famous *mot* on the instigation of the Ionian revolt: 'You made the shoe, Aristagoras only put it on.' This, like other such brief and striking utterances, including maybe that of Gorgo above, could have been faithfully reported in oral tradition.

These cases and numerous others[16] suggest that Herodotos prefers not to rely on a standardised technique but seeks variety. This view is strengthened by cases like that of Aristagoras' visit to Athens where he is given no speech; he had his turn, so to speak, at Sparta. Compare the case of Themistokles mentioned in Chapter 1. At 6.105 Pan's message to Pheidippides as he ran over the Arcadian mountains is reported indirectly, but the runner on arrival in Sparta has breath to utter his appeal! This last case might be linked with another apparent motive for the use of reported speech by the historian; namely that he does not accept, or at least he is sceptical about, the story. A report in indirect speech is subtly removed one degree further from guaranteed authenticity than the quotation of 'actual' words. A prime example, and much the longest passage of indirect speech, is the tale 'Rhampsinitos and the Clever Thief' (2.121ff.), of which Herodotos surely recognised the folk-tale origin. A little further on comes Cheops' prostitution of his daughter, 'as the Egyptians said'; their account was defective anyway, as Herodotos ironically pointed out, for they failed to specify the fee charged by the princess for her services. Similarly at 3.3 an anecdote of the juvenile Kambyses in the harem, beginning in direct quotation, lapses into reported speech; it is a story which the historian does not credit.[17]

A recent study[18] finds that the basic structure of the *History* is provided by twenty-eight individual *logoi* later grouped by Alexandrian 'editors' into nine books; three *logoi* to a book, except for the fifth which comprises four shorter pieces. They are linked in the manner 'here ends the tale of X; now I turn to Y' already mentioned. The aspect of this highly plausible view that now concerns us is not the fairly minor epic mannerism, but the sizeable though manageable chunks into which the history can be bloodlessly dissected. It is not reasonable to suppose that Herodotos would either compress or inflate[19] all of a topic into a single lecture — for surely, such portions are intended as lectures — and there are for example three separate *logoi* for Egypt, with differing subject-matter. Even if Herodotos did not set out on his writing with such a method of pubication in mind, countless 'entertaining' insertions suggest that he adopted it (see Chapter 4); and as his vast quantity of material accumulated, structure was a problem that had to be faced. And when we remember the tradition of his triumphant successes in personal appearance at Athens[20] and Olympia, and the fact that 'prize performances' were a very common method of publicity (the sophists Hippias, Gorgias and Prodikos are all credited with such appearances), it seems probable enough that the general plan of Herodotos' work was modified, if not totally controlled, by the consideration of the appropriate length of a lecture.

In examining the principles for inclusion of material in Herodotos' work, we found that relevance, in our sense, was by no means the sole criterion. One could classify the digressions (using this term in its broadest sense) into 'voluntary' and 'involuntary' types. That the work 'sought additions' is Herodotos' own view (4.30), but while many were dictated by the requirements of historiography many others were included for a variety of other reasons. The author's interest (very like that of Homer!) in all things human and divine, his love of detailed description where the details are, to us, simply inessential (as in some Homeric similes) is not to be overlooked, but the desire to entertain is always present, at least in the background, and affects the arrangement of material. Thus after a stretch of serious historical narrative and interpretation at the opening of the *History* we come upon the 'marvel' of the rescue of Arion by the dolphin. Other, possibly marginal, motives for its inclusion have already been mentioned. Similar cases are the stories about Kypselos and Agariste.

On the other hand, the author was conscious of his own predilections (hardly 'failings'): as already noted he excused the length of an excursus, in the case both of Egypt and of Samos, on the score of 'marvels' or notabilia they had to offer, and at 5.62 says 'I now return to my proper subject' but a couple of pages later has to apologise once more for further digressive material (5.65). We have observed that sometimes the placing of digressions seems to indicate neglect for principles of structure, and to have depended on momentary recall prompted by an incidental mention of an individual or place, of a fancied similarity of circumstances. For example at 8.137ff., the antecedents of the Macedonian royal house should perhaps have been provided at 5.17, before the murder of the Persian envoys.[21] But deliberate structuring is more commonly to be observed; Herodotos wishes to lead us through the labyrinth with a strong thread to guide us. A simple instance appears at the close of the second book. The benefactions of the Egyptian Amasis to Greek shrines lead us to Samos and Polykrates; and Amasis' conquest of Cyprus is immediately followed by Kambyses' second attack on him, which opens the present Book 3. (It will be seen that this book-division is a conspicuously unsatisfactory one.) At 3.39 'while Kambyses was marching on Egypt, the Spartans sent a force against Polykrates' and we have completed a ring.[22]

A demonstration of careful structuring of a different kind may be seen at 7.45f. Here we find a conversation between Xerxes and Artabanos which is in reality a digression on *la condition humaine*. Xerxes has an equivocal or perhaps merely unstable character as shown by Herodotos (see Chapter 10 below), while Artabanos is carefully identified by the historian here as the cautious adviser, or 'Warner' as some critics like to term him — in reality, the representative of the 'peace party' at the Persian court. The topic seems to be one of Herodotos' main preoccupations and will reappear in later discussions. The similarity of what is here said to the observations of Solon to Kroisos in Book 1 cannot be missed. Surely however it did not form part of the traditional Greek version of Xerxes' invasion — though it should be noted that on reviewing his magnificent force Xerxes is reported to have wept for the brief life of mankind, thus eliciting comment from his sententious uncle. What is remarkable, then, is the placing of this conversation for dramatic effect at the point where the Persian king appears at the height of his power, before his forces can suffer any casualties. And a little later (7.53) Herodotos emphasises the symbolic importance of the crossing of the Dardanelles — though in fact this was not the first time an invading Persian army had crossed into Europe (4.1 and 89).[23] Compare the statement at 1.4 that all Asia (and by negative implication, none of Europe) was thought the 'natural' or 'ordained' sphere of Persian power. This emphasis is obtained by placing before it both the strategical debate between Xerxes and Artabanos, and the (second) address by the king to his troops; thus is produced a pregnant pause in the narrative proper, a moment of suspense before the fatal step is taken.

Deliberate manipulation of chronological order takes place even in the last three books, coherent and chronologically precise as they appear. It had been impossible to draw together the diverse threads of Greek and barbarian events before the Marathon campaign of 490 BC. But now, when Xerxes' army is poised on the northern border of Greece proper, we have a 'flashback' to Themistokles' revolutionary naval programme for Athens (7.143); and the historian's judgement on the importance of the war between Athens and Aigina is not given in the context of the actual events related in Book 5, but delayed until 7.144. Using the same delaying technique, Herodotos brings the Persian forces to Therma, near modern Saloniki, before he allows the Greeks to coordinate their defence. Possibly the Greeks did commit the notorious 'democratic' fault of doing 'too little, too late'; the failure to reinforce Leonidas — who should in theory have been able to hold out almost indefinitely — appears to suggest this, and the information conveyed to the Persian king about the celebration of Olympic games (8.26) might confirm it.[24] Obviously a good deal of planning and coordination had been going on. It was 'more dramatic', however, to unleash the barbarian hordes upon an apparently inadequate Greek force; and the sacrifice, no doubt in reality unnecessary, of Leonidas and his 300 Spartans — plus a number of others — at Thermopylai had become too sacred a part of Spartan and Greek mythology for the historian to consider, apparently, that proper intelligence, and wise dispositions by Leonidas, could have halted the Persian advance altogether; reinforcements were in fact already on the way.

The first appearance of Themistokles, just mentioned, is somewhat unusual in its placing and also in its manner. Most individuals of importance receive more than one 'introduction', as it were — they in fact appear in more than one of the separate *logoi*, and not necessarily consecutive sections. Kleomenes is first named and properly identified at 3.148, and appears again up to a score of times down to the fact that he died without a male heir, in 7.205. Polykrates of Samos made his first appearance at 2.182 as an ally of the Egyptian king Amasis — we have seen how that linkage operated — and is repeatedly present during the following book. Periandros of Korinth is introduced twice, at 1.20 by name only and with his position as tyrant in 1.23, then reappears at 3.48 and lastly in 5.92. Pausanias the Spartan regent, victor of Plataia in Book 9, had been introduced incidentally in 4.81 and mentioned (in a context just beyond the scope of the narrative of the war) in 5.32. Such cases seem to confirm the separate composition of various sections of the books.

Themistokles, however, about whom the traditions reaching Herodotos were decidedly ambivalent, does not appear where he first should, and is introduced as the interpreter of the second Delphic oracle to the Athenians before Salamis. More surprising, however, is the fact that instead of the normal 'X' son of 'Y' plus nationality or other identifying label, he is styled as a political newcomer who 'was called the son of Neokles'. The possible implication of illegitimacy is not supported by other evidence; perhaps the lack of a more distinguished ancestry is mentioned to emphasise that he was a political upstart. Whatever the reason for this unusual phraseology, all these cases illustrate that while Herodotos undoubtedly had in the end a general scheme into which the facts were fitted, he worked with one topic in mind at a time.

A number of general principles may thus be seen to have operated in the structural arrangement of Herodotos' narrative, but clearly no strictly defined rules of chronology or relevance. He adopted various procedures in various cases; partly involuntarily, partly through desire for variety. It is not therefore profitable to seek for 'patterns' as some have done,[25] whether of historical processes or of particular events. The reasons for rearrangement of material are always explicable in other terms. Indeed it is insulting to suggest that Herodotos, the industrious researcher of great breadth of vision, would believe that all events he was recording fell into simple patterns. That he was probably influenced in his general thinking, his religious and philosophical notions, by the dominant 'tragic theme' of Greek literature in his day, does not necessitate his having manipulated the data of history to fit such a conception. Herodotean fiction appears only in the dialogue and speeches — fiction by modern criteria, that is, but with both a most respectable literary precedent and a scientific purpose.

Notes

1. The phrase, that of Aischylos, is however by no means appropriate to a great many of the surviving plays, though Homeric subjects are chosen in some cases. In outlook and atmosphere those of Euripides in particular are far from Homeric.

2. Herodotos, spending some time in Sparta, was evidently fascinated by what he saw and heard, but did not unquestioningly believe all he was told, perhaps not even 'official versions' — for example the case of Kleomenes, 6.84.

3. Leonidas, one of the most conspicuous military failures amongst Spartan commanders, nevertheless became a figure glorious in legend. Contrast the reputation of Pausanias, successful in the greatest battle fought on Greek soil, but later suspected of pro-Persian sympathies. The question of his guilt lies beyond the scope of this book, as of the *History*.

4. A number of small items may be found to support such a contention; they include a statement in the Catalogue about the origin of the Ionians, a matter more adequately dealt with in Book 1, and other similar comments.

5. The story of Kyros may be thought to verge on the epic, where it escapes from simple folk-tale — often more a stylistic difference than one of subject-matter.

6. The closing statement which sums up the *logos* normally includes the particle *men*, indicating 'Subject A'; the new topic is introduced in the next sentence with the particle *de*, signifying 'Subject B', or Part Two of a topic, or 'the other side of the coin'. There being no English equivalents, young students of Greek used to be told to render these particles by 'On the one hand . . . on the other hand . . .', a recourse which produced some priceless examples of 'classroom English'.

7. A. Roveri (Ch. 4 n. 1) makes clear the transition from myth to *logoi*, via the honest admission of the Muses themselves in Hesiod's *Theogony* that not everything they tell is truth. See also A. Cook, 'Herodotus; the Act of Inquiry as a Liberation from Myth', *Helios* 3 (1976) 23–66; and H. Verdin (see Chapter 7, n. 30).

8. See further my paper, 'The Purpose of Dramatisation in Herodotos', *Historia* 15 (1966) 157–71; P. Hohti, *The Interrelation of Speech and Action in the History of Herodotus* (1967).

9. There are much more prominent and immediate causes for Kroisos' fall; see Chapter 8.

10. Atossa, daughter of the founder Kyros, and successively wife of each succeeding ruler down to Dareios, almost came with the throne as dowry to the new monarch and continued to exercise great influence. Though Persians would not openly admit to matriarchy, the role of Atossa in the argument about the succession to Dareios (Book 7.2) implies her power behind the throne — as does the 'curtain lecture' more picturesquely.

11. Aristagoras failed in the long run and consequently was damned (like Pausanias) in one tradition, represented by Herodotos' remark about his 'poor spirit', 5.124.

12. A number of scholars since L. Solmsen in 1939 and later years, down to A. Hignett's *Xerxes Invasion of Greece* (1963), have urged characterisation as the main motive for the composition of such speeches. Against this, in addition to the arguments put forward in this chapter, it should be remembered that Herodotos

was not writing a play, nor a series of plays, despite the dramatic skill he displays. See also Chapter 10 below.

13. J. de Romilly, 'L'objectivité dans l'historiographie grecque' in *Proc. 3rd Int. Hum. symposium* (Athens, 1975) 107.

14. R. W. Macan, *Herodotos, The Seventh, Eighth and Ninth Books* (1908), spoke of the 'lower deck informants' available to the historian.

15. Truesdell S. Brown, a sensible critic, unfortunately used the term 'plot' in his article in *Historia* 11 (1962) 259–70. This implies that Herodotos did, or at least could if he wished, manipulate the actual events; not an imputation that can be readily accepted.

16. Other examples of variation between direct and indirect speech are found at 2.162, 4.118, 5.30, 6.50, 7.168, 8.26, 8.65, 9.82, 9.90, 9.96f., etc.

17. An interesting case where possibly a different motive operated is that of Hekataios' account of the Pelasgians in Attica. The conflicting version of the Athenians themselves is reported as if factual, though not in direct quotation. A subconscious wish to score off his predecessor may have guided Herodotos' pen.

18. See above, note 6 to this chapter.

19. See on the Egyptian and Samian digressions, Chapter 4.

20. Not all scholars accept the late and in some ways unsatisfactory evidence for these recitals; most recently A. Podlecki (see note 7 to Chapter 3), who attempts to show that Herodotos had no first-hand knowledge of Athens, and the story of his public appearance there could not be true. When one considers that Herodotos' life spanned the greatest years of Athens' power and brilliance, it is inconceivable that an intelligent man of his wide interests, composing an account of great wars in which the city played one of the chief parts, had not spent some time in the commercial, maritime, intellectual and artistic capital of the world. See also H. W. Parke, 'Citation and Recitation; a Convention in Early Greek Historians', *Hermathena* 67 (1966) 80–95. S. Flory, 'Who Read Herodotus' Histories?', *AJPh* 101 (1980) 12, discusses the non-prevalence of reading in the modern manner, and the problem for Ancient Greek readers presented by the length of Herodotos' work; if read aloud it would occupy some fifty hours.

21. This case could provide further ammunition for those urging the prior composition of the later books. But if the several *logoi* were composed at various times and then tailored to an overall plan, such argument becomes superfluous.

22. Structure within a *logos* is carefully analysed by Laura Boffo, 'Il logos di Orete', *Rend. Acc. Lincei* s. VIII 34 (1979) 85–104, who shows that the various references to Oroites combine to form a unified whole.

23. This is yet another item that might indicate prior composition of Book 7 — but see above, n. 20.

24. However, the abandonment of perhaps the most important of all Greek religious festivals would have risked loss of the favour and protection of the gods.

25. 'Pedimental structure' was suggested in a rather fanciful architectural analogy by J. L. Myres, *Herodotus, Father of History* (1953) as a principle of Herodotean narrative. Less far fetched, but still going beyond the facts, are the 'patterns' of H. J. Immerwahr, *Form and Thought in Herodotus* (1966).

7 SOURCES OF INFORMATION

Oral information dominated quantitatively the source material[1] available to Herodotos to a vast degree. A rough count of his references to type of source and inferred sources would suggest at least five to one in favour of oral communication.[2] The great variety of types of such communication makes a general assessment of reliability impossible: we cannot lump under one heading the statement of a guide to the Pyramids (who could no more read the hieroglyphics than could the Greek inquirer), the popular version of political or military events two or three generations earlier (or more), and the personal reminiscences of a veteran of the battle of Salamis, or the official account of Spartan institutions. (It is generally thought that Sparta had no written constitution, which is perhaps not indubitable, but in any case inquisitive foreigners would not be granted permission to study any such documents.)

The types of source within the main categories differ widely then — perhaps not much less so in written than in oral information — in the degree of authenticity of the original source, in the kind and the intensity of any bias concerned (individual, political, patriotic, racist) and in the amount of unintentional corruption incurred in transmission from person to person, generation to generation, language to language. They also differ in age and especially for oral sources the greater the time elapsed since the events narrated, the larger the number of mediating individuals, and the greater the likelihood of unintentional inaccuracy or deliberate perversion.

Any observant reader of the *History* will have noticed the great frequency of such phrases as 'the Persians say' or 'the Egyptians told me' or, unattributed, 'it is said'.[3] The first two seem to imply an informed authority; in the case of Egyptian priests, their status would have been taken as guaranteeing the authenticity of the information offered, as the temples were the obvious repositories of knowledge of the past. A serious objection to Herodotos' acceptance of their authority will be put later. In the case of the Persians, at their first appearance in the opening section of the history as authorities for the barbarian version of the 'Rapes',[4] they are described as 'learned' — the term is rendered in Powell's *Lexicon* as 'versed in history', no doubt in deference to the context.

However at 1.95 the Persians, whose particular version of the youth of Kyros the historian selects from the four available, are specified not as erudite, but as desirous of not unduly glorifying Kyros, preferring 'to tell the story in accordance with the facts'. Herodotos is acquainted with the other stories, but on this occasion does not include the variants, no doubt for reasons of length (some twenty pages are occupied with the story, up to the establishment of Persian independence). If these variants were conspicuously less credible than the fairy-tale legends of the birth and infancy of Kyros (paralleled by Moses, and within Herodotos' own story rather less miraculously by Kypselos, 5.92) it is hardly surprising that the historian rejected them. At the conclusion of the Kyros-*logos*, he observed that this was the most 'trustworthy' or 'plausible' of the *many* accounts. It has been observed that a special difficulty for Herodotos lay in the fact that many Mid- or Near-Eastern peoples showed little interest in their own past history.

The possibility of a written account — in Greek obviously[5] — of this Persian material is certainly not excluded. But we have no means of proving or disproving its existence. When Herodotos, as frequently, observes that 'there is a *logos* to such-and-such an effect' the probability that it comes from an oral source is very high, and almost absolute in the case of foreign language material. On many occasions the historian expressly says that he 'heard' such an account; while phrases such as 'there is another account current' would seem to carry the same implication.

Direct contact with high-ranking Persians through an interpreter, and occasionally perhaps with Greek-speaking Persians, is almost certain.[6] The note at the end of Book 3 on the defector Zopyros, who came to Athens, makes it probable that the detailed information on his grandfather's part in the second capture of Babylon and the special honour accorded by Dareios was supplied by Zopyros, possibly in person.[7] At 7.106 the report that the descendants of Maskames, the successful Persian defender of Doriskos, still received from Artaxerxes favours like those accorded by Xerxes to their ancestor suggests some personal link; this addendum is certainly not part of any traditional account of Xerxes' march, since it refers to a date later than 465 BC.

The elaboration of the story of the conspiracy of the Seven Persians and the establishment on the throne of Dareios suggests that Herodotos may be reworking, adding to and improving on an existing Greek account derived from one or more Persian sources. No known 'Persika' which could have been available to Herodotos would have been so detailed. It is impossible to determine how much orally-gathered information was added to such a narrative, if indeed one existed.

One of the most contentious points over Herodotos' handling of his sources relates to the constitutional debate (3.80–2), already briefly discussed in Chapter 4. On the liquidation of the 'False Smerdis' the story goes, the Seven Persians held a discussion to consider what form the government should take. To an outside observer, it would seem reasonable that after experiencing a psychopathic despot, and an usurpation (to accept the account as Herodotos must have received it), some more constitutional form of government might well be considered. And to those of his critics who declared that the Orientals would never accept anything but an untrammelled autocracy, Herodotos in 6.43 pointedly reports that Mardonios established democracies in the re-subjected Ionian cities, their quisling dictators having proved so unreliable; the analogy is taken as compelling, though it is hardly exact.

The arguments for democracy, aristocracy and monarchy respectively are placed in the mouths of three of the leading conspirators. These arguments are closely similar to discussions known to have been topical in Greece at the time Herodotos wrote; for almost 100 years some scholars have been able to name their precise source, the sophist Protagoras.[8] It may be that a sophist, Protagoras or another, issued in dialogue form a tract setting forth the rival cases in the persons of three 'barbarians', and that Herodotos accepted a work of fiction either at face value, or by a use of literary convention comparable to that which permitted him to compose these or other speeches 'suitable to the occasion'. However, a composition of such a kind seems more likely to have followed than preceded the familiarisation of Greek educated society with Persian affairs under the guidance of Herodotos. That of the three speakers, Otanes, the proponent of democracy, was subsequently allowed certain special exemptions from the normal feudal vassalage to the Great King (3.83), Megabyxos, who supported aristocracy, was the great-grandfather of Zopyros mentioned above as a possible contact of the historian (3.160), while Dareios was the inevitable candidate for the defence of monarchy, might give some grounds for believing that Herodotos, who protests so loudly that the debate really occured, did have information that made at least a possible basis for historical dramatisation; [9] or, as in the case of Artabanos versus Mardonios in the Persian Council at the beginning of Book 7, he selected appropriate mouthpieces for the several views.

Egypt certainly presents a special case. We know that Herodotos used the work of his predecessor (if that is the appropriate word) Hekataios, since he 'quotes' him at 2.143 and again refers to him unfavourably at 6.137. But by far the greatest proportion, apart from what he himself saw, was verbally conveyed, and unfortunately by often quite ignorant persons. We have already mentioned the imaginative guide at the Pyramids; the so-called 'priests' were no better than might be expected. The proportion of the population in ancient Egyptian towns or villages employed by, or in, or connected with, the temples was very considerable, and Herodotos would not be likely to encounter high-ranking dignitaries among them.[10] Much of the Egyptian *logos* is in *indirect* discourse (on which see Chapter 6 above) not so much for the sake of variety perhaps as to indicate a degree of scepticism in the historian.

Where foreign language sources are concerned, the notorious problems of translation must be borne in mind. Effective rendering of one language into another requires an expert in both languages; many Egyptians and not a few Persians may have had a superficial knowledge of Greek, but that would be quite inadequate for the answering of many of Herodotos' questions. Non-Greek documents suffer the same difficulty; who translated them, and how effectively? (The ridiculous case of the Pyramid inscription merely highlights the problem.) A question is put in Greek; is it fully comprehended by the local inhabitant? (If an interpreter is needed, though actual translation may be more accurate, there is room for yet one more slip 'twixt cup and lip.[11]) The answer is first framed in a 'barbarian' tongue; is it then correctly rendered into Greek?

All study of this writer must proceed in full awareness of the difficulties which he and his informants inevitably encountered in transmitting an accurate account of a particular event or phenomenon to another person. It is to Herodotos' abiding credit that he had more than an inkling of these difficulties and had done his utmost to circumvent them. For this he had forged a powerful, if not infallible weapon, *viz.* historiē (A. B. Lloyd).[12]

Major fountain-heads of information (and also no doubt of mis-information, perhaps on occasion deliberate disinformation) were the great religious centres of Delphi and Olympia. Dodona, Delos and other shrines were also laid under contribution; a curious exception as regards direct personal research would appear to have been the prophetic sanctuary of Apollo, Branchidai near Ionian Miletos, not very far from Halikarnassos — if we accept the implication of the statement at 1.92 regarding Kroisos' offerings there. Much of the mass of material regarding oracular utterances comes no doubt from the functionaries at the shrines; but perhaps not all, since the story of alleged corruption of the Pythia, the god's mouthpiece, by the Alkmaionidai (5.63) and in favour of Kleomenes (6.66), would hardly have had official blessing. Records of victors at festivals also came from individual sources in general, until the compilation by Hippias of his Olympic list.

The shrines could sometimes pervert the truth to increase the glory of their divine patron — and thus their own revenues. The recorded pronouncements of Apollo before the battles of 480 BC suggested no strong anti-Persian policy, and the story of a Persian raid on Delphi and its miraculous rout is clear invention, an attempt to regain credibility (8.34–9). The passing comment that Pheidon of Argos was the most hybristic (or sacrilegious) of all Greeks for trying to 'become chairman of the Olympic committee' should also be noticed.

It has recently been suggested that a good deal of Herodotos' gleanings about Athenian affairs came from these two major shrines. This may well be true, but as I suggest below, a great deal of personal inquiry about the actual Persian invasions seems likely to have taken place in Athens (see also note 7 to Chapter 3). Sparta claimed a good space of time too, not limited to the town itself. In both centres, very careful sifting for tendentious reporting was desirable.[13]

The latter part of the work, dealing principally with the Persian invasions, evidently differs from the descriptions of exotic lands or Eastern history in being compiled to a great extent from the personal recollections of individuals, mostly but not invariably Greek. Most such informants pass unnamed and unmentioned, but a particular instance is the Theban dinner-party given for Persian officers shortly before the battle of Plataia (9.16) where the informant, an eye-witness, is named as Thersandros of Orchomenos. Another named witness from the period is Dikaios, the authority for the vision seen by himself in company with Demaratos before the battle of Salamis (8.65). However, in this case Herodotos does not state explicitly that he had it from Dikaios in person, only that the latter 'used to tell the story', so an intermediary is possible.[14] It has already been noticed that information about Demaratos was plentiful and that by no means all of it was gained in Sparta; Herodotos seems to have encountered a circle of Greek *emigrés* in his travels, perhaps in Ionia rather than in Persia.

Two other examples from earlier periods will suffice. At 5.118 we hear of the sound strategy suggested to the Carian rebels by one Pixodaros, the son of Mausolos, a man of Kindya. The advice was not accepted, unfortunately in the historian's view; why then was it mentioned? Either because its rejection is put forward as the reason for defeat, or because Pixodaros (though not a resident) was connected with the ruling dynasty of Halikarnassos, as his father's name suggests[15] — he also, says Herodotos, married a Cilician princess. (Another reason to 'drop his name'?) A member or connection of the family was surely Herodotos' informant.

Even earlier than the Ionian revolt, in the Spartan intervention in Samos against Polykrates (3.55) one Archias had particularly distinguished himself. When visiting the village of Pitana in Laconia, Herodotos met and talked with his homonymous grandson, whose father had been named 'Samios' in honour of his own father's feats on the island.

The Persian invasions were a constant topic of patriotic not to say jingoistic talk, to judge by Aristophanes' comedies, in the Athenian agora, or at informal reunions of old war-time comrades; there would be few Athenians who did not think they knew a good deal about the battles. Herodotos' account of the campaigns, however, is inadequate in some respects; he seems to have gained little understanding of the strategy and tactics involved,[16] and the accounts tend to be episodic — particularly in the case of Salamis — rather than complete. Omissions are even more conspicuous in the case of the Ionian revolt, with battles taking place between 498 and 494 BC, that is to say at least half a century before Herodotos began to put the *History* together. They are still remarkable in the case of Marathon in 490 and rather less so in the fighting of the invasion of 480/479. (Aristophanes in the 420s is still talking as if 'the men who fought at Marathon' were living, or only recently dead; a twenty-year old 'recruit' of 490 would have reached the age of ninety in 420). Thus it appears that the comparative lack of reliable information is responsible for this gradation; Herodotos did not fill in the gap by fantasy, nor (as was at times his practice) with somewhat irrelevant material. It was not possible to talk, save by necromancy, with the high commanders of 490–480. No doubt Herodotos 'pounded the pavements' of Athens and Thurioi like a diligent detective or newspaper reporter, seeking anyone who might be supposed able to add to his growing files of information; but it is clear that the account of Salamis, in particular, does not depend on people who had a good general view of the battle.[17] The start of the engagement is clear enough, though the reason for the initial tactical withdrawal[18] was not understood by someone 'below decks' tugging at an oar. But very soon tactical formations were broken up and a general mêlée developed. Fighting spread over a wide area and individuals were only conscious of what was occuring in their immediate vicinity. Consequently a number of incidents figure, more conspicuously perhaps than the general course of the battle. And inter-city rivalries are not absent, as will be shown later.

The account of Marathon evidently derives mainly from Athenian sources, and is more coherent, though lacking in detail. A perfectly plausible reconstruction of the tactics and course of the battle is not difficult, though scholars are still arguing over topographical matters. Individuals or family tradition and exaggeration are strongly represented. Indirect oral information — 'I am told that in speaking of it he used to say something like this' (6.117) — is the stated source for the vision and subsequent blindness of Epizelos. A more public tradition might be responsible for noting the death of Kynegiros, a man with a famous brother, the poet Aischylos. A tradition favourable to the Philaid house has made Miltiades the real commander and demoted Kallimachos to a merely honorary position.[19]

'Glorious defeats' always seem to benefit from a favourable tradition. What reports of the disastrous failure at Thermopylai will have reached Herodotos? The official Spartan version, generally accepted elsewhere, endeavoured to camouflage the failure of Leonidas to carry out his mission, with a cloud of patriotic nonsense about devotion to duty and death. In the first place it is important to remember that the historian did not fully understand the strategic plan, brainchild of Themistokles no doubt, which demanded that the land-pass of Thermopylai and the sea-pass inside Euboia be jointly held. He did note that means of communication between the two forces had been laid on, but ignored the implication — he had made up his mind to follow the campaigns on sea and land separately — so that his report of this important fact follows the naval engagements, which are themselves only narrated after the conclusion of the story of Thermopylai (8.21). He did realise that both positions could be outflanked unless proper dispositions were made to prevent this, and reports the failure of the Persian attempt by sea, attributing it however to meteorological (or divine!) causes. 'Afflavit Deus, et dissipati sunt.' The success, on the other hand, of Hydarnes' move via the mountain path does not lead him to comment on the folly of Leonidas' deputing to guard it a contingent who were certain to place first priority on the defence of a route leading towards their own homes. Herodotos instead becomes concerned with the identity of the collaborator who acted as guide for the Persians, and his subsequent fate. Since Leonidas had become a hero, someone else must be found as villain — and the great and possibly undue importance attached by Herodotos to the actions of individuals is also here evidenced.

The Phokians, who failed to stop Hydarnes, would not be likely to offer any detailed account of their inglorious part in the campaign (7.128).[20] Those contingents sent to the rear by Leonidas (7.220) (either to avert their loss, as the historian suggests, or, more probably, to hold up the outflanking enemy force until the reinforcements on their way from the Isthmus should arrive), who also had done little for which to claim credit, would have been equally uncommunicative, and the alternative version which makes deserters of them is surely significant. We are left with the Thespians, who are said to have all fallen, though popular tradition failed to bracket them with the 300; and the Thebans. The Boiotian 'Plutarch' comes down heavily on Herodotos' 'malice' for the calumny perpetrated on his countrymen in the *History*. Malice there undoubtedly was, but not on this historian's part. Thebes and Athens were at loggerheads and several times at war in the period between the repulse of Xerxes (when Thebes figured on the wrong side at Plataia) and the outbreak of the Peloponnesian War which began with a Theban act of treachery to pay off an old score. Was not the slanderer of the Thebans at Thermopylai an Athenian informant or tradition?

We come now to the Spartans. The official version and that generally accepted conformed to the 'myth' of Spartan devotion to duty, death before surrender. An oracle had duly been produced 'forecasting' the death of one Spartan king as the price of survival. The 'duty' notion was reinforced by Simonides' famous two-line epitaph, which simply claims that the 300 died 'carrying out orders'. There were survivors, and versions which did not discredit them too greatly will have competed with the official account (they were all three allegedly absent); but public opinion quickly obscured such seditious offerings. Various 'trimmings', for example, the part played by the soothsayer Megistias, came perhaps from individuals rather than official sources. An honours list, comprising three Spartans and one Thespian distinguished for outstanding valour, presents the intriguing question as to whose evidence, among the 297 dead, supplied the citation for awards? Could Theban judgement have been considered worth canvassing?

Salamis and Plataia, however, were battles in which a large number of Greek contingents were engaged. In the latter, Spartan tradition is conspicuous; detailed information from someone close to Pausanias is probable, and perhaps one might name Teisamenos the diviner, for whom there is great detail. (But observe that the same goes for his opposite number in the camp of Mardonios, one Hegesistratos: an example of the great popular fascination with augury.) Sectional interests and inter-city jealousies which make an undisguised appearance in the lengthy dispute between Athens and Tegea (9.25ff.) set in the early stages of the Plataia campaign, produced variant versions denying achievement to rivals. The most conspicuous of all these perhaps is the allegation, made by the Athenians alone, that the Korinthian fleet took no part in the fighting at Salamis (8.94). The rest of Greece, Herodotos admits, supports the Korinthian claim.[21]

The varying stories about the manoeuvring before Plataia again display the lack of comprehension, not so much by Herodotos, but by the ordinary man in the ranks (who often suspects, not without reason, that he is being 'mucked about' by the generals). The parallel with Salamis is clear; in both cases, the engagement of forces of such magnitude and consisting of diverse contingents was beyond all Greek experience. Eurybiades the Spartan and his chief adviser Themistokles of Athens (with Adeimantos of Korinth too no doubt, who has come down to us in the role of devil's advocate) deserve the greatest credit for not losing control over the many small and large squadrons which made up the fleet. At Lade in 494 BC the opposite situation had prevailed (6.7–17), where

Dionysios had had difficulty beforehand in briefing his fleet in practice, while in the engagement itself one contingent after another deserted.[22]

Similarly Pausanias, though Plataia was 'a damned near-run thing' must be duly commended for not losing control except possibly over some of the lesser contingents — if it is true that they failed to contribute materially to the victory (9.52 and 69). The anecdote about Amompharetos reports disregard of orders quite contrary to the Spartan 'image' — and he is later named for conspicuous valour! The story is a combination of misunderstood tactics[23] with the myth of Spartan refusal ever to retreat.

Such are the contorted congeries of true and false reminiscences, legends, popular beliefs, not without an occasional supernatural intervention,[24] that *historiē* amongst oral sources presented to Herodotos, for the climax of his work, the major battles of BC 480 and 479. We may criticise him for failing to notice all the tendentiousness of his informants, and for failing to correlate the accounts, discarding totally what was demonstrably untrue, as in the slander on the Korinthian fleet.

For the Persian side of the campaign, Persian sources need not be premised. Demaratos the Spartan exile and his connections will have been responsible for a good deal of information, establishing the routes, progress and conduct of the land forces with Xerxes; Halikarnassians who served with Artemisia at sea, or their descendants, will have provided a sizeable quarry for the historian's investigation; many other Greek contingents were also incorporated in the Persian fleet, coming from all around the coast and islands of Asia Minor from Cilicia to the Bosporos.

The account of Xerxes' march, with its detailed anecdotes (for example that of Pythios (7.27f. and 38ff.), and Antipater of Thasos on the cost of Xerxes' rations (7.120), and 'marvels' such as the rivers that ran dry), suggests popular tradition, whether based on fact or on fancy. It is impossible to determine whether any written document regarding the march itself or the campaign generally came into Herodotos' possession. An example of the historian's use of popular tradition may be found at 7.43, the reported panic in the Persian forces near the site of Troy; no cause is suggested, nor any comment forthcoming from the historian. The phenomenon immediately follows the narration of Xerxes' 'chiliatomb' (sacrifice) to Athena; for a fifth-century Greek the tacit implication is that the goddess was not pleased by the extravagant offering, being of course aware of the Persian's hostile intentions towards her regular worshippers — and perhaps particularly her own city of Athens.[25]

There were indubitably however written sources for the Persian War period in general. Almost all authorities agree that some sort of official document underlies the catalogue (7.60ff). The opening statement that 'no one has left a record' of the numbers of the respective contingents confirms the suspicion that the list is that of the forces available from the various provinces of the Empire, not one specific to the Greek campaign. However, the commanders are named, and ethnographic and other notices are appended, perhaps from some Greek compilation of 'Persika' — 'Persian matters'.[26] It is urged by some scholars that one or more such Greek 'accounts of Eastern History' was written before that of Herodotos.[27] (Hekataios is quoted as an authority on the Ionian revolt — and indeed he was a participant therein — at 6.137). Such accounts *probably* dealt with both sides in the war, as did, for example, the Tale of Troy, but suffered from *interpretatio Graeca* to a greater extent than the *History*.

For Eastern matters in general, Herodotos appears to have acquired, or worked out for himself, a chronological scheme, based no doubt on some sort of generation reckoning.[28] He gives precise figures for the duration of the Lydian, Assyrian and Median dynasties — but over Egypt has gone 'wild', encouraged no doubt by those informants who realised how deeply impressed the visitor was by the antiquity of their culture.

Foreign sources reduced to writing in Greek need not be regarded as authentic. Much criticism has been directed at the account of the reign and particularly the end of Kambyses, where Egyptian prejudice is evident, and of the conspiracy which placed Dareios in power; here pro-Dareian propaganda played a large part, and it has even recently been suggested that there never was an impostor, a 'False Smerdis', but that he was an invention of Dareios who actually liquidated the 'Real Smerdis' (Bardiya), brother and lawful successor of Kambyses.[29] Thus even documentary sources of Persian or other barbarian origin, probably taken at face value by Herodotos, were by no means totally reliable.

Documentary sources on the Greek side were much to be preferred to literary works. For the earlier period to which Herodotos' account reached back, myth, as enshrined in literature as much as in popular tradition, demanded stern examination; and as we have seen, the historian gave early warning that he was wary about accepting mythology as evidence. More serious than the somewhat light-hearted remarks about the 'Rapes' in 1.3 is the elaborately reasoned discussion of the 'alternative version' of the Trojan War story given to Herodotos by Egyptian 'priests', at 2.120. This, which we need not here examine, seemed more historically plausible to him for a number of reasons; and though his argument concludes with a profession of his belief in divine punishment for great wrongs, which was active against the Greeks for their behaviour in the matter, the rest is totally acceptable on purely rational grounds. Poets have too much licence, it appears to Herodotos.[30] This scepticism, which placed him a long way ahead of his predecessors and even most contemporaries, exceeds perhaps that of Thukydides. It is possible that the latter is more scientific, and more in accord with modern fashion, in seeking to extract a kernel of truth from the legendary data.

Written sources in Greek include of course the epigraphic material, frequently quoted, and perhaps such items as a list of the Spartan dead at Thermopylai (which he knows but does not publish). The 192 Athenian dead at Marathon were also probably on public record, unless the Persians had destroyed the memorial at the Soros in 480–479 and it had never been restored — but Herodotos, despite his encomium upon the Athenian feat of arms, did not pay them a similar compliment. Also probable seems a catalogue, whether in an earlier written account or as some form of public document, of the Greek forces by land and sea who opposed the Persian invasion of 480.[31] The two lists of ships at 8.1 and 40ff. are circumstantial, and in most cases not suspiciously 'round'. The lists of land forces too are detailed, and whereas the small number of separate contingents at Thermopylai permitted oral trans-mission, the thirty-odd groups participating in the Plataia campaign — though rounded, as normally, to hundreds or thousands[32] — seem more likely to have been committed to writing — unless I do too little justice to popular memory.

The discovery of the famous Troizen inscription, purporting to be a 'Decree proposed by Themistokles' before Salamis seems to show that Herodotos failed to study all the available epigraphic material, since his account does not entirely coincide with it.[33] But some have doubted its authenticity, and even if (and the condition is weighty) such a decree was not only passed, but actually inscribed and set up in Athens, it may very well not have been visible when he was there. In general, he was keen to inspect epigraphic evidence (for example, 4.88, 5.77), even if it was in an indecipherable script or tongue. He states in the latter passage that he saw and copied the inscription celebrating the Athenian victory over the Boiotians and Chalkidians, scorched as it was by the Persian burning of the Akropolis.[34]

Ranging further afield, some credence must be given to the view that a written account of 'Skythia' was available to Herodotos (see Chapter 3 for his travels). And of course much of the geographical excursus on the Nile for example, and *en passant* remarks (1.202 on the Caspian, 203 the Caucasus, 2.12, 4.8 on the 'River Ocean') indicate the works of earlier geographers. As for Skythia, so with Libya; at 4.99ff. the second description of Skythia is not consistent with the first (4.16–20) and is artificially schematic — a tendency which he deplored elsewhere (4.36). In the same way the Libyan area which apparently he had not visited is laid out in far too schematic a manner (for example, oases at intervals of ten days' march). This suggests a pre-Herodotean Greek account.[35] But one should not be led into supposing that once Herodotos in such an excursus passed the bounds of knowledge, he then indulged in fantasy.[36] As in Book 3, 115, Herodotos can find no eye-witness for the seas to the north of Europe, and disbelieves the story of 'one-eyed Arimaspians', so at 4.16 he is unable to produce visual evidence, only hearsay, of what lies beyond Skythia. Reason certainly predominates over fantasy here! At 4.24f. both Skythians (evidently coastal inhabitants questioned by the historian through interpreters) and Greek traders travel as far as the 'bald' Argippaioi, so that 'knowledge' of the area is held to be reliable. But beyond, Herodotos admits, there is no sound information to be had. Epic poetry is the only 'evidence' for the existence of Hyperboreans — and with an ironic hit at the purveyors of schematic geography, he says there should be 'Hypernotians' (beyond the South wind) to 'balance the northern creatures'. In 5.9 we hear that *nobody* can given accurate information on what lies to the north of 'Thrace'. In the digression on the Russian rivers, fairly correct information is forthcoming on their lower courses, familiar to enterprising Greek traders, as far east as the Dnieper; beyond, all is fabulous. But are we to suppose that this is Herodotean fantasy, or criticise him for including it? Believe it if you like, as he says elsewhere.

In the Libyan *logos* too, which overambitiously reaches towards

Mt Atlas, there is an admission of ignorance of what lies beyond. Note that Mt Atlas 'is said to be' (4.184) so high that its summit is never seen, and its inhabitants 'are said to be' vegetarians, and never to dream! The first of these ethnological points at least is plausible enough, the second offers an interesting byway for psychological anthropology. The monstrous beasts reported by the Libyans, again, are qualified by the ironic particle 'if you please!', while at the end of the two *logoi*, Skythian and Libyan, which contain so much implausible material, the historian repeats, rather sadly 'I do not know if this is truly so; but all things are possible'.

The tendency however to see things from a Hellenocentric viewpoint (the *interpretatio Graeca*) influenced the description (by Herodotos, or his forerunners, or informants) of areas where sound information was scanty or totally lacking.

Herodotos, like most people, may have been prone to see and hear what evidence he subconsciously wished to find. In the case of Egypt he strains the information given him in his anxiety to prove the priority of all things Egyptian; note the statement 'I will not say that the Egyptians adopted this or any other practice from the Greeks' (2.49), and such far-fetched notions as that the Danaids brought the rites of Demeter from Egypt to Greece (2.171). Further, in his enthusiasm for the brilliance of Egyptian culture, he insists not only on their different manners, but on the superiority of many aspects of Egyptian life, from the size of their buildings to social legislation (2.148, 177). But occasionally, however, the 'philobarbarian' attitude is dropped, as when Demokedes proves superior to all the Egyptian doctors in his treatment of the injured Dareios; here, clearly, the source is Greek, the context Persian, and Herodotos' pro-Egyptian tendency is forgotten. In 7.23 it is the Phoenicians who show their superiority in civil engineering, though one might expect the Egyptians to be the most experienced canal-builders.

Not only the researcher, but the interviewee or the interpreter may have been affected by a complementary weakness, in wishing to supply the type of answer which would please the inquirer. Few travellers who take the trouble to pursue inquiries (*historiē*) will have escaped the sometimes unfortunate effects of this tendency. At 2.118 occurs a wonderfully illustrative but by no means unparalleled example: the Egyptian priests averred that they, or their ancestors, got their information regarding the Trojan War at first hand — from Menelaus![37]

A late source informs us that Herodotos spent a period of exile from Halikarnassos on the island of Samos. He certainly seems to be particularly well-informed about this island and its recent history — consider, on the other hand, the scanty remarks about Naxos, an island of nearly equivalent importance both economically and in the strategy of the Persian advance — the reason I have suggested for emphasis on Samos! Both the internal and external history of Samos figure prominently, and political divisions within the community are also conspicuous. Here then is a case where availability, indeed voluntary offering, of information has certainly influenced Herodotos' acceptance of it; confirmation of what he was told.[38]

Herodotos was, to be sure, often aware of tendentiousness in the answers of his informants, and not infrequently expresses his doubt, or straight-out disbelief. For the Egyptian *logoi* in particular, hearsay evidence is a primary source of the account, and he admits it (2.123). He sets up, not explicitly but implicitly by the way he distinguishes various categories of information, a scale of authenticity. Genuine knowledge, at the top of the scale, is generally a matter of autopsy, or a study of sources with the application of reasoning. Next comes hearing, and eye-witnesses, who may be presumed to *know*, are best to hear from, since sight, as Kandaules remarked (1.9) is a more trustworthy sense than hearing. When inquiry has produced sufficient satisfactory evidence, he says 'I find by inquiry' or 'I have come to know' — in cases too numerous to mention — one illustrative example is the reported equivalence of Kroisos' offerings at Branchidai with those to Delphi. The third degree is mere hearsay; at 2.99 we have the most formal expression of the scale: 'Up to this point I have limited my account to the results of autopsy and *historiē*, and the views I have formed therefrom (i.e. by reasoning). But from this point my narrative will be based on what the Egyptians themselves told me . . .' The fact of multiple versions in itself declares that 'what people say' 'what is said' or 'as the story goes' cannot be accepted as gospel; sheer common sense at times dictates their rejection.

Reasoning comes into play not only at the second level but also at the third. The historian's personal opinions are stated: 'as it seems to me' or 'I prefer the latter story as more plausible.' On occasions the report, though not rejected outright, had a deprecatory particle appended: 'They said, if you please, that . . .' Reasoning, *gnomē* applied when *historiē* has gathered the data or reports, is sometimes *a priori.* On a number of occasions Herodotos tells us what is 'reasonable' or 'probable' (*eikos*) or is a 'plausible view' (some part of the verb *dokein* = to seem, seem likely, seem right, gain acceptance). But more common — perhaps in the ratio of two to one — is the refusal to make a judgement: 'I cannot say precisely' or the outright rejection of a story, with or without reasons given.[39] A case of elaborate statement of reasons given is the defence of the Alkmaionidai against the charge of communicating with the enemy (6.121f.).

The case of Egypt was no less thorny for Herodotos, despite his sojourn there, than that of the unvisited parts of Russia and North Africa. True, he could rely on autopsy for existing monuments — though the oral 'information' gained on visits could be rather worse than useless; social and religious practices could be observed, but reasons offered for various observances and customs must depend again on inquiry, and to check the accuracy of any such information was almost impossible. (There is an interesting case of cross-checking by the researcher at 2.3.) On more than one occasion he defends himself against the possible imputation of falsehood by stating 'I can only repeat what I was told' (2.123, 131, 155). As noted previously, his own predisposition may underlie not only the disproportionate emphasis on certain aspects[40] (especially religious) and the interpretations he placed on reports received. But it becomes a matter of subjective judgement to examine such tendencies in depth, and the likelihood that, like Herodotos, the modern scholar may well find what he is looking for is a serious danger. That Herodotos was both selective and non-selective at different times in his choice of material was shown in Chapter 4.

A more serious defect, however, is the patent failure consistently to correlate information from different sources. At times, this may be due to lack of revision (the possibility that the work was never fully completed has long been canvassed; see Chapter 5). Also there is on occasion apparent neglect to obtain precise information which should have been available. An example of the latter is the question of the precise status of the Athenian polemarch and the ten 'tribal' generals at Marathon (6.110), surely readily ascertainable at Athens. Again, Hippias the exiled tyrant appears to be in command of the Persian forces before Marathon (6.107) but the preceding narrative has left no doubt that (as always) the high-ranking Persian Datis held the supreme command, Hippias being an 'adviser' as Demaratos later to Xerxes; yet Hippias is actually made responsible for the battle-order of the Persian troops! The Marathon narrative also presents us with the astonishing claim that the Athenians on that occasion were the first Greeks able to face the terrifying aspect of the Persian battle-dress. One problem is why the inferior personal armament of the Persians should produce apprehension rather than confidence in a hoplite force, another is that Marathon was not even the first encounter of Athenians with Persians, as they had participated in the Ionian revolt which had seen several engagements between Greek and Persian land forces.

A contemporary continental scholar has this to say on the general subject of the historian's treatment of source material.

> It has been perverse judgment of Herodotos, and the first appearance of historiography, to limit the first historical work within an excessively narrow schema, that of rational explanation of the past replacing mythical explanations. After the conclusion of the archaic period history appears much more in the guise of a collection of data, followed by a classification, with the aim of reconstituting the past; principles of checking the accuracy of information are far less important therein than the utilisation of the greatest quantity of data that can be acquired.[41]

Herodotos' attitude of scepticism, strongly displayed at times, did not apply itself to every piece of information he acquired, but not all modern critics have shown the desirable tolerance and understanding of the writer just quoted.

It is also necessary to bear in mind what has been shown in this discussion; that a vast amount of inaccuracy, often impossible to check, infected the oral information; tendentiousness and mere lapses of memory caused great historical unreliability, and when criticising Herodotos for failure always to detect these faults, it must be remembered that it is far easier for us at this distance to see the wood; not only the trees, but some pretty dense undergrowth impeded the historian's view and made it difficult for him to disentangle himself from perversions and prejudices.

Notes

1. On the whole question see G. Schepers, 'Source Theory in Greek Historiography', *Anc. Soc.* 6 (1975) 259; D. Fehling, *Die Quellenangaben bei Herodot*

(1971); A. Momigliano, 'Greek Historiography', *History and Theory*, 17 (1978) 1.

2. The figures given by Powell for λέγω λόγος and congeners tend to corroborate such an estimate, when checked rather arbitrarily for relevant usage.

3. Comparison with Thukydides' usage in H. D. Westlake, *Mnemosyne* 30 (1977) 345.

4. But Herodotos dismisses all such tales and proceeds to state what 'he knows for a fact'; the epithet may be ironic. At 2.3, however, the people of Heliopolis are said to be the 'most versed in *logoi*', while at 2.77 the Egyptians are 'the most skilled in memory' (or 'in recording the past') of the whole human race. In 4.46 the adjective, there used nominally, appears to signify 'man of letters, educated person'.

5. The Persians did not write history; the boastful pronouncements of kings clearly do not qualify. If Herodotos ever heard of the Behistun, Naksh-i-Rustum and other Persian memorials, he would still have to depend on oral information as to their contents, and this might have been no more reliable than that offered him on the Pyramid inscriptions. His account nevertheless has some features in common with the inscription of Dareios.

6. See especially J. Wells, 'The Persian Friends of Herodotus', in *Studies in Herodotus* (1923).

7. The 'record-book' nature of the final paragraph could suggest that it had been acquired otherwise. There is much reference to honours and rewards bestowed by Persian kings, whose munificence was impressive to the Greeks; e.g. to Mandrokles, engineer of the Bosporos bridge, 4.88.

8. Protagoras of Abdera, a contemporary of Herodotos, was suggested as the source by Maas in 1887; J. A. Morrison took up the thesis in 1942, and it has recently been supported by F. Lasserre.

9. Of the quantity of studies on the 'constitutional debate' I mention only a few: P. T. Brannan, 'Herodotos and History: the Constitutional Debate', *Traditio* 19 (1963) 427; C. W. Fornara, Appendix I in *Herodotus; an Interpretative Essay* (1971); D. Hegyi, 'The Historical Authenticity of Herodotus in the Persian Logoi', *A. Ant. Hung.* 21 (1973) 73; K. Bringmann, 'Die Verfassungsdebatte . . .', *Hermes* 104 (1976) 266; F. Lasserre, 'Hérodote et Protagoras; le débat sur les constitutions', *MH* 33 (1976) 65; J. Bleicken, 'Zur Entstehung . . . , *Historia* 28 (1979) 148.

10. For recent discussions, see R. Drews, *The Greek Accounts of Eastern History* (1973), and especially A. B. Lloyd, *Herodotus Book II: Introduction* (1975), Ch. 3, from whom the quotation on p. 79 is taken. When Herodotos does specify the rank of a particular interviewee, the man is only a 'grammatistes', records- or accounts-clerk, of no high or privileged status.

11. A recent personal experience on a tour of China will illustrate the problem. At the famous 'briefings' which, with tea, begin every visit to any commune, factory or other institution, the interpreters are usually proficient. However it was not rare for a question put to the PR person to receive a partial, unsatisfactory or indeed irrelevant answer. Two causes may be operating here: (i) the question has been misunderstood, or it and/or the answer mistranslated; (ii) the PR person clearly wishes to show the particular enterprise in as favourable a light as possible, and also has excellent reason not to criticise government policy. In a somewhat different context, Egyptian priests were in a similar position.

12. See n. 10 above. The quotation is from p. 81, and is followed by a useful study of *historiē*. See also Schepers (n. 1 above).

13. See Chester G. Starr, 'The Credibility of Early Spartan History', *Historia* 14 (1965) 257; H. Verdin, 'Notes sur l'attitude des historiens grecs à l'égard de la tradition locale', *Anc. Soc.* 1 (1970) 183.

14. 'Dikaios, son of Theokydes, who had become well known in Persia.' Demaratos then was not alone, even apart from such involuntary arrivals as Demokedes. But where and to whom, if not Herodotos, did he tell this story? He

surely would have been no more welcome back in Athens than was Demaratos in Sparta.

15. The name Pixodaros recurs in the Halikarnassian royal house in the next century; Mausolos of course is also the name of the famous fourth-century dynast, builder of the Mausoleum.

16. Apparently Herodotos, unlike Thukydides (and suffering from the comparison) has little personal knowledge of warfare. If the story of his participation in an attempted coup against Lygdamis is true, a small-scale guerrilla-type raid only seems to be indicated, and we hear of no other military experience.

17. Demaratos was perhaps the best placed witness, and one of the most expert. Was he the original source for the behaviour of Xerxes during the battle?

18. This was to negate the superior seamanship and sailing qualities of the Phoenician and Ionian squadrons by drawing them into tight formation.

19. Herodotos may be censured for not checking up on the easily verifiable constitutional situation — and thus averting the spilling of much scholarly ink. On the variability of accounts of Athenian history of this period see e.g. C. W. Fornara, 'The "Tradition" about the Murder of Hipparchus', *Historia* 17 (1968) 400.

20. The picturesque detail of the sound of feet shuffling through oak leaves seems likely to have been fictional, since it was not yet autumn, and oak-trees are (now) lacking; in any case armed men on the march at night were likely to become audible in other ways.

21. So too, apparently, does an epitaph discovered on Salamis which confirms Plutarch's version. Herodotos' information on Korinth seems to have been at best patchy and often hostile; see Chapter 5 above on Kypselos and Periandros. Though fragmentary, the inscription (ML no. 24) confirms the first couplet of Plutarch's quotation. It is generally accepted that the Korinthians had the duty of guarding the western entry to the Salamis channel and thus were absent from the main action in the east.

22. The Ionian fleet commanders had been tampered with by Persian agents. The imperialists knew well the value of financial and other material inducements, and may indeed have attempted the same method at Salamis, where, however, the core at least (Athens, Sparta, Aigina and perhaps Korinth) proved incorruptible.

23. The 'Saturday afternoon' inter-city conflicts had never envisaged such an oddity as a rearguard! The Spartan army was at this stage the sole 'professional' force in Greece.

24. The mysterious voice at Salamis criticising the initial retirement, the 'vision' of Dikaios, the non-violation of the precinct of Demeter in the rout at Plataia, and the rumour of victory there that encouraged the Greek force at Mykale. But note that neither the number nor the incredibility of these events is high.

25. An alternative explanation, if one is needed, would be that the panic was caused by the thunderstorm reported in the previous paragraph, and the report has been misplaced. That is perhaps too facile.

26. *Persiká* is reported as the title of such compositions; it may imply concentration on the wars, as with *Troiká*, the Tale of Troy, though the common later expression for the Persian Wars was *ta Mediká*. The nonsensical 'etymological' linking of the Persians with Perseus and of the Medes with Medea 'according to their own account' (*sic*!) are surely not Herodotean in origin. They contrast strongly with his attitude to myth at the opening of Book 1 (though some of the 'connections' discovered in Egypt suggest extreme credulity in such matters) and are not to be found there; either Herodotos failed, as elsewhere, to correlate sources, or was unable to complete a revision.

27. See especially R. Drews (n. 10 above). Charon of Lampsakos and Hellanikos of Lesbos are both known to have written on the general topic, though it is not possible to identify any positive contribution from either to the Herodotean

account. It is not quite certain that the work of Hellanikos preceded that of Herodotos; they were it seems close contemporaries.

28. The obscurities produced by generational dating have not been noticeably lessened by recent studies of the problem. That Herodotos should have bothered with precise chronological calculations over ancient Oriental kingdoms may surprise; less astonishing is an apparent internal inconsistency about the duration of the Median kingdom. It should be mentioned that the MS transmission of numerals in ancient Greek was extremely liable to corruption.

29. Most recently, E. J. Bickerman and H. Tadmor, 'Darius I, pseudo-Smerdis and the Magi', *Athenaeum* 66 (1978) 239.

30. See H. Verdin, 'Les remarques critiques d'Hérodote et de Thucydide sur la poèsie en tant que source historique', *Historiographia Antiqua* (1977).

31. The list of those who 'warred the war' on the 'Serpent Column' from Delphi (removed to Constantinople by its founder) records only the names of the states, not naval or military strengths. It is quoted against Herodotos by Plutarch, *de Hdti. Mal.* 39. The slight differences of Herodotos' list are easily accounted for; see How and Wells, *Commentary, ad loc.* ML no. 27. Other dedications recorded by Herodotos at 8.121 and 9.40 are no longer extant.

32. The almost incredibly large number of helots reported as accompanying the 5,000 Spartiates (itself an absolute maximum strength), if true, can only have been intended for supply and other services. The only further mention of them apart from the catalogue occurs at 9.80, after the battle, when they are instructed to gather the loot.

33. The Troizen Inscription, first published by M. H. Jameson in *Hesperia* (1960) 198, has acquired a huge bibliography — at least seventy items within ten years. Some have urged that it is based on, or compatible with, the version of Herodotos, but it appears, to most, implausible. See the commentary in ML no. 23.

34. Discussed in ML no. 15.

35. Excessive tidiness, the desire to find order in all things, was a besetting sin of the Greek intellect, to which Herodotos occasionally succumbed.

36. The view of the otherwise sensible critic D. Hegyi, 'The Historical Authenticity of Herodotus', *A. Ant. Hung.* 21 (1973) 73–87.

37. Note that the Egyptian priests had adopted at least in part Herodotos' own rules of evidence; their concluding statement runs 'where Menelaus went after he left Egypt they were unable to tell. They told me that they had learned of some of these matters by *historiē*, but spoke with accurate knowledge of what had happened in their own country'.

38. On the 'Samian informants' of Herodotos see especially now R. Tölle-Kastenbein, *Herodot und Samos* (1976).

39. There are some forty or more expressions using forms of *dokein*, and nearly half that number with *eikos*, all meaning something like 'It is reasonable to assume'.

40. Why, for example, should Sesostris receive such extensive treatment? M. Pohlenz, *Herodot*, 2nd edn (1961), suggested that his conquests are seen as a parallel to those of Dareios, and there is an explicit comparison at 2.110.

41. F. Lasserre (in French), 'Hérodote et Protagoras', *Museum Helveticum* 33 (1976) 65ff.

RELIGIOUS AND MORAL ATTITUDES

The religious ambience of Greece in Herodotos' formative years was one of rather superstitious belief in divine influence in, or control of, human affairs. At the most unsophisticated level, it had hardly advanced from that of the Homeric poems where direct intervention of deities both on a community scale (for example the epidemic visited by Apollo on the Greek forces) and in the individual case (a spear-cast turned aside to protect a favourite — or indeed a relative!) was the controlling influence upon single events. History as a whole, however, appeared rather to be determined by a very vaguely defined force, Fate or Necessity, against which even Zeus, Father of gods and men, on one occasion declared his impotence. (Compare the reply of the Pythia to Kroisos, 1.91 which has close epic parallels.) As we have seen in another context, the Homeric poems, the basis of primary education, continued to affect or even to shape the intellectual attitudes of fifth-century Greeks.

Religious observance formed an important, if not the major component of community life; every state festival was held in honour of one or more deities; the great athletic and literary/musical contests were staged at religious festivals, and every city had its own divine patron and protector. Art, especially in the form of architecture and sculpture, was particularly dedicated to religious purposes.

The majority of Herodotos' contemporaries, as the majority in many other societies both ancient and modern, were unthinking acceptors of the traditional religion, and duly observed its forms. Religion in ancient Greece did not demand either conformity with a given set of beliefs, or a particular strict code of ethics. The 'recorded', that is to say, legendary, behaviour of the gods themselves — vain and jealous females, arrogant and bullying males — resembled that of spoilt children rather than that of ideal humans. The Greeks had indeed made gods in their own image, as Xenophanes had ironically pointed out before Herodotos was born — but his message went largely unheeded. Social conventions owed little to religious teaching; for instance Zeus, not alone amongst deities, cohabited with his own sister, an example considered undesirable by the Greeks (until they came into contact with certain Oriental cultures). Nor were the deities monogamous in 'practice', while in Greece it was not generally considered advisable to ape the sexual feats of Zeus or Herakles — even were it humanly possible! This intellectual climate had not remained entirely unchallenged, apart from Xenophanes' destructive criticism as noticed in Chapter 2. Not only had a nobler concept of divinity developed among thinking persons who were still believers, on the other hand the whole fabric of belief came under fire from agnostics and atheists.[1] These no doubt received no less than their fair share of publicity, though of course among the younger generation of the Peloponnesian War period — about which we have some information from the contemporary but very different works of Thukydides and Aristophanes — it was fairly fashionable to pour contempt on traditional tenets in all fields. (The ambivalent attitudes induced by the plague at Athens are noted in Thukydides 2.47 and 53.) The 'silent majority', however, were little affected and showed their reactionary power a few years later in the condemnation for irreligion, or nonconformity, of one of the most devout men in the city, Sokrates. Religion is perhaps the most conservative area of human activity, and no great change in the attitudes of the majority is observable in the following century either. A typical representative of such conservatism is Xenophon, himself a would-be disciple of Sokrates, who found it necessary to consult the oracle at Delphi before embarking on his eastern adventure with the attempted coup of the young Kyros. Xenophon also records faithfully the consultations of the omens before each stage in the military moves, such as crossing a river, in his account of 'The March Up-country'.

Hence it is not surprising that the supernatural plays a considerable part in the *History*. As pointed out in earlier chapters, Herodotos was not writing for a select, intellectual readership, but — in the first instance at least — an audience in the literal sense, consisting of ordinary citizens of the Greek *poleis*; at times perhaps particularly Athenian, at others the more cosmopolitan gatherings at Olympia, Delphi or the Isthmus of Korinth.

Such people were indeed able, despite the prevalent irrationality of their beliefs, to appreciate the more advanced theology — perhaps more accurately, presentation of the divine powers — in the plays of Aischylos and Sophokles. In the same way, people of very little theological knowledge or indeed quite lacking in religious conviction can enjoy on more than a merely aesthetic plane Handel's *Messiah* or even Bach's *Passion according to St Matthew*. Tragedy, religious poetry, may be taken to represent 'the spirit of the age', in its more advanced manifestation. In contemporary comedy the gods were often laughing-stocks; no ordinary Greek viewed the deities as transcendent, and deep feelings of religiosity appear to have been confined, in general, to worship at the great shrines, or the mysteries, and on great occasions. But none the less formal religion predominated, even though there was no 'religion of the Book', no mandatory creed, no Ten or Three Command-ments. Certain types of 'wrong-doing' tended to attract divine displeasure and punishment, but there was no general supervision of morality by deities or religious agencies; no priest had a moral tutelage over laymen.

Herodotos' reports or criticisms of irreligious wickedness are few. He personally maintains an attitude of respectful piety, both in the reliance on *nomos* noticed in Chapter 4 and in such phrases as the last sentence of 2.46. At 2.111 Pheros behaved with reckless impiety[2] in hurling a spear into the Nile (Greeks too were very conscious of the divinity of rivers and other waters) and thereupon went blind — or so it was said. The reason for Herodotos' inclusion of this item is not only that it is a 'marvel', but that it provides a peg on which to hang the fable of the faithless wives. However at 7.35 Herodotos himself describes Xerxes' order to rebuke the Hellespont for destroying his bridge as not only 'barbarous' (i.e. un-Greek) but impious. So was the behaviour of Xerxes' officer Artayktes who not only stole treasure from the shrine of the hero Protesilaos but used to fornicate within the sacred precinct (9.116). Greek *nomos* forbade the latter, as did Egyptian (2.64); but Herodotos notes in the latter passage that 'nearly all other peoples' impose no such ban. Herodotos had encountered forms of temple prostitution (such a practice is reported to have been current in Korinth, but Herodotos does not refer to it) in addition to the 'disgraceful' Babylonian custom mentioned below.

Kambyses' treatment of the corpse of Amasis was sacrilegious (3.16), like the trapping of Polykrates with intent to murder by Oroites (3.120). Other personages to incur the blame, apparently, of Herodotos, as well as the wrath of heaven were the Macedonian king (but in a legendary passage, 8.127) and Astyages, who sealed his own fatal destiny by deputing the command of his army to his wronged enemy Harpagos (1.127). At 8.129 Herodotos approves the attribution by the people of Potidaia of responsibility for the drowning of the Persians in tidal waves to their impiety at the shrine of Poseidon (whose role in seismic disturbances Herodotos elsewhere somewhat hesitatingly accepts, 7.129). At 9.78 the proposal by Lampon of Aigina to impale Persian prisoners is labelled 'most sacrilegious' — though its author regarded the measure as fitting retribution for what he in turn described as the impiety of cutting off the dead Leonidas' head. But in more cases Herodotos makes no assertion of blame, though his personages may; and he notes the savage atrocities of the Greeks against Artayktes without comment.

It is extremely important, if one wishes to arrive at an unprejudiced assessment of Herodotos' moral views and religious attitude, to exclude from consideration what is 'said' by the many personages whose fictitious words are reported. The same mistake has regrettably often been made by modern would-be interpreters as was committed by some Athenians in respect of Euripides; the tragedian was pilloried for remarks put in the mouths of certain of his characters.[3] An eminent commentator once claimed that Solon's words to Kroisos represented the very core of Herodotos' own thought. Why should this be the case? The argument is completely circular; Herodotos 'must have' regarded human happiness in a certain way. Solon's words are to be taken as expressing this, therefore (!) Herodotos is speaking here in his own person and with his own voice. But in fact Herodotos makes Solon say what is appropriate to Solon. This was put clearly by M. Miller, 'It *cannot* be supposed that Solon's speech was intended by Herodotos to set forth his own conclusions on the nature of history . . . but . . . stating what a Greek *sophistes* of Solon's time would have said'[4] (my italics). There may be other reasons why Solon's words have seemed important in the context of the *History*, but the sayings were well known, in substance if not in the now familiar phraseology, before Herodotos wrote. The reasons for the inclusion of, and the alleged emphasis on, this whole passage are discussed later in this chapter.

The major components in the mental attitude of those for whom the *History* was intended were belief in the power of the gods to intervene if they wished (but quite arbitrarily), and in the possibility of gaining favour, protection or assistance from them by carrying out appropriate rituals, in common with the practice of most other religions. A more individual aspect, and one extremely prominent in Herodotos' narrative, was the possibility of gaining advice, or approval for a course of action, from a particular deity in whose honour an 'oracular' shrine was maintained. Herodotos is only reflecting the facts of contemporary Greek life when he so frequently reports that such-and-such an individual or community acted as a result of some 'divine pronouncement'.

When Herodotos came to write universal history, he had to consider the causes of events. While he had no intention of dismissing the divine entirely from his calculations, he attributed to by far the largest proportion of actions a specific human, and often individual motivation. All the less attractive manifestations of human nature play their part; greed, envy, revenge, ambition, lust — as well as some more admirable traits. The case of Kroisos will serve as a general introduction to the 'pattern'; 'Kroisos began his invasion of Kappadokia for the following reasons: he wanted to increase the size of his existing domain, but more particularly he placed trust in the oracle, and he wanted to exact vengeance from Kyros on behalf of Astyages' (1.73). Human motives are rarely simple; the oracle of course is only a confirmation of his resolve, for this is the notorious pronouncement in reply to Kroisos' query about his already proposed 'defensive war' against the hegemonists of Susa, to the effect that if he crossed the frontier he would destroy a mighty empire. Readers will recall that Kroisos was fated to lose the throne anyway, being the fifth successor to the usurper Gyges[5] — and that he had incurred the potential wrath of heaven by his arrogant claims to unequalled prosperity. Thus there are at least two, if not three levels of causation in this complex; but the trigger, as always, is the character and behaviour of the individual.

On a much simpler level, it appears that the satrap of Egypt, Aryandes, used the pretext of sympathy with the wronged Pheretime to order the invasion of Kyrene (4.167), but the historian regards the pretext as implausible, and believes the real motive was the conquest of the North African coast. No divine agency is involved. Nor is a specific deity mentioned in the case of Oroites, another Persian governor whom we have already met; he was visited by 'vengeance' for the crime against Polykrates perpetrated for personal gain — and perhaps, to further the basic programme of Persian expansionism (3.120 and 139).

But a simplistic *reductio ad hominem* would not satisfy the restless enquiring mind of Herodotos, any more than constant divine intervention. Vengeance is perhaps a special case, falling between the human and superhuman spheres of control — as implied in the case of Hermotimos (8.106) (see below). At 2.120 the historian, discussing the case of Helen, says the Trojans could not have returned her to the Greeks, since the gods had prepared their total ruin as a paradigm to mankind of the mighty divine retribution for great wrongs. At this juncture Herodotos seems to be accepting the orthodox, Homeric view of the Trojan War.[6] We have already mentioned the case of Persian imperialism, a *nomos* of the Persians and especially of their kings; the desire for revenge against Athens is picturesquely put forward, but the King's Remembrancer was in historical fact quite superfluous as the constant attempts at conquest beyond the coasts of Anatolia[7] make clear, even had not Atossa and Mardonios, and Xerxes himself, expressly stated the policy. The queen, on the occasion previously discussed, urged a number of reasons why Dareios personally should follow the *nomos*. Multiple causation is common, as we saw in the case of Kroisos above. Not too often, however, is there an explicit divine factor.

Herodotos appears to use the terms 'the gods', 'the god' and 'god' almost interchangeably.[8] Sometimes it is clear that he is referring to a particular deity, especially Apollo, whose prophecies figure so largely in the narrative, when we find 'the god ordered them to . . .' and the like. He does not reveal any personal devotion to a particular deity, a fairly common phenomenon in Greek piety. His interest in individual deities lies largely in the comparative sphere, where he is rather too eager to make facile identifications; under a polytheistic system, where no omnipotent god prevails completely over all the rest (though the senior deity may well endeavour to control the juniors), the most important features of any divine personages are their functions, or spheres of influence. Hephaistos is the god of crafts, Apollo of music, Aphrodite of sexual relations, Demeter of agriculture and so on. One such system was likely to bear at least a superficial resemblance to another, since most of the important areas of human activity obviously were common to the several societies. The supposed personal characteristics of such deities, kind and merciful, fierce and intolerant, might however differ wildly, without discouraging identifications. Thus Herodotos finds no difficulty in saying 'The Assyrians call Aphrodite, Mylitta; the Arabians, Alilat; the

Persians, Mitra' (1.131), the last a most astounding error, since Mithras, a male deity and god of light, had nothing whatever in common with female sex-deities. He clearly does not expect his audience to find anything strange in this comparison. Furthermore, a civilised degree of tolerance regarding the cults of foreigners prevailed; religious exclusivism belonged particularly to the Hebrews, from whom it descended into Christian churches.

Now the gods, collectively, do seem to exercise a degree of control over human affairs. But unlike the Homeric situation, it is only occasionally that they appear as responsible for the outcome of human endeavours. Two particularly noteworthy passages in this respect are at 7.139: 'It was the Athenians — after Heaven — who saved Greece' (from subjection to the Persians); and on a slightly less global level at 8.13: 'Everything possible was being done by god to bring the Persian fleet down to the strength of the Greek.' Thus the gods are on the side of the Greeks; naturally, since they are the Greek gods — no need to remind readers that they have been identified with Egyptian and other invading barbarian deities![9] Slightly less committed is the remark at 9.65: 'My opinion is, if one should have opinions about superhuman matters, that it was the goddess herself who kept her precinct free from the pollution of bloodshed.' Notice also, at 9.91 'the *possibility* that, by coincidence, god made Leotychidas ask the man's name'. It turned out to be a name of favourable omen, Hegesistratos — 'leading an army' — but Herodotos also allows that idle curiosity rather than divine prompting could have inspired the query. '*If one believes* that Poseidon is responsible for earthquakes' (7.129) is remarkably non-committal. Herodotos accepts that seismic forces produced the gorge of the Peneios (*Tempē*) and allows the pious to attribute such forces to the Earth-shaker, Poseidon. The defeat, disgrace or moral destruction of Xerxes has sometimes been attributed to his 'irreligion' and hybristic actions. 'In Aeschylus', says J. de Romilly' 'these deeds are the main reasons for Xerxes' ruin, whereas in Herodotos no connection is ever suggested, not even by a hint. We can read it into his text if we wish, but we certainly do not do it with much encouragement from him.' And again '[Herodotos] shows a clear tendency to adopt more rationalistic explanations and attitudes' (*The Rise and Fall of States* (1977) 46).

Coincidence is not rare; a truly Dickensian example finds Demaratos happening to turn up in Susa just when the argument

over the succession is raging — and he is one of the few men with
personal experience of such a situation (7.3). The first wife of
Anaxandridas, previously barren, 'coincidentally' fell pregnant
soon after the second wife, irregularly wedded for the purpose of
child-bearing (5.41). It was a coincidence, or lucky accident, that
enabled Kleomenes to dislodge the Peisistratids from the Athenian
Akropolis (5.65). But such fortuitous events are often described as
'divine', 'supernatural' or 'emanating from [a] god'. The adjectival
form of *theos*, *theios*, is used to qualify *tychē* (chance) or is itself
used as a noun, resulting in a phrase meaning something like 'by
divinely-ordered chance'. It was by such chance that the baby
Kypselos smiled at his would-be murderers and temporarily at least
melted their wicked resolve (5.92). By 'divine escorting' the Seven
Conspirators passed the guards unquestioned, on their way to
liquidate the usurper (3.77). (However the omen used to decide
which of the Seven should rule was rigged by human agency (3.85).)
The 'divine' adjective appears twice in the remarkable story of the
Spartan envoys Sperthias and Boulis and their envoy-sons, Nikolas
and Aneristos; the fate of the latter was a 'supernatural affair',
while the courage of the first pair was 'most supernatural'.[10] (One
might therefore water down the rendering of *theios* to something
less colourful, such as 'remarkable' or 'extraordinary'.) At 9.100
our historian admits that 'there is much evidence to show that
supernatural occurrences do exist'. He is referring to the report of
the victory at Plataia, which was supposed miraculously to have
reached the forces about to fight at Mykale on the same day.[11]

Divine providence, *Pronoia*,[12] makes but a single appearance in
the *History*, where it is responsible not for any human event but for
preserving the ecological balance between predators and the species
on which they prey (3.108). Since no other trace of a benign
providence is to be found, but as regards mankind in general the
divine powers show a negative attitude, it is likely that Herodotos
has obtained this very modern view from one of the fifth-century
philosophers, yet in his eclectic manner does not follow it
consistently.

Fate however has a definite part to play. Though actual
occurrences of terms for fate are very few, there are a dozen cases
of a phrase implying fatal necessity, such as 'Kandaules was fated
to turn out badly' (1.8). I once argued that this was only a rather

meaningless formula, like that of the nineteenth-century novelist 'Little did he know that . . .', but I no longer maintain that view. The phrase does imply, most probably, the workings of a supernatural power; certainly the implication is that man's fate is not entirely of his own making. The Greek language habitually used the verb related to *tychē*, fortune or chance, 'to happen' as it is usually rendered, in all sorts of contexts where English speakers would not normally refer to 'chance'. It serves very much as a kind of modal verb,[13] not necessarily emphasising fortuitous occurrence — 'as fate would have it' may still be too strong a rendering for the literal 'he happened to be present'. Herodotos is naturally no exception and numerous examples are to be found in other historians such as Thukydides and Xenophon. We do not expect such writers to expound their philosophy, determinism or whatever, concerning apparent chances. Thukydides, while excluding any divine intervention in human affairs, lays considerable emphasis on the factor of chance or the unexpected in warfare. In that particular area of human activity chance has a more obviously dramatic impact; the 'lucky' hit or miss may considerably affect the outcome; and perhaps that is one reason why epic poets entrusted this role to particular deities.

Fate, it would seem, works on the principle that favours must not be channelled too constantly to any one individual. Whether Herodotos had consciously elaborated a consistent theory in this regard is far from certain. A number of observations made by historical or quasi-historical[14] personages have been thought to imply it; these include, notoriously, Solon's 'Call no man blessed till he is dead' (1.32) and the letter of Amasis to Polykrates (3.40) on 'unnatural' prosperity. (The letter, which of course cannot be said to depend on any actual document, is as much a composition of the historian as any speech.) As argued earlier, these opinions are not to be taken as necessarily those of the historian; they are those he thought suitable to the occasion, and in fact like his attitude to religious matters reflect the unconsidered views of the average Greek citizen. Solon's 'wisdom' had been widely publicised, and his 'slogans' become common property. Amasis was an Egyptian, but irrespective of whether Herodotos had informed himself correctly on the beliefs of the Egyptians in general and the king in particular, Egyptians, Skythians, Persians in their speeches all share the common views and phraseology of fifth-century Greece. Note for instance the comments of Kyros at 1.86 (indirectly reported) and the specific statement of Artabanos that 'god blasts the tallest living things' (7.10ε). God, on this occasion, not fate or necessity; in the case of Kroisos 'the gods' punish not his prosperity but his presumption in boasting thereof — a distinction without a difference in the result (1.34)!

We should however pay close attention to whatever the historian has said in his own person. First in order of appearance is the statement at the end of the prologue (1.5) that, historically, small cities have become great, and great fallen to insignificance; and, he infers, human prosperity or happiness is never stable. No word of fate, the envy of the gods or punishment, however. This expression may also be first in importance, since standing where it does, it may well have been written last, when the evidence as to instability had all been set out; it could be the final considered judgement of the historian. The precise term by which this activity of fate is referred to — and by Kroisos! — is the 'cycle' or 'wheel' in human affairs (1.207). Having himself experienced the height of prosperity and the depth of misfortune, the ex-king, miraculously saved by Apollo from the funeral pyre (it is said) has now a comfortable position as adviser to the Persian king.[15] What other opinion could Herodotos have represented Kroisos as holding? As for the context of the passage, it precedes the defeat of Kyros in a crucial and indeed fatal battle. Before it, according to the literary (and practical military) convention, he would have taken advice — and he clearly accepted the wrong arguments, for he was beaten.

A similar view, more crudely expressed, made the jealousy of the gods responsible for the downfall of the great. Herodotos himself comments on the fall of Kroisos that 'one might reasonably guess that it was the king's boastful claim to being the most fortunate of men that caused the gods' to bring him down (1.34). Solon had previously been made to say that the divine power is a jealous one (1.32). Amasis issues the same warning to Polykrates (3.40) and Artabanos to Xerxes (7.46). The warning by Amasis is necessitated by the folk-tale of the Ring of Polykrates — clearly too good a story to be left out, whether or not the moral is being underlined by the historian. That of Solon needs no further discussion, and Artabanos' avuncular advice to the 'young' and 'impetuous'[16] Persian king, who like Kyros is headed for defeat, is also inevitable, whether it was Herodotos' opinion that the gods were jealous or not (for he does not personally say so).

Vengeance[17] is on the human level a frequently occurring

motivation or justification for individual action. Dareios seeks
revenge on the Skythians for the Kimmerian invasion (4.1), and on
the Athenians (5.105) as also does Xerxes (7.8β) — but these are
mere propagandist pretexts, the real motive being Persian
imperialism (6.95 al.). It is rejected as an adequate pretext in the
case of the rapes of Helen and Io (1.3), but is naturally 'in
character' in the case of irresponsible despots. But vengeance is
sometimes perhaps to be given a capital letter: the vengeance of
Hermotimos upon the professional castrator Panionios is practically personified in the concluding phrase of the episode 'Thus it
was that Panionios was overtaken by Vengeance and Hermotimos'
(8.106). The abstract noun is here plural, as also in the case of
retribution upon Oroites for his trapping and murder of Polykrates
(3.128). In 1.13 the Pythia foretells that vengeance will come upon
the Mermnads in the fifth generation. Like necessity and chance,
vengeance may be a supernatural agency as well as a human failing.
Personification[18] in this manner is of course very common in Greek
tragedy, where two concurrent levels of thought are constantly
required. Herodotos' own ability or tendency to think in such an
ambivalent way is displayed in his comment on the death of
Kleomenes: 'In my opinion Kleomenes had to pay this retribution
to Demaratos' (for depriving him of the throne). The word translated here as retribution is the same Greek word *tisis* as that
rendered above as vengeance.

The quite remarkable prominence of oracles in the work of
Herodotos may encourage the belief that he was of a highly superstitious and credulous nature. Indeed he himself gives more
credence to the view by a direct statement of his own belief in the
validity of oracular pronouncements: 'I cannot refute the truth of
oracular utterances since I do not wish to discredit them in view of
the following [eight lines of verse by Bakis, not a diviner but a
professional 'oracle-monger'] and I will not allow others to do so'
(8.77).[19] This compares with his statement on the portents sent to
signify future disasters (6.27). However a total lack of scepticism
did not prevail here, any more than in other areas. We find
recorded, for example, a 50 per cent failure rate in the matter of
Amasis' kleptomania (2.174); at 2.152 Buto had 'the most veracious
oracle in Egypt' — so not all could be totally relied upon! — and
there is the notorious case of Kroisos' universal consultation-

test.[20] In this, Amphiareus successfully gave the correct answer, along with Delphic Apollo, but was not, it seems, rewarded with Kroisos' future custom (1.46ff., 53). A Delphian source for the Herodotean version of Kroisos seems certain. Also, Apollo could be asked to revise his estimate, and did so for the Athenians, through the intermediary services of one Timon (7.141). Herodotos does not fail to record the corruption of the Pythia on two occasions, once by the Alkmaionids (5.63) and also by Kleomenes (6.66). Thus Herodotos' statement given above must not be taken as a declaration of faith in the infallibility of oracles; his great interest in Delphi, together with the large amount of information gathered there, may well have coloured his view.

In this area too we find mere conformity by the historian with the mental attitudes of his own society. All societies have indulged, more or less, in various devices for foretelling the future; none have had, according to Fontenrose, so permanent, universal and constantly approached institutions as the oracle of Apollo at Delphi.[21] Therefore it is reasonable to expect in Herodotos' own narrative a reflection of its importance (not forgetting its lesser rivals, and individuals such as Bakis, Mousaios and more historical practitioners like Onomakritos (7.6)). This statement needs no modification in view of the somewhat startling findings of an eminent authority on the Delphic oracle.[22] Of the pronouncements recorded or referred to by Herodotos, he lists none as historical but fifty-five as 'quasi-historical'. Herodotos obviously did not apply the same criteria; if the consultations or replies were in the tradition, they were included in his narrative. The overwhelming majority of his auditors undoubtedly believed in the veracity as well as the existence of such pronouncements. Legend is full of the efforts of misguided individuals to avert the fulfilment of an oracle, like Kroisos with regard to his son Atys; in the legend, of course, such efforts never succeed. Herodotos' audience would find quite unsatisfactory an account which disregarded the oracular shrines, and there is no doubt that in some cases action followed from the consultation, whatever the status of the actual pronouncement; therefore *historiē* and *gnomē* justified, indeed demanded, their mention.

It is noteworthy that oracles tend to appear in clusters in the narrative. One largish group concerns the invasion of Xerxes, when all the cities were seeking, if not always advice, then at least a propaganda cover for the course they intended. No doubt many consultations did take place, and were subsequently edited, cosmeticised or camouflaged, often in the conventional oracular verse. The episode of the foundation of Kyrene is thickly festooned with oracles — no less than nine in number — equalling the quantity related or referred to in the Kroisos story (not counting multiple consultations!) (1.46–91). In Book 2 there are few, but though the subject is Egypt one Delphic oracle is included. Another cluster is found in the obviously part-fictional account given by Soklees of the Korinthian tyranny (5.92). Since the material of these clusters varies from recent Greek history to legend and to other societies, the inference about Herodotos' inclusion thereof is that he simply incorporated what his sources offered, being well aware of the interest taken by his hearers.[23] And Delphi, as noted earlier, was one of Herodotos' main sources of information.

The dreams, the portents, as well as the oracles 'true' or false, clear and imperative or ambiguous and misleading[24] have a pre-eminent claim for inclusion as being both an integral part of the common versions of the past and as a reflection of the mental attitudes of the society. But in addition another factor, important in the eyes of Herodotos, was their colourful and picturesque nature. 'Why are you sitting idle (waiting for this response), you miserable folk? Flee to the ends of the land!' (7.140). Thus the Pythia to the Athenians when they consulted the god as to the imminent Persian invasion — a fine piece of dramatisation of history.[25] When Kleisthenes the elder, tyrant of Sikyon, wished for political reasons to reallot the honours paid to the hero Adrastos, the priestess declared 'Adrastos is rightfully king, you are a mere terrorist' (5.67).[26]

Dreams and Portents

In addition to the oracles Herodotos mentions a score of dreams (not invariably specifying their content) and about twice the number of portents. Already mentioned is his observation, in the context of the double disaster that befell Chios — not however relevant to the main narrative — 'There is a natural tendency, it seems, for important signs to indicate the coming of great disasters for a city or a nation' (6.27). That dreams are of supernatural origin is a belief quite commonly held in many societies, of course mainly those less sophisticated, but prominent in literature almost everywhere. Dreams are 'sent' to give counsel or warning. That scepticism about the origin and meaning of dreams had made some progress in Herodotos' day is shown by the remark attributed to Artabanos explaining visions as arising from the mental preoccupations of the day (7.16ß). However this ill suits the folk-tale atmosphere of Xerxes' repeated dream and the naïve attempt to deceive the 'phantasm' by dressing the uncle up in his nephew's royal robes and placing him in the royal bed — an unsuccessful attempt, naturally. It should be noted that the Magi, though professionals, but like Artabanos wishing to promote a particular view, also deprecate the importance of dreams (1.120). In neither case does the historian offer his own opinion. Even Artabanos' rationalism is overcome by his experience, as the phantasm sees through the deception and rebukes Artabanos for giving the wrong advice.[27]

Such dreams often involve a superhuman but anthropomorphic form; the phantasm is 'seen', 'comes' and 'goes', and may appear repeatedly, as in the Xerxes episode. The final dream of Xerxes (7.19) of the crown that fades is pretty clearly an invention of a moralising kind, paralleling the counsels of Amasis and of Solon in the early books: it is painlessly incorporated by Herodotos along with the more picturesque and dramatic events that precede it. The source is to be found in the imagination of some Greek; I do not regard it as possible to identify the original source of the major dream-story, dressed as it is in Herodotean form and language. More than a dozen other such occurrences are reported, the majority being vouchsafed to kings or other rulers.[28] They are not usually deceptive or riddling, in the manner of several oracles. Kroisos, an addict of supernatural agencies, received a direct warning (1.34) about danger to his son Atys against which of course he failed adequately to guard, with the inevitable result.[29] At 2.141 the Egyptian monarch has a dream pledging divine aid against Sennacherib, and receives it in due course. (Compare 2 Kings 19!) Thus a dream is not always a warning, as when Kyros' dream foretells the future extension of the Persian Empire under Dareios — a dream that is said (by Herodotos or by his learned Persian informants?) to have been sent by 'the god' (1.209f.). However, the daughter of Polykrates is enigmatically warned by a dream of her father's sad end (3.124), and Astyages' two dreams (1.107f.) portended the overthrow of his throne by his daughter's son. Hippias' Oedipal dream before Marathon is first interpreted

optimistically, but after the portent (*sic?*) of his lost tooth reinter-
preted less hopefully (6.107). The subject-matter of Datis' dream
while at Mykonos during the subsequent withdrawal of the
Persians is not recorded but the sequel suggests a threat of punishment if a looted image were not restored. Similarly the repopula-
tion of Samos by Otanes followed not only a dream but a sickness,
which he clearly interpreted as a warning (3.149). Lastly one may
mention, though it occurs only in a minor 'footnote', the pregnant
Agariste's dream of giving birth to a lion. Whether this was a
warning, given the malignant potentialities of lions, or a prophesy
of future quasi-regal status for Perikles, the lion being the kingly
beast, depends on the view taken of that politician. Herodotos'
attitude to Perikles, and Periklean Athens, has been in dispute;[30] it
was not, in my opinion, a very favourable one, but the historian
would no more comment on Periklean matters than he did, for
example, on the eventual palace-assassination of Xerxes, which lay
less far outside his own chosen boundaries. (This latter fact
provides a telling argument against the imposition of a 'tragic
pattern' on Herodotean history.)

On moral questions Herodotos maintains, on the whole, a quite
remarkable objectivity. An outstanding example is the human
sacrifice alleged to have been performed by the invading Persians at
the crossing of the Strymon (7.114). A parallel is offered in a
similar sacrifice supposedly offered by Amestris, Xerxes' consort,
much later, on the grounds of which it seems to Herodotos to be a
nomos of the Persians, and therefore hardly to be criticised. A
different method of human sacrifice, burning rather than burying
alive, was proposed by Kyros for Kroisos and fourteen Lydian
prisoners (whose fate, unlike the king's, remains unrecorded), and
equally draws no adverse comment. Nor does Xerxes' somewhat
excessive punishment of Pythios (7.39) — the latter had infringed
the Persian *nomos* of absolute obedience to the king. At 1.151 we
find no comment, but possibly an implication, when it is reported
that the people of Methymna enslaved the people of Arisba 'though
they were of related stock'. After a tale full of aggression and
ruthlessness, the despot of Syracuse is hailed as 'a mighty tyrant'
(be it remembered that for Herodotos *tyrannos* is no derogatory
term, specifying merely an unconstitutional monarch[31]). However,
from a Greek point of view (and here Herodotos may be too easily

accepting a nationalistic opinion) it was *adikos*, unjust or wicked of Kroisos to attack the Ionian Greeks, though there is no criticism of his predecessors for similar aggression; perhaps his crime consisted in exacting tribute (taxation). At least in the view of Astyages, an injured party, it was 'most unjust' for Harpagos to enslave all the Medes, by the agency of Kyros — and stupid as well, since Harpagos could have made himself ruler! The moral issue seems somewhat clouded (1.129).

The opposite attitude is shown in the condemnation of the ritual prostitution of Babylonian women as 'the most disgraceful of practices' (1.199). On the other hand he expresses admiration for the sensible manner in which marriages used to be arranged at a kind of auction (1.197), while reporting without comment the more recent general prostitution of poorer girls to gain a dowry. Elsewhere, all manner of sexual *nomoi* pass uncriticised, even the *droit de seigneur* exercised by the king of the Adrymachidae (4.168). This attitude perhaps stemmed from the normally 'clinical' posture of ethnographic writing, which accorded with Herodotos' own procedures elsewhere in his work. Neither the Nasamones with their plurality of common wives and the 'pack rape' of brides, nor the Gindanes whose women add a band to their anklets for every man they have taken to bed, excite adverse or any comment (4.172, 176). Greek 'macho' views of the proper subjection of women (still strongly held by the majority!) would be outraged at this last. Nor could common approval be expected for the complete sexual freedom allowed unmarried girls among the 'Thracians beyond Kreston'. The dispassionate attitude of the researcher is shown equally by his report of the no doubt apocryphal 'test' conducted by Dareios which proved the sovereignty of *nomos* (3.38), and by his account of the many social and domestic practices of the Egyptians which are the opposite of Greek behaviour (2.35). His general equanimity with regard to diverse mores[32] appears also in his quotation of foreign (barbarian) criticism of Greek practices; at 4.79 the Skythians condemn Bacchic orgies conducted by the Greeks — 'Surely no god would induce people to go crazy.' (Yet these were heavy drinkers themselves, who had taught Kleomenes to drink neat wine and so brought on his madness (6.84).)

Did Herodotos intend, in his capacity as educator, to convey any moral teaching at all? The principal arguments in favour of such a view stem from the recognised didactic status of the 'maker', *poiētēs*, and in particular from the prominence of Solon's 'wisdom' quite early in Book 1; from the recurrence of several motives common to Attic tragedy, especially that hubris is punished (or the non-moral version in which mere eminence brings disaster), and certain fables, in particular the strangely-positioned observation attributed to Kyros which concludes the extant text of the *History*.

The interview of Solon and Kroisos was not necessarily included for its moral teaching, as has often been assumed. Kroisos, we have seen, provided the chosen starting-point for the consecutive historical narrative of the hostile relations between Greeks and Orientals, and he for various reasons had become a legendary figure for the Greeks in the next century. His reputedly inordinate wealth is emphasised by the cataloguing of his offerings at Greek shrines (1.50f. and 92) especially Delphi. The contacts between the king and the oracle of Apollo were the very stuff of popular tales; the tendency of his court, like that of other potentates, Greek or barbarian, to attract eminent visitors made it inevitable that there would be, in tradition, a meeting between Solon and Kroisos. An added attraction was the historical fact that so prosperous and powerful a monarch lost his kingdom, and according to one version was led away in captivity, albeit honourable, by the Persian conqueror — exactly in accord with the 'home-spun philosophy' of Solon. (A perhaps more plausible version would discard the miraculous rescue of Kroisos from the pyre and his captivity; it is found in the poet Bacchylides (Od. 3.23ff.) and conflicts with the version sanctioned by Delphi which Herodotos has combined with other information.[33]) Two major themes appear; one, that material riches do not produce happiness, a thought neither unique to Solon nor startlingly innovative to a man of Herodotos' wide knowledge; and two, that the uncertainty of human life renders hazardous any premature estimate of 'prosperity' or 'success'. Herodotos could use the setting of the supposed meeting to incorporate two picturesque anecdotes; that of Tellos the Athenian, inconspicuous but dutiful and honoured for his patriotic death in battle; and that of the two devoted sons Kleobis and Biton, so renowned that they figure in sculpture as well as literature. With his 'ironic smile'[34] he could present the 'catastrophe' of the intransigent refusal to flatter by the Wise Man, for the entertainment rather than the instruction of his audience. Few of them could congratulate themselves upon enormous wealth or power; the downfall of the mighty, whether farcically upon a banana-skin or grandiosely in tragedy, may not purge us with pity and fear so much as offer a feeling of warm satisfaction that we are no tall poppies to be cut down; the proverbs are simply a reflection of the subconscious wish of the ordinary person. Let us not belittle Herodotos' intellect by supposing that he elevated the Solonian maxims to a text for his sermon; it just happened — a 'divine chance'! — that they fitted reasonably well with what he had observed in his researches. The repetition of similar ideas in the case of Amasis and Polykrates is necessitated by the folk-tale of the Ring, which is included solely for the sake of the story. As with Kroisos, Polykrates' excessive prosperity ended in a miserable death; this too is factual, perhaps not in its details, but is not needed simply to reinforce the 'lesson' of Solon and Kroisos.[35]

Neither the length of the digression nor its position in the first quarter of the first book provide support for the argument that it contains Herodotos' 'message'. At some three and a half pages of the Oxford Greek text it is a little longer than the story of Gyges and a little shorter than that of Rhampsinitos and the Thief. The Solonian digression could not occur anywhere but in the main account of Kroisos, and its placing is therefore not emphatic. What is more, it follows, after an appropriate interval (for we cannot have all pure entertainment!) the story of Kandaules' undue admiration for his wife's physical charms and the luck of Gyges in profiting from it to the extent of obtaining this beautiful woman (and no fool either) as his wife and the throne of Lydia to boot. Hardly a great moral lesson here! Maxims such as 'opportunity only knocks once' and 'save your own skin' are not regarded as highly elevated morality. All that can be salvaged is the regrettably amoral view that the sins of the fathers may be visited on the children, in the fifth generation. Fate, fortune and necessity have little to do with morality.

What Herodotos himself says about the downfall of Kroisos is that he seems to have (it is only an opinion) aroused the ire of the gods by his claim to the height of prosperity. 'Vengeance is mine, saith the Lord'; a whole pantheon of Hellenic deities might challenge Jehovah in this respect. Once again, we find our historian reflecting the common view of the society, partially enshrined in the maxims of Solon. No sermon was required. Vengeance perhaps is not a moral issue.

The final paragraph (9.22) of the *History* presents Kyros, dead two generations before the context, suggesting that the Persians would have a better chance of maintaining their empire if they continued to reside in the harsh mountain country of their homeland rather than emigrate to the milder climates and more fertile soils of conquered lands. This observation fits none too well with the facts of Persian history as recorded by Herodotos. Kyros himself, at the time of his alleged conversation with Artembares, was not content with the large empire he had already gained, since he met his death on the northern frontier fighting against the Massagetae. This was a war of aggression, despite a revenge pretext, with motives similar to those expressed by Atossa to Dareios and by Xerxes. The advice says nothing about material wealth which some people see as a motive strongly emphasised by Herodotos for the failure of the Persian attempt to conquer Greece. They adduce the amazement of the defenders at the luxury of the Persian king and high command on campaign (9.82). Pausanias is made to express surprise that 'the Mede, on this standard of living, should want to rob us of our penury'. Kyros then was not moralising about the debilitating effect of wealth; he had acquired the riches of Lydia, not to mention Nineveh and Babylon, so it hardly befitted him to urge restraint in living standards. Nor did the Persians lose their empire in Herodotos' lifetime, nor show signs of it; such a conclusion would have been balm to the spirit of those who wish to force a tragic pattern onto Herodotean history.

It emerges therefore that Kyros is only talking about environmental conditions, and the advice is due originally not to a Persian king but to someone like the contemporary author of *Airs, Waters, Places* (Chapter 2 above). And it does not form a moralising tailpiece to the work not only for this reason; its unsatisfactory nature as an ending has puzzled scholars for seventy years.[36] It is not, however, an interpolation, falling as it does into the category of many anecdotes and gobbets of information which are attached to an individual mentioned in the course of the narrative (see Chapter 5). Artembares was an ancestor of Artayktes, subject of the preceding episode; recollection has recovered an interesting anecdote concerning this ancestor. There is in fact no proper conclusion to the work, and though I have accepted the capture of Sestos as a logically reasonable end-point, other material could well have followed and some kind of 'epic' conclusion might well have been expected. In any case, no moral inference can be drawn from the position of Kyros' advice, any more than in the case of Solon. Even worse, from the moralist's point of view, is the immediately preceding story. Artayktes had just been most barbarously executed by the Greeks; their resentment against him used the pretext of his sacrilege, but was probably occasioned more by his obstinate defence of Sestos which delayed their own return home. The savagery of the Greeks in stoning to death his innocent son before his eyes was certainly no less impious or unjust than any action of the Persians. If Herodotos meant his auditors to learn a moral lesson, he has scrupulously refrained from underlining the moral. He does the same in regard to the lynching of the sole Athenian councillor to propose the acceptance of Mardonios' peace-terms, and the utterly appalling complementary action by the Athenian women against the blameless wife and children of the murdered man. Nor is there explicit blame[37] of the Greek and Karian mercenaries who ritually murdered the sons of Phanes, against whom they bore a grudge, and drank their blood mixed with wine. For those who remembered what the historian had observed about the internal struggles of his own life-time, and were perceptive enough, his unspoken thought could perhaps be retrieved. But the absence of any condemnation is better referred to his normal practice of objective reporting of behaviour, even extraordinary behaviour.

Notes

1. J. P. Vernant, 'L'evolution des idées . . .', *BAGD* (1964) 308, points out that philosophy brought religion into the full light of day as a subject of rational inquiry. But Herodotos' religious thought was not caught up with either the atheism of certain sophists or the transcendentalism of a Sokrates; it appears slightly tinged with agnosticism.
2. Recklessness or rashness is a prime feature of tragic characters on the Attic stage; this fault rather than deliberate wrongdoing often brings about their downfall.
3. Notably the trapped Hippolytos, in the play of that name, saying that the oath he had taken was mere words, not his own conviction.
4. M. Miller, 'The Herodotean Croesus', *Klio* 41 (1963) 58(90). Contrast G de Sanctis: 'Solone (and Artabanos) i veri portavoce di Erodoto' in 'Il logos di Creso', *RFIC* 54 (1936) 1 [= *Studia di Storia* (1951) Ch. 3].
5. In the view of T. N. Gantz, 'Inherited Guilt in Aischylos', *CJ* 78 (1982) 1, Herodotos too was a believer in inherited guilt, but the argument is not compelling.
6. This statement is at first glance inconsistent with the ironic denial of 'great wrong' in cases of abduction at 1.3; but note that this latter view is that of 'the Persians', not of the historian.
7. Oroites' unsuccessful attempt on Samos by the trapping of Polykrates, 3.123ff., and Dareios' subsequent annexation of the island 3.142ff.; the attempt on Naxos suggested by Aristagoras and eagerly supported by Artaphernes 5.31; and the conquest of a portion of the north coast of the Aegaean as a pendant to the Skythian

expedition of Dareios 4.144. all confirm the Persian intention of Aegaean and European expansion.

8. I. M. Linforth, 'Named and Unnamed Gods in Herodotus', *UCPCPh* 9 (1928) 201, is still useful.

9. Perhaps the main lines at least of the narrative of Xerxes' invasion had been compiled before Herodotos' visit to the East aroused his interest in comparative religion.

10. It appears to be the remarkable nature of the coincidence that the sons of the two original (but unsuccessful!) envoys were selected for a similar mission, and also the fact that the wrath of Talthybios fell, most unjustly, upon the second generation that provoked Herodotos' comment. The translation by de Selincourt in the Penguin edition, 'clear evidence of divine intervention', is much too strong for πρῆγμα θειότατου.

11. Coincidence of battles are not rare in ancient history; the battle of Himera was said to be fought on the same day as that of Salamis, 7.166. Since the normal Greek campaigning season was limited to the period between the grain harvest and the vintage, the number of appropriate dates is also comparatively limited.

12. Divine providence, *Pronoia*, first appeared in the writings of Xenophanes and later of Anaxagoras; in the third century BC the Stoic philosophers elevated it to the supreme position.

13. *Tuchein* (this aorist form shows the root appearing in *tychē* more clearly than the present) may be either the principal verb or a participle; 'he happened to come' might appear literally either as 'he happened coming' or 'happening, he came'.

14. Solon in Herodotos is not really a historical personage and has no direct influence on events; in the remarkable work done at Athens the historian shows no interest; though he mentions the attempted coup of Kylon this is in reference to much later history; his Athenian political history begins with Peisistratos, perhaps a generation after Solon's reforms. The reformer is mentioned twice, apart from the Kroisos story, in non-Athenian contexts, once as having borrowed an Egyptian law (2.177) and the other in a reference to affairs in Cyprus which Solon was also said to have visited (5.113).

15. Bacchylides' version (3.23–63) is that Kroisos intended to immolate himself, and that Apollo transported him to the far north, to the Hyperboreans. The suicide seems to be confirmed by the famous vase-painting in the Louvre, of a date earlier than the *History* of Herodotos. See now J. A. S. Evans, 'What Happened to Croesus?', *CJ* 74 (1978) 34; Kyros only pretended to have kept him at court! The relationship with the tragic motive of 'learning through suffering' is discussed by H.-P. Stahl in 'Learning through Suffering?', *YCS* 24 (1975) 1.

16. Xerxes refers to his own youth in his apology to Artabanos (7.13); 'impetuous' is Aischylos' word, *Persians* 73.

17. A full discussion in Jacqueline de Romilly, 'La Vengeance comme explication dans l'oeuvre historique d'Hérodote', *REG* 74 (1971) 314–37.

18. The usage in 2.152 has less definite personification, since the vengeance is there specified as '[consisting] of bronze men'.

19. It can be suggested that this strong affirmation of belief was made in opposition to the destructive criticism of Protagoras; in particular the choice of the terms ἀντιλογίαι ἀληθεές and καταβάλλειν suggest the known titles of the sophist's tracts. (I owe this observation to the publishers' reader.) It would then provide a further example of Herodotos' eclecticism (see note 8 to Chapter 7).

20. One might have expected that the testing of the oracles would have been Kroisos' most offensive action to the gods.

21. See especially J. Kirchberg, *Die Fonktion der Orakel im Werke Herodots*, Hypomnemata 11 (1965). J. Elayi, 'Le rôle de l'oracle de Delphes dans le conflit greco-perse d'après les histoires d'Hérodote', *Iranica Antiqua* 13 (1978) 93.

22. J. Fontenrose, *The Delphic Oracle* (1978).

23. Of the nearly ninety oracular pronouncements mentioned, the books containing the greatest proportions rank as follows: 1, 4, 6, 5, 7, 8, 2, 3, 9. These figures seem to give no ground for any conclusions; examination of Cagnazzi's '28 *logoi*' (see Chapter 5 above) might be more productive.

24. Fontenrose (n. 22 above) argues that ambiguity lay not so much in the oracular response as in the mind of the recipient.

25. The two responses are discussed by J. Elayi, 'Deux oracles à Delphes', *REG* 92 (1979) 224; J. A. S. Evans, 'The Oracle of the "Wooden Wall" ', *CJ* 78 (1982) 24.

26. The signification of the Greek term has been disputed; if, as commonly thought, it means 'stone-thrower' the implication is that Kleisthenes, so far from aspiring to royalty, did not even qualify for inclusion in the regular armed infantry; the unarmed 'rabble' utilised the plentiful rocks of Greece as ammunition, while persons of standing used metal weapons.

27. Important recent discussions of the whole passage are to be found in G. Germain, 'Le songe de Xerxes', *REG* 69 (1956) 309; P. Frisch, *Die Träume bei Herodot* (1968), and R. G. A. van Lieshout, 'A Dream on a καιρός of History', *Mnemosyne* 23 (1970) 235.

28. Frisch (n. 27 above) points out that ten Herodotean dreams appear to kings. The possibility in primitive thought of a royal prerogative as to warning dreams cannot be excluded.

29. The Kroisos-Adrastos-Atys affair undoubtedly conforms with tragic ideas and, almost, format; but that is not to say that Herodotos put the story into tragic form, though he is responsible for the manner of the narration of the dialogue.

30. The basic arguments against a pro-Periklean Herodotos were put by H. Strasburger in *Historia* 4 (1955), 1 (also now in Marg, *Herodot* (1965) 574). An opposing view is offered by F. D. Harvey, 'The Political Sympathies of Herodotus', *Historia* 15 (1966) 254; my own view remains that presented in 'Herodotos and Politics', *Greece and Rome* 19 (1972) 136. That Herodotos, if previously attracted by the glamour of Periklean Athens, became disenchanted by the harsh suppression of the revolt of Samos, his early refuge, is a reasonable supposition.

31. Despite recent criticisms I remain unrepentantly of the view that Herodotos used the three terms (*mounarchos*, *tyrannos* and *basileus*) interchangeably. See F. D. Harvey, 'Political Sympathies of Herodotos' and A. Ferrill, 'Herodotos on Tyranny', *Historia* 27 (1978) 385; also S. I. Oost, 'The Tyrant Kings of Syracuse', *CPh* 72 (1976) 224.

32. See J. A.S. Evans, 'Despotes Nomos', *Athenaeum* 43 (1965) 142.

33. See n.15 above.

34. The phrase is that of A. Piatowski, 'Le sourine ironique d'Hérodote', *Studii Clasice* 10 (1968) 51–62. 'Like a mirror reflecting all the current ideologies, while remaining firmly attached to the old-fashioned ideology of the preceding century.'

35. H. J. Immerwahr, *Form and Thought in Herodotus*, 154 writes 'The figure of Croesus is treated in so much detail that it seems to typify, in the manner of a parable, the whole fate of man. Unfortunately, the commentators are not agreed on the contents of the message thus conveyed.' An obvious inference would seem to be that there is no message.

36. F. Jacoby, whose monumental article in PW suppl. v. 2 is still influential, first raised objections; P. Legrand in his Budé edition (1946–56) regarded it as an interpolation, and recently Cagnazzi, 'Tavola dei 28 logoi', *Hermes* 103 (1975) 385 denies that it is a fitting ending for the history. However T. Krischer, 'Herodots Schluss-Kapitel', *Eranos* 72 (1974) 95, accepts it as a 'rounding-off'. See also T. Sinko, 'L'historiosophie dans le prologue et l'épilogue de l'oeuvre d'Hérodote d'Halicarnassos', *Eos* 50 (1956/60) 3.

37. The Penguin translation renders the literal 'the following deed' as 'a dreadful revenge' — thus attributing to Herodotos a condemnation which might well be expected, but which he does not voice.

Amongst the many and varied criticisms levelled against Herodotos one of the more prominent has been that of undue prejudice, of not even attempting to write 'without fear or favour' as historians sometimes claimed. Like some other accusations, this count too results from failure to take a general view, and selecting one or two items which seem to indicate favourable or unfavourable bias in his treatment of nations, groups or individuals. Examination will show that in most areas Herodotos shows a greater objectivity than the majority of ancient historians; he has not prejudged the character and behaviour of the participants in historical (and even non-historical) events but shows several, if not all, facets of peoples, institutions and personages.

One of the major counts in the indictment, which has already come to our notice, is his excessive fondness for barbarians. The author of the pamphlet *On Herodotos' Malignity*,[1] as a good, honourable if somewhat narrow-minded Greek, considered the Hellenic character and institutions superior to those of the rest of the world, excepting perhaps the Roman masters who had 'inherited' Greek culture in his day. But Herodotos shows that he can recognise merit displayed, in any area, by non-Greeks; and this apparently offended. We have noticed the historian's fondness for things Egyptian and his frequent attempts to father Greek institutions, religious or legal, upon Egyptian sources. This tendency may have resulted in part from a (subconscious) 'diffusionist' theory of culture, as Lloyd suggests. On the other hand by 'Plutarch's' time Egypt had succumbed in turn not only to the Persian but to Macedonian and Roman conquerors, and was regarded as effete and contemptible.[2] For these reasons the term *philobarbaros*, pro-barbarian or unpatriotic, was applied by the hostile critic; we of course, at the distance of over 2,000 years, may find a positive virtue in the fact that Herodotos regarded all the nations of the world simply as members of the human race. His broadmindedness on varying moral standards has been shown in the previous chapter. Whatever influences brought him to the realisation that a *nomos* is a *nomos*, wherever it is found, and that it is natural, if not inevitable, that societies formed in environments unlike that of the

Hellenic should have different laws and customs, Herodotos deserves commendation for it. Neither the *physis* (mod: genes) nor the *nomoi* of the Egyptians are understood, he believes, by the Greeks; and the differences are the greater because the land is so utterly different. The Nile behaves in a way unlike, indeed the reverse of, all other rivers, and the inhabitants who depend upon it also behave differently (2.35). The Nile's behaviour is its *physis*; although some physical characteristics of the Egyptians may show variation from those of the Greeks or their other neighbours,[3] the really remarkable divergence is in their *nomoi*.

In fact it is unlikely that for Herodotos the term *barbaros* had fully acquired the derogatory significance which we normally associate with it.[4] Its archaic connotation was merely 'non-Greek'; perhaps non-Greek-speaking and therefore unintelligible; probably, stupid. Herodotos had wider experience of barbarians, that is, non-Greeks, than most other members of his society, and was indeed one of very few who had set out to learn as much as possible about the other societies, from the most primitive to the most highly developed. He therefore declined to accept the popular view, one that had gained general acceptance since the Persian Wars, namely that in all respects non-Greeks were less civilised than and generally inferior to the Hellenes. Such a refusal invariably excites the anger of racists — modern examples leap only too readily to mind. However a contrast or distinction between Greek and barbarian occurs some sixty to seventy times in the history.

Sometimes Herodotos is accused of inconsistency, a charge that is neither without substance in certain areas nor unexpected when the difficulties of handling his vast mass of materials are recalled. In the present instance, the statement in point is at Book 1.60, commonly rendered 'the Greeks in the past were cleverer and less liable to such silly foolishness than the barbarians'. Unfortunately, a number of the manuscripts, by a very simple exchange of a couple of letters, render the reverse meaning; and the likelihood is that the second version is what Herodotos actually wrote.[5] The context is the deception practised by Peisistratos on the Athenian populace by dressing up a tall and handsome woman as the goddess Athene, come to support his claim to political ascendancy. How could the Athenians, 'said to be' (an ironical touch, surely, in view of Herodotos' attitude to what is merely 'said') the cleverest of the Greeks, fall for such a trick, even allowing for the fact that 'in the old days' the barbarians were much more sophisticated? The evidence from the rest of Book 1, and 2, and elsewhere, is that the barbarians were responsible for all manner of clever inventions; the Lydians invented coinage and the games Greeks play, the Phoenicians alphabetic writing, the Egyptians the calendar and many other 'firsts'. Such knowledge gave Herodotos firm ground for his opinion that the world was not divided into Greeks and non-Greeks on the basis of merit, but into groups and individuals who were each capable of both good and ill. The historian only appeared *philobarbaros* to a *misobarbaros* or racist mentality. He does not, however, appear to have gone as far as to have formulated the concept of the 'Unity of Mankind', but laid an implicit foundation for its subsequent development.[6]

The Athenians played a disproportionately large part in the repulse of the Persian invasions; almost single-handed they defeated Dareios' forces at Marathon and made the largest contribution, both numerically and strategically through Themistokles, to the naval victory at Salamis. Their effort continued on both land and sea in the great triumph over the Persian army at Plataia and in the destruction of the Persian (i.e. Phoenician) fleet at Mykale. Then we have noted the transfer to Athens of leadership in anti-Persian activity of which the capture of Sestos represents the initial stage — and the close of the Herodotean narrative.[7] Thus any dispassionate narrator of these events would be bound to reach a conclusion similar to that of Herodotos, that notwithstanding indispensable Spartan generalship, steadfastness and ability to lead other states, it was the Athenians who were mainly responsible for the repulse of the Persian invasions. The author of the pamphlet already mentioned, taking a somewhat anti-Athenian stance,[8] objects to the undue favour shown to the Athenians. Also, it has often been thought that Herodotos aimed his work particularly at an Athenian audience and was careful to flatter their patriotic sensibilities. That he descended from his normal position of Olympian neutrality 'above the fray' to utter in his own person this pro-Athenian declaration (7.139) is said to reveal that he suffered from prejudice. Typically perhaps of Herodotean structure (cf. Chapter 5 above) it does not stand as a summing-up at the close of the history — there is, as we have seen, no formal closure — but is introduced by the statement that while the king's stated aim was revenge upon

Athens, his real intent was the conquest of all Hellas. His demand
for symbolic 'earth and water' had been obeyed by some; those
who refused were extremely apprehensive of the consequences,
especially because of their inadequate force of warships, and many
were glad to 'medise'. It was the thought of such non-resisting
surrender to the invader which reminded the historian that Athens,
though the recipient of terrifying pronouncements from Delphi,
stood firm and provided the backbone of the naval resistance. He
does not tell us here, but in due context later, that after their land
had been ravaged and their city despoiled, they were offered
favourable terms by Mardonios, who knew what Herodotos here
urges, that without the Athenian fleet the rest of the defenders had
no chance of successful resistance. The Athenians refused the offer
out of hand, and what is more lynched the one councillor who
ventured to suggest that the offer be debated (9.5) even though its
rejection meant a second Persian ravaging of Attika and Athens.

Herodotos' argument here is impeccable. He examines the
strategical weakness of the Peloponnese in face of a superior navy,
and believes, no doubt correctly, that no amount of bravery on the
battlefield would have saved the Spartans; they would have been
isolated by the piecemeal reduction or surrender of their allies in
face of the great Persian fleet, its numbers not reduced by battle
but perhaps even augmented by the Athenian ships. (Several Greek
states fought, under greater or less compulsion, on the 'wrong' side
at Plataia, and the invading fleet of course included the naval
contingents of the Greek and semi-hellenised cities around the
coasts of Asia Minor.) Herodotos gives due credit however to
Spartan valour and there can be no question of anti-Spartan
prejudice. The historian admits that his judgement will not be
popular (outside Athens, of course; therefore he was not merely
considering its reception by Athenians). He is only too well aware
of the jealousies and hostilities between individual *poleis*, some
arising from opposing participation in these struggles, others
provoked later by Athenian imperialism or mere local quarrels. He
may indeed have paid too great heed to tendentious accounts of
some episodes in these Persian Wars, as witness the allegation that
the Aiginetans had offered the tokens of submission to Dareios
before the invasion of 490 (6.49). It seems that there were (as might
be expected) two opposing groups in Aigina; the patriotic party
certainly prevailed ten years later, and the Aiginetan squadron
distinguished itself at Salamis. But Athens had earlier quarrelled

with Aigina, and one might suspect the story of an Athenian origin.[9] However, it is bound up with the rivalry and machinations of the Spartan kings Demaratos and Kleomenes, and some non-Athenian source certainly provided information about the former. The calumny on the Korinthian part in the battle of Salamis (cf. Chapter 7 above) is stated to be of Athenian origin and rejected elsewhere; to report it hardly indicates especial favour to Athens!

As with other matters, it is an erroneous procedure to pick on one Herodotean passage and deduce a general attitude therefrom, while ignoring other references. The digressions on Athenian history do not reflect great credit on either the leading individuals or the city as a whole; it was the total dedication of the Athenian state to the patriotic defence effort that inspired Herodotos' praise.[10] His guarded remarks about the struggle for hegemony in the ensuing half-century (6.98) and the possibly derogatory implication of the gratuitous report of Agariste's dream (6.131) do not imply approval of the role played by Athens after the Persian invasions. Moreover her most successful military leaders, Miltiades and Themistokles, both indulged in imperialist ventures in the euphoria of their triumphs, against Paros and Andros respectively (6.133ff., 8.111ff.), neither of which attempts reflected credit upon their authors, who are said to have acted from personal motives of revenge or greed. (See further Chapter 10.)

The historian displays, it would seem, enthusiasm for Athenian democracy in the statement that the city flourished greatly after ridding itself of the Peisistratid tyranny (5.66). But the statement carries limitations: 'Athens was already a considerable city; increased growth came after the removal of the tyrants.' Herodotos then proceeds to tell of internal power struggles between the aristocrats, and further Spartan intervention, to say nothing of an attempt to gain alliance with Persia. In the last case, it is true, the volatile Athenian populace discredited the envoys on their return — perhaps because of their failure to gain advantageous terms. None of this reads like the version of a reporter biased in favour of Athens.

Evidence more convincing to some, perhaps, is the short digressive paragraph (5.78) in which the Athenian victory over their neighbours in Boiotia and Chalkis is hailed as the proof that free men fight better than the subjects of a despot. This myth, disproved so many times in history from Kyros to Napoleon and beyond, was of course reinforced by the many feats of war achieved by Athens in the great days of the fifth century. However both the course and the purpose of the paragraph are the praise of freedom rather than of Athens; freedom, it is clear enough, Herodotos preferred to slavery, whether or not one accepts his inference that success in war is related to political status. As for democracy, one should not forget the cynical comment on Aristagoras' success in 'fooling' the Athenian assembly, after being rejected on the advice of a precocious child at Sparta (5.97). It is also recorded that the Athenians refused further help to their Ionian relatives despite repeated appeals; only a commendation of Athenian pragmatic wisdom, not of their courage or unselfishness, if one accepts that Herodotos was convinced the revolt could not have succeeded even with naval assistance from the Greek mainland.

In the case of Athens, a particular bias in favour of the leading clan of the Alkmaionidai is a frequent charge against Herodotos. This, like some other allegations, depends on a single passage; namely his defence of the family against the charge of treasonable communication with the Persians after the battle of Marathon (6.121–4). The charge against the Alkmaionidai presents so many difficulties that the weightiest item of the accusation of bias in the historian is that he appeared eager to offer a somewhat superfluous defence. Obviously however there was a pro-Persian, or more correctly pro-Peisistratid party still alive and well in Athens, even twenty years after the expulsion of the tyrants, and an attempt by some of its members to supply intelligence to their former leader Hippias was not incredible. The main argument too of Herodotos' apologia is flawed; evidence that the Alkmaionids were at times, like most aristocrats, hostile to the tyranny leaves political opportunism out of court, despite his own reports of the erstwhile alliance between Megakles and Peisistratos, and the former's dynastic marriage with the daughter of the Sikyonian tyrant Kleisthenes.

Other references to the family include one credit mark, the rebuilding of the temple at Delphi to exceed the specifications of their contract (5.62) — the motive for which generosity he does not infer; piety it was not, as shown by their corruption of the god's mouthpiece in their own interest; there shortly follows his report of the allegation, still current in the 30s of the fifth century, that the Alkmaionidai had been responsible for the sacrilegious killing of Kylon and his partisans (5.70). Two further anecdotes show how they gained their wealth and prestige; the first, owing to friendship with a foreign potentate (6.125), and the second, to the marriage of Megakles to the daughter of the tyrant of Sikyon (6.131). Both of these are humorous stories, the former not particularly creditable to Alkmaion; the latter certainly no support for Herodotos' impassioned defence of the clan in the earlier passage.

Lastly, Megakles allowed his daughter to marry the tyrant Peisistratos (1.61). Herodotos may be inconsistent, but he is not pro-Alkmaionid; the fact that he rejects the allegation of treason is due to faulty reasoning, but faulty reasoning does not always arise from prejudice.[11]

Herodotos lived as a neighbour of the Ionians, benefited enormously from their studies in geography, genealogy and much else, and wrote in their dialect. It would accordingly be surprising to find his work full of anti-Ionian prejudice. Such however has been the received opinion. At Book 1.143, after an enthusiastic recommendation of the climate of Ionia and a short digression upon dialects, Herodotos provides a reason for the isolation of Miletos in face of the threat from Kyros by saying that while the whole of Hellas was weak, the Ionian towns[12] were particularly so. Only Athens was of any repute 'in the old days', i.e. the early years of Ionian settlement east of the Aegaean. It is because of this ancient weakness that the Athenians from whose city the Ionian colonists traditionally set out (1.146) do not refer to themselves as Ionians. And what are we to make of the fact that 'Herodotos of Thurioi' (according to Aristotle and others) fails to mention Thurioi in his references to Southern Italy? We must be cautious about presuming bias on such an inadequate basis.

More serious is the attitude taken by Herodotos to the Ionian revolt. An enormous literature[13] has recently accumulated on the manifold problems; of the sources (deliberately omitted from our discussion in Chapter 7), of Herodotos' treatment of the available information, the deficiencies of his account (which unfortunately can only be minimally repaired from other writers), his attitude to the principal characters Aristagoras and Histiaios (see Chapter 10 below), and his apparent condemnation of the whole undertaking as a piece of folly. Now this condemnation undoubtedly appears pragmatic; the revolt failed, therefore it could not have succeeded. Surely this is unnecessarily naïve. While Herodotos was collecting his material and writing his history, Ionia was, if not free, at least free from Persian rule; and this comparative freedom was due to the command of the sea maintained by Athenian sea-power. This lesson can hardly have been completely lost on Herodotos, whose grasp of the basic principles of strategy was not as abysmally weak as is sometimes suggested. One only has to glance at the speeches of Artabanos and of Demaratos on strategic matters (7.49 and 235) to see that its major problems are present in his mind. Even the anecdote about Bias' dissuasion of Kroisos' intended attack on the Aegaean islands is relevant evidence (1.27).

The failure of the Ionians to form a more cohesive confederacy and to present an unbroken front against the Persians caused the breakdown of their resistance. Was it the case that they lacked the desire for freedom, or at least the intensity of fervour that impelled the Athenians? Now Herodotos attributes the instigation of the revolt not to any stirring urge for liberty amongst the Ionians, but to the personal ambitions and individual machinations of Aristagoras and Histiaios (5.35f.). The former had fallen foul of Megabates, the Persian admiral of the force collected at his instance to conquer Naxos, the most powerful of the central Aegaean islands. In a huff he warned the Naxians that they were to be the object of the attack; he had either hurriedly to leave the sphere of Persian control or, a more attractive, nay, glorious alternative, remove that control from Ionia. His predecessor and uncle Histiaios meanwhile was chafing in honourable confinement *chez* Dareios, and perhaps urged revolt to give himself a pretext for return to Ionia. Our present question is not the degree of individual responsibility (and irresponsibility) genuinely to be attributed to these individuals; it is clear that individual initiative is needed to touch off a revolt, and that some organisation by a dynamic personality is essential.[14] Aristagoras seems to have displayed plenty of energy at first.[15] It is clear from the ease with which pro-Persian quislings were got rid of in the other Ionian states that there were pressing public as well as private reasons for desiring a change. Not everyone however thought the proposition timely. Hekataios, sometimes styled as the predecessor of Herodotos (but not cited as authority for the account), strongly urged its abandonment in view of the overwhelming might of Persia. Finding no support, he then made the sensible suggestion of using the temple treasures of Branchidai as the necessary sinews of war (5.36).[16]

Initial success at Sardis was followed by a serious reverse near Ephesos which apparently led to the withdrawal of Eretria and Athens from the war. Undeterred, says Herodotos, the Ionians carried on; the revolt spread north and south, to Byzantion and Cyprus, whither with daring initiative the Ionian fleet sailed to face the Phoenicians. They fought, we hear, particularly well and won the naval battle (5.112), but the land battle went against their allies, not without reports of treachery, and the island was lost. Persian counter-measures on land against the Ionian towns succeeded gradually — evidently, but Herodotos does not report this — because of lack of support by sea. It appears there was no Phoenician fleet in the Aegaean till three years later, and had Ionian dominance of the sea ensured supply and reinforcement for the maritime towns their resistance could have been prolonged. But the impetus of the revolt had faded away; it was always difficult to keep a combined fleet operational — as later events proved — and Persian agents had been offering a mixture of threats and inducements for return to Persian vassalage. But Aristagoras is now made the scapegoat (5.124 and 6.1). Only nine cities contributed ships to the fleet at last assembled to raise the siege of Miletos, two of them sending only three vessels apiece. The supposed anti-Ionian bias of Herodotos relies heavily on his account of the energetic admiral Dionysios of Phokaia in Aiolis (an unprejudiced appointment by the more numerous contingents) and his strenuous training programme, against which Ionian crews went on strike (6.12). It is clear that this story (inconsistent with their earlier performance) was put about by persons interested in finding an alibi for their own defection in battle[17] — most likely the aristocratic Samian acquaintances of the historian. He has not been able to discount the report; certainly the indisputable disunity amongst the squadrons at Lade could well have been reflected in a refusal to act under the command of 'a man without a city'.[18]

The events of 498–494 were regarded by Herodotos as typical of the struggles for freedom of the Eastern Greeks against Lydian or Persian overlords.[19] One important difference was the involvement, brief as it was, of mainland Greece in the war — 'the beginning of the troubles', in Herodotos' notorious and often misinterpreted phrase. If he in fact thought the Ionian revolt was the *cause* of the invasions of Greece proper under Dareios and Xerxes, it is strange that he has gone to the lengths already discussed to emphasise Persian expansionist policy, and to explain that 'Athens and Eretria' were a mere pretext in the expeditions of Mardonios and of Datis. He has not used the Ionian revolt and its failure to display a vindictive bias against the Ionians.

The cooperation of Ionians, willingly or not, in the invasion of Xerxes does not lead to wholesale condemnation of them either. A rebuke may be seen in the statement that some of them 'welcomed' the expected defeat of the patriotic Greeks (8.10), whom Herodotos several times terms 'those who had chosen the better course'. Accusations of medism, the equivalent behaviour to the compliance of the Ionians, were flung about on the mainland of Greece also. Herodotos distinguishes between unavoidable surrender, like that of the Thessalians (7.172), and the voluntary defection of Thebes (apart from the 'hostages' taken by Leonidas to Thermopylai, for the report of which the historian is in hot water with 'Plutarch'). Argos, enabled by its glorious legendary past to make claim to joint command of the Greek forces with Sparta, but motivated by justifiable suspicion of all Spartan activity since the inroads of Kleomenes, used this pretext for refusal to join; but unlike Thebes, did not have to contribute forces to Xerxes owing to its situation within Fortress Peloponnese. Herodotos provides a variant version, remaining impartial — and to illustrate the folly of recrimination offers a parable about exchange of evils (7.152).

Greek society in the fifth century was male-dominated to a high degree, in most cities. Wives in particular it seems were kept out of public view, except perhaps in Sparta. It is possible that Herodotos was influenced by the prevailing male chauvinism, yet he obviously considered women important in decision-making, as well as admirable for various other qualities. Long ago his philosophy of history was epigrammatically if inaccurately summed up as 'Cherchez la femme, mais n'oubliez pas le dieu' (Macan).[20] The real influence of Atossa in Persian politics, like the alleged importance of Artemisia in Xerxes' council, may be exceptional cases. The legendary feats of Semiramis, Nitokris and Tomyris are merely part of romantic history, but certainly Herodotos pays them due regard.

It is noticeable that a number of women who are prominent in minor episodes remain anonymous — the wife and widow of Intaphernes, the consort of Kandaules and later of Gyges — but both of these may have a non-historical origin, and like 'the princess' (and also 'the prince') in fairy-tales do not require a name. These omissions should not therefore be taken as implying that Herodotos was anti-feminist. There are however more solidly historical ladies who remain nameless; the daughter of Hegetorides of Kos who appealed to Pausanias after the battle of Plataia (9.76) — apparently sufficiently identified for contemporaries by her father's name — and more surprisingly the unfortunate wife of Masistes,[21] the object of Xerxes' lust and victim of Amestris' savagery (9.108). Her daughter, however, to whom the king transferred his affections despite her marriage to his own son, and less faithful than her mother, is named as Artaÿnte. I cannot offer anything but speculation about sources to explain this inconsistency. Another pawn in Oriental harem diplomacy, the daughter of Apries, is named, Nitetis (3.1–3). The historian's sources, not his prejudice, are to be blamed for such inconsistencies.

The tongue-in-cheek comment about the willingness of girls to be abducted has recently been urged as showing that Herodotos approved of rape.[22] But this he presents as the view of the Persians. Certainly the historian was not averse to the modern recipe for popular literary success, 'sex and violence' in his *History*,[23] and it is perhaps noteworthy that he seems to have a considerable interest in prostitution, and does not condemn it in principle; indeed he admires successful practitioners of this as of other *métiers* (2.134f.). The only explicit 'editorial' judgement on sexual behaviour is that already referred to, on the ritual fornication of the Babylonians (1.199). The most flagrant example of sexual misbehaviour is that of Xerxes in regard to Masistes' wife and daughter and no doubt Xerxes stands condemned without Herodotos pronouncing sentence; it is to be noted that neither does Amestris receive any comment on her unjustifiable and atrocious vengeance on the innocent wife of her brother-in-law.[24] Her sadism had already appeared in the reference to her living sacrifice (7.114).

As with men, Herodotos finds women capable of both good and ill; their capacity for cruelty is further exemplified by the case of Pheretime (4.202), and collectively, the women of Athens who in one generation use their dress-pins vindictively, and in another stone to death the innocent wife and children of Lykidas (5.87 and 9.5). (This from a 'pro-Athenian' historian!)

The insult 'worse than a woman' (9.107) is specified as being a Persian jeer, and may be discounted. But the myth of female inferiority is revealed also in the alleged exclamation of Xerxes as a spectator at the naval battle, on mistaking for particular valour the quite unscrupulous deed of Artemisia. That Amazonian lady herself puts the view that men are far stronger — one thinks of that 'weak woman' Elizabeth I! — and this is no doubt of Greek origin, part of the Artemisia legend if not the original composition of Herodotos (8.68). The popular view is also reflected in Euelthon's gifts to Pheretime; and the *logos* of the Amazons shows some orthodox opinions about women, despite the unusual character and martial prowess of these females; they are unable to handle a boat, but they pick up a foreign language quicker than the men; their relations with their female in-laws are not happy (4.110ff.). The faithlessness of all wives (2.111), a scandal to the unliberated masses, appears only in a folk-tale.

In women Herodotos admired not only masculine bravado in Artemisia (and the legendary queens, Semiramis and Nitokris) but intelligence. Gorgo at the age of nine is a somewhat precocious example (5.51) but in maturity the wife of Leonidas, she reappears as the only person intelligent enough to solve the problem of a secret message (7.239). Was this little digression included as a 'record', a genuine tribute to female intelligence, or a jeer at the male Spartan population, popularly if erroneously supposed to lack initiative? Other Spartan royal wives are beautiful perhaps, but rather passive, and do not affect government like Eastern consorts.

Herodotos then is certainly not a male chauvinist though he may not have progressed as far in feminist thinking as Euripides; he tends to reflect, rather than to endorse, current Greek attitudes which are perhaps well illustrated by a phrase in the mouth of Themistokles, 'we have left our children and wives', making clear the 'normal' priority of the society.

Political prejudice might well be expected in a keen student of societies who was also a patriot and a believer in freedom.[25] However, as we have seen, theoretical politics were only in their infancy, and while 'freedom' is to be preferred to 'slavery', a realist becomes aware that 'freedom' is highly conditional and that 'slavery' is not entirely abhorrent in all its forms. 'The Spartans [says Demaratos to Xerxes, 7.104] have a master, the law — *nomos* — which they fear more than your subjects fear you.' In truth, most moderns view classical Sparta as a totalitarian state, in which little political freedom was enjoyed by the 'peers', and even the kings, since the Five Commissars kept a tight rein on their political and military conduct and even interfered in their marital affairs. Yet Herodotos accepts the *Eunomia*, the 'Good

Institutions', at face value (1.65). We have already noticed his qualified support for democracy, Athenian style; and qualified approval, reserved disapproval, so typical of the historian apply also in the political sphere. It is remarkable that the most detailed account of how a particular form of government came into being (apart from that of the Peisistratid tyranny, which loses its impact somewhat by being related in stages from Books 1 to 6) is that of the Medes under Deiokes (1.96ff.). Deiokes graduated from being a local magnate through demagoguery to despotism; the process by which he was 'elected' by his own supporters does bear resemblance to the little known from sources other than Herodotos about Greek tyrannies. One may therefore suspect an *arrière-pensée*; the type of government of the Medes was only distantly relevant to the main historical narrative, and perhaps the reason for its inclusion is parabolic. Considering the arguments against democracy in 3.81 and 82, and the fact that Thukydides was later to define the vaunted Athenian democracy as 'in reality, the rule of the First Citizen', it is possible that Herodotos viewed the eventual establishment of despotism as inevitable. But the type or ideology of government did not concern Herodotos over much; it was the impact on historical events that was important. Thus Artemisia's despotic rule is ignored, and an encomium on her offered at 7.99. So for Athens the development of tyranny and subsequent advance to Kleisthenean 'democracy' are recorded, but the organisation and methods of government are almost entirely ignored.[26] Hence no discussion of Solon's earlier reforms, considered epoch-making by others.

At Sparta Herodotos was not given access to the arcana of Spartan government, and the earliest description of its institutions and procedures is to be found in Xenophon, half a century later. However the nominal extent of the powers of the dual kings and limitations thereon were relevant to the external political and military events, and therefore included. Adequate tribute to Spartan military prowess and courage is given both in the historian's narrative of Thermopylai (obviously based on popular accounts), in the remarks attributed to Demaratos and in the observation on the primary defence role of Athens (7.139).

A considerable portion of the *History* deals with tyrants and their doings; over fifty are mentioned, and some play an important part.[27] But the reason for this is not that tyranny, or the despotism of Oriental monarchs, was either ideologically interesting or detestable to Herodotos. In face of this phenomenon he maintained his usual scholarly detachment, recording both good and bad deeds with impartiality. Tyrants received attention in the first place because some of them played leading roles in the history of the sixth and early fifth centuries. Two in particular were of great importance to the developments leading to the Persian invasions of Greece, as shown in Chapter 7; Polykrates, whose naval power in the Aegaean had to be neutralised before any Persian advance beyond the land of Asia Minor could be contemplated; and Peisistratos, who played a slightly more equivocal role in the rise of Athenian power. Of lesser stature and notoriety were the group of Persian-supported rulers of Asiatic Greek cities, all concerned positively or negatively in the conflict between Persia and Greece. Histiaios and Aristagoras stand out amongst these, not only because of the eminence of their fief Miletos, but because they appear in Herodotos' account as responsible for the outbreak and some of the conduct of the Ionian revolt. Others who gain top billing, but whose historical activities were marginal to the main stream, are Periandros of Korinth and Gelon of Syrakuse; the reason in their case is that (like the two first mentioned) they were impressive. That is (more or less) the term used by Herodotos in his comparison of Polykrates to the Sicilian dictators (3.125). They and their like gathered, by fair means or foul (and Soklees would claim the latter) great riches, and in a poor country like Greece, where individuals can still become inordinately wealthy, their opulence was a matter of prestige, envy — and news value! They were talked about, stories became attached to them, sometimes with a factual basis, others like the advice of Periandros to Thrasyboulos (5.92) and the Ring of Polykrates (3.41ff.), folk-tale motifs. And of course personal scandal was spread, with authenticity about equal to that concerning the British royal family in the popular press.

With their wealth, they either built up large military and naval forces or engaged in great construction projects, as did Gelon and Polykrates.[28] Neither of these policies results in a 'bad press' in the *History*; even Polykrates' habit of robbing friends and enemies alike, or Gelon's ruthless forced migrations of populations, elicit no adverse comment. The latter tyrant, in the meeting with the envoys from mainland Greece, has plenty to say, showing both good sense and a deal of humour. Both of these ingredients are probably the contribution of Herodotos himself, the latter perhaps in view of the name Gelon, 'Smiler' (7.158ff.).

Thus there are several reasons for the prominence of tyrants in the history, none of which are ideological or moralising. Herodotos is not hostile to them on principle, and where they rule well he says so, as in the case of Peisistratos (1.59). It was a well-known fact of political life that tyrants expelled their chief opponents, the leading aristocrats who resented their own loss of power; the same was often true also of political groups of any colour who gained control as well as of individuals. Taxation was inevitable, though perhaps unknown as a direct impost in some cities before the dictatorships (an early *polis* had no budget): one rather excessive example of an extraordinary levy is detailed in the tendentious speech of Soklees (5.92); the shade of Periandros' wife had to be pacified by the sacrifice of all their finest array stripped from the women of Korinth. But this speech, from which incidentally we learn that the founder of the tyranny after a rule lasting thirty years was able to hand over peaceably to his son, is a political tract and ought not to be taken as representing the Herodotean view.

Eastern despots too are treated equitably. It was the *nomos* of Orientals to be ruled by an autocrat. Why should Herodotos, one of whose main principles was the supremacy of *nomos*, criticise this institution? Again, we are not to take the criticism of despotism by Otanes (3.80) as the view of the historian, in preference to the attacks on aristocracy and democracy which figure in the same debate. Herodotos was something of a pragmatist, and in view of the fact that the Persian despotic monarchy seemed as firmly entrenched as ever in his own day,[29] he could not invent any other conclusion to the debate than the triumph of the arguments of Dareios. All he is conveying, apart from the enjoyment of a nicely-packaged set of rival political theories,[30] is that according to his information (which he had verified as best he could) the Persians at that time of troubles looked at possible alternatives to their traditional monarchy, but rejected them.

Oriental despots, like tyrants and private individuals, display faults of character, vices even, and may even be psychopathic, like Kambyses (3.25). They are not condemned in general; as individuals, merits and demerits are attributed to them. Lust, cruelty, cupidity are not uncommon, and owing to their situation of power they have more opportunities to indulge these vices, but no monopoly of them. Herodotos retains his moral as well as his political objectivity in the face of their exploits. That a late anecdote has the youthful future historian participating in an attempt to overthrow the local tyrant has nothing to say about a political prejudice in his *History*.

Notes

1. The attribution of Plutarch may be erroneous, as there are some stylistic differences, and the bitter tone of the work hardly suits the otherwise mild and fair-minded author of the Lives. See the thesis by J. W. Boake, 'Plutarch's Historical Judgement, with special reference to the *de Herodoti Malignitate*' (Diss. Toronto, 1975), and the older article by P. E. Legrand in *Mélanges Glotz* vol. II (Paris, Presses Universitaire, 1932) 535. But the authorship question hardly affects the present discussion.
2. The poets Horace and Juvenal, a little over a century apart, both reflect such an attitude in early Imperial Rome.
3. Herodotos informs us that (3.12) that one could tell Persian from Egyptian skulls upon a battle-field, not by their cephalic index but by an environmentally-induced difference in thickness.
4. H. Diller, 'Die Hellenen-Barbaren Antithese im Zeitalter der Perserkriege', *Entretiens Hardt* 8 (1961 (1962)) 37; Ingomar Weiler, 'The Greek and the non-Greek World in the Archaic Period', *GRBS* 9 (1968) 21–9; R. Rtskhiladze, 'La specificité de l'Orient dans les histoires d'Hérodote', *A. Ant. Hung.* 22 (1974) 487 (in close agreement with my view): so too D. Hegyi, 'Die Begriff barbaros bei Herodot', *AUB* v–vi (1977/78) 33.
5. The change is one that might have been intentionally made by some copyist more patriotic than honest, or unintentionally by one merely expecting the 'obvious' praise of the Greeks. See Rosa Lamacchia, 'Erodoto nazionalista?' *Atene e Roma* 4 (1954) 87.
6. Relevant is F. Stoessl, 'Herodots Humanität', *Gymnasium* 66 (1959) 477.
7. Other indications of latent Athenian imperialism had been given by Miltiades' ill-fated attempt on Paros (6.133), paralleled after Salamis by Themistokles at Andros (8.111) — and earlier still by aspects of Peisistratid policy, e.g. the support of Miltiades the elder and his successors in the Gallipoli peninsula (6.36 and 39).
8. Easily explained if the author really was Plutarch of Chaironeia in Boiotia, whose people were naturally jealous of their more powerful southern neighbour.
9. The forcible subjection of Aigina under the Athenian empire might account, through guilty conscience, for attempts to blacken the reputation of the island in Herodotos' day.
10. See J. A. S. Evans, 'Herodotus and Athens; the Evidence of the Encomium', *AC* 48 (1979) 112.
11. On the whole question see D. Gillis, 'Marathon and the Alcmaeonids', *GRBS* 10 (1969) 133; V. M. Strogecki (English résume: Herodotus and the Alcmaeonids), in *VDI* 41 (1977) 145 (R. Develin, 'Herodotos and the Alkmeonids', forthcoming).
12. He uses here the term *polismata*, signifying a much less impressive organisation than the *poleis* 'city-states' which are usually designated. See G. Maddoli, 'Erodoto e gli Ioni: per l'interpretazione di 1.141.2', *P.d.P.* 34 (1979) 256.
13. A selection of recent work on this topic; D. Hegyi, 'The Historical Background of the Ionian Revolt', *A. Ant. Hung.* 14 (1966) 285; G. A. H. Chapman, 'Herodotus and Histiaeus' Role in the Ionian Revolt', *Historia* 21 (1972) 546; P. Tozzi, 'Erodoto e la responsabilità dell' inizio della rivolta ionica', *Athenaeum* 55 (1977) 127; J. A. S. Evans, 'Herodotus and the Ionian Revolt', *Historia* 25 (1976)

31; P. B. Manville, 'Aristagoras and Histiaios: the Leadership Struggle in the Ionian Revolt', *CQ* 27 (1977) 80; Laura Boffo, 'Gli Ioni a Micale', *Rende. Ist. Lomb.* III (1977) 83; D. Lateiner, 'The Failure of the Ionian Revolt', *Historia* 31 (1982) 129.

14. Recent history provides ample examples; one need only cite Lech Walesa.

15. However when the revolt was failing, Aristagoras is described as being 'no keen spirit' (5.124); thus a further reflection of a pragmatic approach in the sources.

16. This reference to Hekataios is obviously not denigratory, since it appears that Herodotos shared his view of the impracticability of the revolt, independently or derivatively. Hekataios' useful advice is quoted again at 5.125, where also it is rejected.

17. It is an interesting problem to unravel the conflicting strands of evidence, from Samos in particular: see B. M. Mitchell, 'Herodotus and Samos', *JHS* 95 (1975) 75 and R. Tölle-Kastenbein, *Herodot und Samos* (1976).

18. A similar denigratory tactic was used by anti-Athenian elements before Salamis; Themistokles 'had no city' because the Persians were in occupation of Athens — but on that occasion common sense prevailed (8.61).

19. J. W. Neville, 'Was there an Ionian Revolt?', *CQ* 29 (1979) 268.

20. See J. Annequin, 'Remarques sur la femme et le pouvoir chez Hérodote', *DHA* 2 (1976) 387.

21. See E. Wolff, 'Das Weib von Masistes', *Hermes* 92 (1964) 51.

22. P. Walcot, 'Herodotus on Rape', *Arethusa* 11 (1978) 137.

23. See P. G. Maxwell-Stuart, 'Pain, Mutilation and Death in Herodotus, Book 7', *P.d.P.* 31 (1976) 356.

24. Cutting off the breasts of a female appears to be the equivalent to castration of a male, i.e. 'defeminisation'.

25. The meaning of 'freedom' for Herodotos is discussed by K. von Fritz in *WS* 78 (1965) 5. J. de Romilly in *Rise and Fall* (Jerome Lectures 11, 1977) finds in Herodotos 'a definite idea that democratic institutions are the best conditions for the rise of a state, because in a democracy every citizen feels directly responsible for the success of the state, and is directly concerned in its success' (p. 31).

26. The limited interest in politics and administration has produced puzzles for modern historians; e.g. 'the prytaneis of the naukraroi' 5.71, or the command-structure at Marathon, 6.109.

27. Studied at greater length in my *Herodotos on Tyrants and Despots* (Historia Einzelschriften, 15, 1971). Some opposing views have been expressed by F. D. Harvey, 'The Political Sympathies of Herodotos', *Historia* 1, 15 (1966) 254 and A. Ferrill, 'Herodotus on Tyranny', *Historia* 27 (1978) 385.

28. We know from other evidence that Peisistratos undertook a great building and public works programme; it is rather a surprise that despite Herodotos' admiration for the dictator's mild rule, he says nothing of these constructions. An Athenian audience would of course need no reminder.

29. The proponents of the tragic theme as the basis of Herodotos' history seem unable to explain why only the actual defeat of Xerxes and some tales of distress and dissipation figure, without mention of his eventual assassination. They also ignore the fact that the 'evil deeds' and hubris of Xerxes are never connected in any way with his defeat by the historian, whereas a tragedian would have emphasised the connection. See J. de Romilly, *Rise and Fall* (1977), and my monograph, *Herodotos on Tyrants and Despots* (1971), Sec. III.

30. Perhaps the word should be 'realities' rather than 'theories'. It is not impossible that there is an alternative to the sophistic source suggested in Chapter 7, namely the historian's actual experience of diverse political institutions within Greece itself.

10 THE IMPORTANCE OF INDIVIDUALS: CHARACTERISATION

Herodotos has little or nothing to say about the impersonal forces which predominate in the causation postulated by modern historians, except for purely national movements against invaders or internal revenge against dictators. Individuals play the most important roles, so much so that the historian has been described as the founder of biography.[1] His theory of causation, which is elastic, normally includes a personal motive; that is to say, an individual is made directly responsible for a historical event. Other factors, including even the supernatural, are not excluded, but the general impression is that the activities or emotions of individual persons provide the immediate triggers for events.[2]

There are a number of reasons for this feature, which sometimes causes readers to regard Herodotos as unsophisticated, naïve and incapable of historical analysis. The first of such reasons undoubtedly is literary; earlier chapters have detailed the influence of narrative poetry on the technique and even the form and content of Herodotos' work. Although Greek epic may deal with what at times appear to be national struggles — the Greeks against the Trojans — the interest centres from beginning to end on the heroes, the champions (and perhaps also the gods) rather than on the generality of the armed forces concerned. Individual combat, and face-to-face interviews on and off the battlefield, receive far more attention than mass conflict or mass emotions. In his opening statement Herodotos has expressed the close relationship of his work to the epic, stating the aim of keeping alive the deeds of mankind and the fame of great achievements, of Greeks and non-Greeks. (He excludes of course the deeds of supermen, i.e. heroes, and of gods, except indirectly.) One should therefore expect biographical history — accounts of the achievements of individuals and the part they played in bringing about national or international events. No analysis of economic, social or other vague factors was either probable or possible. Dramatisation, in formal speeches or in dialogue, emphasises the prominence of the individual; it is not however confined to individuals, since groups or societies are permitted a common voice.

Next, the conditions of the societies principally concerned threw great weight upon the individual, who was often in a position to influence or indeed control the actions of the city or nation concerned. On the Greek side, a very large number, hundreds indeed, of small independent 'city-states' made up Hellas, the lands where Greeks lived, not a single large national state. Now even in the super-states of today, individuals may have very great power, or exert influence on populations of many millions through the mass media; recent and contemporary examples spring easily to mind. In the little *poleis*, consisting mostly of a few thousand down to a few hundred citizens, mass media, if invented, would have been superfluous; frequent face-to-face contact with leading individuals made their impact on fellow-citizens no less effective. Athenian aristocrats or Spartan kings could exercise an influence proportional to their political intelligence and skill in oratory. We have already observed the prevalence of dictators or 'tyrants' in a number of states, and it hardly needs saying that in such situations those particular individuals counted for almost everything. Apart from this undeniable historical fact, other factors noted in the previous chapter tended to increase the attention paid by our historian to such personages.

On the barbarian side, autocracies of various types prevailed. Hence the prominence of a number of monarchs in the *History*: first, Kroisos of Lydia, resembling some of the Greek tyrants both for his notoriety in respect of wealth and the tales attached to his person and throne, and also for the historical importance of his kingdom and its overthrow in the westward thrust of Persian imperialism. Next Kyros, founder of the Persian power, and his successors Kambyses, Dareios and Xerxes, each of whom played a part of the highest relevance to the clash of Persian expansionism with Greece. These mighty figures tower over the pages of the *History*, as their autocratic rule, their almost unimaginable wealth and military power dominated the imagination of Greeks, to whom in the fifth century BC the title 'king' *tout court* indicated immediately the King of Kings, the Persian potentate.

'Second class' in the matter of importance to the main narrative are other impressive monarchs, such as Deiokes the Mede, Sesostris the Egyptian or the Skythian chief Idanthyrsos, not to mention the nearly-mythical queens Semiramis and Nitokris; a long list of minor monarchs could be added, individuals whose importance owes most to their position or their notoriety.

The kings in Herodotos do not, however, act entirely upon their own whim or judgement. Advisers play a considerable part; deliberations, whether in council or *à deux* are frequently found. This results from the device of dramatisation (see Chapter 6) which enables the historian to put forward appropriate considerations on a proposed action without editorialising. Thus the miraculously preserved Kroisos becomes an adviser to Kyros, and is still alive in the next reign to accompany Kambyses to Egypt and flatter him — an ability perhaps learned from his own ex-courtiers, which might have been responsible for his survival. Dareios, on his seizure of the throne, consults with his fellow-conspirators; later he is advised by his experienced consort Atossa in the famous bedroom scene. Xerxes holds a regular council before undertaking the invasion of Greece;[3] subsequently he seeks advice — which of course he does not always accept — from Artabanos, Mardonios, Demaratos and Artemisia. Histiaios, in preventive detention at Susa, proffers advice to Dareios. Thus these individuals too gain further prominence in the story, in addition to the respective importance of their own actions. (In the cases of Artabanos and Demaratos, *vis-à-vis* Xerxes, as of Kroisos after his defeat and capture, their only role is as counsellors; Artabanos is disqualified from more active participation nominally perhaps by age but in practice by his opposition to the whole enterprise, Demaratos by his status as a political refugee, and Kroisos by total dependence on his captor.)

Thus a mythical Herodotean favourite, the 'wise adviser', has been invented, to fit the prominence in the narrative of these counsellors.[4] But much of their advice is not particularly wise, whether or not accepted. Kroisos gave an opinion which led to the defeat and death of Kyros — a fact brought up against him by Kambyses on receipt of some unpalatable advice from the Lydian. Atossa advised Dareios to invade Greece, and it would be hard to imagine that the pragmatic historian regarded this as sound advice, from either a Greek or a Persian standpoint. Mardonios and Artabanos gave opposing counsel; Artabanos was proved right by the event (though Mardonios would have been the bookmaker's odds-on favourite); Artabanos' views, as already mentioned, represent both the likely existence of a 'peace party' at Susa and Herodotos' own hindsight. Dramatic, i.e. epic, technique required such mouthpieces. Artemisia and Demaratos were not primarily cast in this role, though in the latter case it predominates, since his reign at Sparta was brief and overshadowed by the more forceful and aggressive Kleomenes. The 'wise adviser' is said to be a figure from tragedy — which does not automatically exclude his or her appearance in real life — but as we have already observed Herodotos is not influenced in the *structure* of his history by the supposed tragic theme, and should not be expected to borrow conventional characters from the Athenian stage either. Advisers, wise or foolish, were and are a fact of political and military life.

Herodotos did not always attribute historical action to the design, desire or impulse of an individual.[5] As shown in an earlier chapter, he avoided an oversimplified view of historical events, and causation appears on more than one level. On a few occasions divine agents or agencies play their part; omens and oracles impel individuals to or deter them from action; strategic or political considerations affect the judgement of rulers and communities. 'The Argives' make an unacceptable offer of terms on which they will join the patriotic alliance; the valiant but vain defenders of the Athenian acropolis have reasons other than personal motives for their stand; the reasons for the choice of Thermopylai and Artemision as the first line of defence, like the despatch of an advance guard only to the former, are communal, not individual. 'The Athenians', no one person, make the consultation at Delphi — though a single Delphian suggests and facilitates their second approach to the deity. The reasons Herodotos provides for the Persian defeat at Plataia typically combine individual behaviour with a general consideration: Mardonios was overconfident,[6] and thus lost control of his forces; while the inferiority of the Persian arms and armour for close infantry combat certainly contributed to the Greek victory. Sometimes Herodotos gives not joint but alternative reasons and cannot decide between them — an example occurs at 9.18. Individuals too may have a number of motives: Dareios has three separate reasons for postponing action against Oroites (3.127) and three also for undertaking the Skythian campaign, none of them strictly personal (4.1). No less than four personal motives are adduced for Aristagoras' decision to revolt (5.35), together with the coincidental arrival of the man with the tattooed head bringing its secret message from Histiaios. Kambyses' invasion of Egypt was personally motivated according to the Persians — 'if you can believe it', implies the historian using the ironic particle *dē*. But a study of the stages of Persian expansion recorded by Herodotos reveals the high priority that was bound to be accorded to the annexation of Egypt.[7] Thus the alleged motive is practically superfluous, though in keeping with the character attributed to Kambyses in the *History* (see below).

Sometimes, particularly in dealing with legendary material, Herodotos treats individual motivations ironically. For example the Argonauts, 'having completed the other business which took them to Colchis' decided to abduct Medea (1.2); and Paris, 'having heard of this' — two generations later! — decided to abduct a Greek female in retaliation (1.3). The majority of decisions and actions, however, are indeed taken by individuals, a situation which most modern readers tend to find implausible. But to fifth-century BC Greek audiences it seemed perfectly natural and reasonable.[8]

What a vast number of individuals figure in the *History*! Very approximately, they number a thousand, the vast majority of whom appear or are named once only (a fair number being fathers, used to identify a son in the usual Greek manner). A rough classification into five groups would find the largest number by far in the two groups least important historically; a dozen or fifteen are of absolutely prime importance, a similar number claim secondary rank, and a score or more are very prominent though not of essential relevance to the main narrative.[9] This third group includes quite conspicuous characters such as Adeimantos, Gobryas, Syloson, who made a definite historical contribution, but excludes many individuals who do not, yet are unlikely to be rapidly forgotten by readers; frequently these are quasi-legendary, such as Kleobis and Biton the devoted sons, the clever thief who robbed Rhampsinitos, or the shepherd responsible for saving the life of the infant Kyros. Gods and semi-divinities and all figures of mythology are not here considered.

There is no fixed proportion between the amount of space devoted to a character and his historical importance. The reasons for this have been shown in earlier chapters, and we may take the case of Gelon, tyrant of Syrakuse, as an example. The total contribution, other than verbal advice, of Gelon to the struggle between Greece and Persia was nil, according to Herodotos; he failed to observe the probability of a link other than chronological coincidence between Xerxes' invasion and the Carthaginian invasion of Sicily.[10] Nevertheless the unproductive embassy to Gelon is related in great detail, as have been the antecedents of the man and his power; what is more, a degree of characterisation may be observed in the remarks he offers (7.153ff.). Deiokes, founder of the Median kingdom, is another who receives detailed, if less lengthy, treatment. No direct influence of Periandros of Korinth on the history is explicit, and perhaps only implicit by hindsight in the naval power of Korinth at the time of the invasion; yet in addition to three incidental mentions in Book 1, a number of pages are devoted to his political and personal affairs (3.48ff., 5.92ξ). The dramatisation of the Gelon and Periandros episodes displays the enjoyment the historian experienced in narrating these matters, but the depiction of character, so far as it is found at all (note that Deiokes utters no speeches) is an accessory or adjunct to the tale, never an end in itself.

Much of the material concerning real persons is far from being genuinely historical. Biographers have often tended to romanticise their subjects (though the opposite tendency is not unknown!), and an inclination in Herodotos to include the striking and indeed the marvellous has already been documented. Thus we have personal stories such as that of Zopyros, the dedicated schemer for the recapture of Babylon (3.135ff.); the meeting of Syloson in his flame-coloured cloak with the young Dareios and the eventual royal recompense for the Samian's gift (3.139ff.); the birth and providential escape of the infant Kypselos (5.92), and the parallel folk-tale motives in the account (selected, be it remembered, from three different versions) of the birth and boyhood of Kyros (1.108ff.). To this brief list may be added the more plausible narrative — 'oral history', perhaps — of the birth of the Spartans Dorieus, Kleomenes and Leonidas. Slight suspicion may be cast on its authenticity by the fact that myths about these three personages tended to develop later, to the discredit of the two former but to the fame of the last.

Herodotos, it may appear, is not particularly consistent in dealing with the character of his personages. The mistaken view that his speeches were composed to display character has already been disposed of; minor characters need not be depicted in full, as their traits, virtues or vices, have no real impact on events. A number of major figures are employed largely in presenting political and military arguments presumed to have been considered at the time, while some persons of importance are given no opportunity to speak and thus, supposedly, to reveal their characters. A notable example of the last group is Leonidas, the hero (or villian) of Thermopylai. His bravery is commended indeed, not least by the editorial comment that Xerxes was particularly resentful of

Leonidas' intransigent resistance (7.238),[11] and it might be thought that in his case deeds were enough. He is the very archetype of Spartan *aretè*, the warrior's virtue. But other Greek commanders more successful in fact though less bruited in legend have plenty of opportunities to speak; notably, Miltiades, Themistokles and Pausanias — the last said to have won 'the finest victory of which we know' (9.64).

Some characterisation of these major Greek military men there undoubtedly is. Much of the utterance attributed to Pausanias (9.45–82 *passim*) shows an officer of traditional Spartan rectitude, diplomatic in dealing with his allies, difficult as they could be, and restrained in victory. An anecdote shows his consideration for an unfortunate lady, and can hardly have been included for any other purpose than to praise the victor.[12] Similarly, his criticism of Persian luxury, though it might have been uttered by any Spartan, seems to have been deliberately allotted to him. Herodotos must have known of the later accusations against Pausanias, since he hints at them (8.3) saying that the Athenians used the 'intolerable behaviour' of the Spartan commander as an excuse for taking over the 'hegemony'. Thukydides thought Herodotos had been misleading on this account and mentions the arrogant inscription set up by Pausanias,[13] but those events fell outside the scope of the *History* and the fact that no reference is made to Pausanias' sins and sad end, any more than in the case of Themistokles (see below), is further evidence against the imposition of a tragic pattern on events by Herodotos. If Solon's advice to Kroisos to 'look to the end' were the basis of Herodotos' philosophy, then not only the disgrace of Miltiades but that of the two architects of the defeat of Xerxes should have been recorded and underlined. (However, as discussed earlier, the historian as a rule avoided mention of events subsequent to 479 BC, especially perhaps when they were well known to his audience.)

The case of Themistokles however is difficult. Long ago the Herodotean Themistokles was styled a fifth-century Odysseus, brilliant, courageous, resourceful but unprincipled. No reader of Herodotos doubts that Themistokles was responsible for both grand strategy and naval tactics (even allowing for helpful hints from a Mnesiphilos). He appears also as a good orator and effective politician, able both to persuade the Athenian voters to build a fleet instead of lining their own pockets, and to overcome the petty isolationism of Peloponnesian commanders. But emphasis is continually laid on his trickery, dishonesty and greed. On two occasions he sends secret messages to Xerxes; neither of these is actually essential to the proposed defence plans,[14] and the second in particular is highly implausible.[15] But of course Herodotos did not invent these stories. He is to be blamed for not employing his critical acumen upon them, a lapse apparently due to his acceptance both of the hostile and the favourable views of the admiral current during his researches.[16] Trickery, duplicity, may be justified by their ends; the base element in Themistokles as shown by Herodotos is his greed for personal profit. The extraordinary tale of the bribe offered him by the Euboeans (8.4) after Eurybiades the Spartan admiral had rejected their appeal for protection can possibly be rationalised[17] but it is quite incredible that 'no one knew' of the source and magnitude of the funds with which Themistokles was able to suborn both his superior and a colleague. Equally implausible is the statement that it was Themistokles personally, 'always on the look-out for profit', who blackmailed some of the island states which had failed to resist the Persians, the other fleet commanders remaining in ignorance of his demands (8.112). How did Herodotos' informants get to know? Clearly Herodotos has included libellous statements because he was inclined to accept the character given Themistokles by Athenian sources after his disgrace and banishment. On the other side, however, due credit is readily given; Herodotos' personal statement (the product of reflection rather than of street gossip) is 'His earlier reputation for skill had now been proved beyond doubt, as also for good advice; the Athenians were now totally prepared to accept whatever he proposed' (8.110).

While the Greek commanders are, naturally, dominant figures in the last three books, earlier sections give most prominence to Eastern potentates. Book 1 is shared by Kroisos and Kyros, Dareios preponderates in Books 3 to 6 (to the extent that some have thought him the central figure of the whole composition), and Xerxes competes, rather successfully, with the less elevated personages in Books 7 to 9. Kambyses receives concentrated attention in the first *logos* of Book 3; his is the most simplified of the portraits of Oriental monarchs of prime importance. By 3.29 he is already half-crazed, in his attack on the Apis, and later completely insane, embarking on both fratricide and incest (the latter, however, perhaps not barred by Persian royal *nomos*, as certainly not by Egyptian). His behaviour continually displays ruthless and pointless savagery. A possible 'rational' explanation of his mania is offered in 3.33. Further editorial comment to back up the horrific account of his actions is supplied at 3.38, the passage already discussed about the supremacy of *nomos*; it is the wild attacks of Kambyses upon the *nomoi* of the Egyptians which elicit this digression. Yet Kambyses has lucid intervals and makes a remarkably sane final speech of repentance (3.65). He had treated Ladike, the former wife of Amasis, generously (2.181) in returning her to her native city; while for certain of the dire punishments he inflicted there is some justification in the circumstances or in the Persian *nomos*, for example the case of Sisamnes (5.25).[18]

More complex is the picture of Kyros, father of Kambyses.[19] In the account of his birth and early years romance rules — a picture to be filled out later, no less fictionally, by Xenophon the follower of his descendant and namesake. Kyros as man and king, though more plausible, shares certain stock characteristics such as regal generosity and love of power — obviously! — but a number of diverse characteristics are presented; that type of 'cleverness' (rather than 'wisdom'), shared also by Greek dictators, verging on cunning (1.77); in strategy, his skill combines with ruthlessness (1.211). He possesses the speed of a Julius Caesar, and the luck — a factor emphasised by the king himself (1.84, 204). A better side is shown in magnanimity towards Astyages (1.130). A vein of humour is associated with his 'wisdom', showing a sardonic streak; the 'parable' at 1.141 which has a close relative in St Matthew 2.17, the comment on Kroisos' relations with Apollo at 1.90, the satirical description of Sparta at 1.153, and his reply to the summons of Astyages (1.127).

Kyros in due course meets his fate, but is not forgotten, nor remembered as a tragic figure. He is referred to in later passages as giving the Persians their freedom (*sic*!) and has as it happens the last word in the *History*, in which his 'wisdom' is not mere cunning or cleverness but the result of rational inference from observation. That it is not necessarily correct hardly matters.[20]

Dareios represents most strongly and at the greatest length the force of Persian imperialist expansion; not one but several campaigns are recounted, while he is 'on stage' from Book 3.70 to the opening of Book 7. In addition he appears incidentally in all three early books; the first reference is unfavourable, when he is said to have wished, but lacked the audacity, to purloin a solid gold statue from a Babylon temple (1.183), and a couple of pages later is reported to have broached the gateway-tomb of Nitokris for similar motives. However, this popular explanation has an alternative; the gate was a traffic hazard, and Dareios' interest in public works and utilities is shown both by his reopening of Necho's canal from Nile to Red Sea (2.158) and the curious irrigation system (3.117) among the Chorasmians.

Dareios is unscrupulous, typically of despots, and proffers a defence of expedient lying (3.72); he usurps the lead amongst the Seven Persians and profits by the courageous devotion of Gobyras in killing the pretender, as also by the strategem of his groom — this last a purely derogatory piece of scandal (3.85ff.). Relentless in punishment (see above) he was insisting on *nomos* in dealing with the evasion of military service by Oiobazos and his sons (4.84), a precedent precisely followed by Xerxes in the case of Pythios (7.39). He ruthlessly sacrificed 'cannon-fodder' both at the siege of Babylon and in the Skythian campaign (3.157, 4.134). His drastic punishment of ill-behaved satraps is mentioned on pp. 150–1, n.18.

A hostile, derogatory type of source seems to be represented in two anecdotes portraying the king as naïve. One of these is the famous and clearly apocryphal tale in which the king enquires 'Who are the Athenians?' and appoints a special officer to remind him of their existence. All intelligent persons, from Herodotos on, knew well that Greece was high on the list of proposed conquests, and indeed that some Athenians had been intriguing for Persian support in their own political aims. The other is the case of the knotted rope at the Danube; again, Dareios had entrusted the vital task of bridging the Bosporos and Danube to Ionians, but here he does not think them capable of counting up to sixty days. Both of these are picturesque stories and their inclusion has in fact nothing to do with any intended characterisation of Dareios.

However, the main impression is of a level-headed organiser (though the Greek term *kapēlos* may be derogatory in intent) with care for the interests of subjects, whether 'howling' Chorasmians or defeated and transplanted populations; his warning to his general not to damage Samos in returning it to Syloson's rule exemplifies this. The great list of the revenues (3.90ff.) is intended to emphasise not only the wealth of Persia but the king's organisational ability. The Skythian expedition does him less credit; this too clearly comes from hostile sources and it seems Herodotos has not been concerned to harmonise these in order to produce a consistent portrait, for that was not his purpose.

Dareios' successor, Xerxes, is often taken to be the villian of the piece. But such a dramatic metaphor is out of place. Like his counterparts, Xerxes has a wide range of characteristics, and does not consistently follow a set pattern of behaviour. Much writing on this subject seems to have been unduly influenced by the play of Aischylos, produced at Athens in Herodotos' youth, and evidently of considerable influence on the naturally hostile public opinion of fifth-century Greece — or perhaps the drama was the encapsulation of the low popular estimation of Xerxes stemming both from his attack on mainland Hellas and from its failure. Thus Xerxes is thought to be depicted as hubristic, sacrilegious, irresolute, cruel and lascivious. But the hubris of attacking Greece, exceeding the bounds of his allotted sphere, Asia, and transgressing nature's water-frontier are all deeds also perpetrated by his predecessor. The love-affairs of Xerxes, whether included as a moral lesson or as a piece of scandal-sheet reporting, are without any impact on the historical events occurring after his retreat from Greece; it is his deceived wife, Amestris, who figures most villainously.[21] The harem life of the Persian court naturally intrigued the Greeks, but no other excesses are recorded, save of Kambyses. Dareios had several wives, but only the lecture by Atossa gives any indication of his marital relationships.[22] On the other hand Xerxes intended condign punishment for Sataspes when convicted of rape (4.43) but was persuaded by his aunt to send him on a perilous journey of exploration instead.[23] However we do not hear of female counsellors in his palace; the virago Artemisia, an apparent exception, was seemingly treated merely as a particularly outspoken naval commander of exceptional intelligence.

Xerxes is prone to sudden onsets of emotion which certainly make him a more human character than monarchs with merely royal characteristics. The elaborate council-and-dream-sequence of the early pages of Book 7 does indicate a certain lack of resolution, but in carrying out the campaign he betrays no such weakness. His decision not to remain in Greece after the defeat of Salamis is indeed attributed by the historian to apprehension, but since his withdrawal was also advised by Mardonios, whose counsel was independently reinforced by Artemisia (8.100ff.) a reader may well surmise that Herodotos realised there were good political reasons why Xerxes should not absent himself too long from Susa. And the historian, while apparently accepting the view that Xerxes was anxious for his personal safety, explicitly rejects the more colourful version supplied to him of Xerxes' 'flight' and tyrannical procedures therein (8.118). Aischylos' poetical account shows the extent of popular exaggeration; a version, which Herodotos rejected, has the defeated king reaching Abdera on the north Aegaean coast before changing his clothes, while Aischylos actually has him back at Susa (three months later?) in the same clothes in which he had viewed the sea-battle from Aigaleos.

Thus Herodotos' interest in the personalities of the Eastern potentates never dominates, but is subordinate to the 'facts' of history. One possible exception is Kroisos of Lydia; did Herodotos treat him as the canon of historical process, and give him a character which would support the thesis? On general grounds we have already rejected such a theory; a brief look at the principal traits evidenced by the speech and actions of Kroisos should confirm that judgement.

Kroisos suffers from excessive imperialist ambition (1.26, 73ff.) but the major reason, though not the immediate impulse, for his attack on Kyros is the reasonable wish to pre-empt the dominance of Persia in Anatolia. His other excess is pride in his own position; it was, 'presumably' says Herodotos, because he thought himself the most prosperous of mankind that divinely-inspired Nemesis fell upon him (1.34). But the historian later informs us that the destruction of his kingdom was in expiation for the crime of his ancestor Gyges (1.91); his own hubris had not involved crime or punishment, it seems. Despite his ambivalent attitude to oracles and the blame he laid on Apollo for 'misleading' him (1.87), he actually received divine favour, by a three-year postponement of ineluctable fate[24] and by the rain-storm which extinguished his pyre; thus his attempt, by no means unique, to purchase the favour of heaven by magnificent offerings would appear to have paid off!

Though foolish in interpreting the oracles by wishful thinking, Kroisos could at times take sound advice, that of Bias (1.27), though later he rejected that of Sandanis (1.71) which in fact came too late. Also he dismissed Solon's pessimistic theory of *la condition humaine*; if optimism be a crime, that was the crime of Kroisos, a gambler whose luck ran out.

An emotional character, he variously displays anxiety, over his dream about Atys (1.34), pity, for Adrastos (1.36) and the son of Psammenitos (3.14), despair at the fall of Sardis (1.85), amusement at the ungainly greed of Alkmaion (6.125) and scorn at Solon's incredible choices (1.33). Generosity is shown not by the too obvious self-interest of his offerings at shrines, but to Alkmaion (above) and the gift to Sparta (1.70); not so pleasant is his threat to Lampsakos on behalf of Miltiades (6.37). As a giver of advice he is again ambivalent; Kyros receives from him good, dubious and bad advice (1.90, 155, 207) and he flatters both Kyros and Kambyses. Not then an impressive personality, designed to drive home a lesson on the inevitability of rise and fall.

Inconsistency has been found in the treatment of Aristagoras, a principal in the Ionian revolt. He first appears as a collaborator in Persian rule over Ionia, like his uncle and father-in-law Histiaios, and one might well expect ambivalent traditions regarding him. Herodotos of course took no stance against such collaborators — his laudatory attitude to Queen Artemisia should make that clear — where the power situation made such a policy preferable to annihilation. It is not until the failure of the revolt appears probable that Aristagoras is condemned as 'rather poor-spirited' for abandoning the undertaking (5.124). His previous successes and failures, especially in diplomacy, have left the impression of a fast-talking salesman, not above bribery — hardly to be considered a fault in Greek political life! — with considerable organisational ability. The speed with which he transformed himself from Persian-supported tyrant to leader of a 'national liberation army' was remarkable (5.37) — all the more for the reported reprisals in a couple of cities against his deposed counterparts there; and the fact that he remained at his headquarters in Miletos instead of leading the initial attack on Sardis may show greater than usual strategic sense.

Histiaios first comes to notice as mainly responsible for keeping Dareios' communications open at the Danube during the Skythian campaign, convincing his fellow-commanders as to which side their bread was buttered. This entire scene, in which Miltiades, tyrant in the Gallipoli peninsula, plays the patriot urging the opposite view, may have been invented and transmitted to Herodotos by the Philaid clan (of which Miltiades was then the chief personage) or their supporters; Miltiades certainly gets no less credit than his due for the victory at Marathon.[25] But as mentioned earlier, Herodotos does not fail to record his subsequent error, disgrace and death. It is more likely that what Herodotos received was the factual information that Ionian ships made the crossing possible, and that an explanation was needed as to why the Ionians did not take advantage of the opportunity to maroon Dareios and his army, and proceed to throw off the Persian yoke then, instead of waiting fifteen years or so. Herodotos therefore dramatised the incident in his manner, showing the type of considerations he thought would have been canvassed, and selected two suitable candidates, one a trusted adviser of Dareios, the other subsequently victor over invading Persian forces, to present the opposing views.

Histiaios appears throughout as a scheming adventurer; like his son-in-law, a fast talker but unable to persuade all those he dealt with. The city of Miletos, first among the Ionian group, was considered of importance by the Persians only second to their 'Western capital' Sardis, formerly the seat of Lydian power; its collaborating rulers consequently possessed great influence, but even if trusted at Susa were suspect at Sardis. However Histiaios, no doubt on account of his especially close collaboration, was not trusted by his fellow-countrymen either, a fact which led to his capture and death. Herodotos however goes so far as to betray his own admiration for the intelligence of Histiaios by saying that Dareios would have spared his life. For neither of these figures, crucial to the complication of relations between Persia and Hellas, do we have a comprehensive portrait: both share the characteristics common to most Herodotean 'tyrants'; cleverness,[26] ambition, power-seeking, unscrupulous self-interest.

The large number of 'thumb-nail sketches', extending from legendary heroes through barbarian chieftains to near-contemporary Greeks, forms one of the many endearing aspects of the *History*. There was neither need nor possibility of fully characterising such persons; often a single act, incident or remark prompted their only appearance, but all are recognisable human beings even if they display but a single trait. For Herodotos' all-embracing interests, not restricted to the human race, nevertheless were dominated by his fascination with mankind. Mankind *en masse* was the subject of his ethnology; mankind as individuals provided the subject of fictional tales and amusing anecdotes, of the account of remarkable achievements and records, and of course of narrative history itself. In this respect the normally anthropocentric view of the world taken by Greeks is represented at its most comprehensive and liberal by the most typically Greek of writers.

Notes

1. H. Homeyer, 'Zu den Anfangen der griechische Biographie', *Philogus* 106 (1962) 78–85. However, Herodotus in no case compiles a reasoned biography of an individual; see below on (e.g.) Leonidas.

2. See also H. R. Immerwahr, 'Aspects of Historical Causation in Herodotos', *TAPhA* 87 (1956) 241; A. E. Wardman, 'Herodotus on the cause of the Greco-Persian Wars', *AJPh* 82 (1961) 133; J. de Romilly, 'La Vengeance comme explication dans l'oeuvre historique d'Hérodote', *REG* 74 (1971) 314; Hunter Rawlings, *Prophasis in pre-Thucydidean Literature*, Hermes Einzelschr. 33 (1975); P. Hohti, 'Die Schuldfrage der Perserkriege in Herodots Geschichtswerke', *Arctos* 10 (1976) 37.

3. No doubt the decision had long been made and the troops mobilised; the logistics and engineering required much advance planning. Did Xerxes feel it necessary or at least advisable to obtain a rubber-stamp from the council?

4. See R. Lattimore, 'The Wise Adviser in Herodotos', *CJ* 51 (1955/56) 83. Cf. D. Grene, 'Herodotus; the Historian as Dramatist', *JPh* 58 (1961) 477.

5. See n. 2 above.

6. Overconfidence, Selbstsicherheit, also is a trait shared by many tragic heroes — but obviously need not be borrowed from them, since it occurs regrettably often among the human race.

7. The material resources of Egypt as well as its naval potential necessitated its acquisition before any drive westward, either into Europe or North Africa; and Xerxes postponed his invasion of Greece until some years after the suppression of the Egyptian revolt, which had been planned by Dareios (7.107).

8. Other views exist, e.g. P. Hohti, 'Die Schuldfrage der Perserkriege in Herodots Geschichtswerke', 37.

9. Such classification is however both arbitrary and highly subjective, and I forbear to detail my lists here.

10. If it is going too far to posit concerted action by Persia and Carthage as some have done, the likelihood that Carthage took advantage of the preoccupation of metropolitan Hellas with her own defence to attempt to gain the upper hand in Sicily is considerable. The intention of Persia had long been well advertised.

11. But the Persians in general, says Herodotos, particularly honoured brave men — note Zopyros above, and Pythias on the Greek side (7.181).

12. A possible alternative explanation is that a person of consequence from Kos (which lay within Artemisia's power) may have been known to Herodotos; compare the story about Pixodaros of Kindya, 5.118. (n. 15 to Chapter 7).

13. The details are given by Thukydides in his most Herodotean digression, 1.131.

14. The Persian attack on the Greek fleet at Salamis was necessitated by Xerxes' position at the end of a long line of communications late in the sailing season. Persian intelligence, through the likes of Demaratos, well knew of potential disunity in the Greek fleet and no doubt hoped for a repetition of the desertions at Lade. It was not practicable to maintain a blockade, and therefore Xerxes must attack.

15. If the Persians had been naïve enough to allow Themistokles' emissary to depart after delivering his first message, they certainly would have arrested him on sight when he turned up again, the first message having proved deceptive.

16. Thukydides endeavoured to counter the unfavourable, and perhaps especially the Herodotean, account in his lengthy excursus. (A politician who has been banished automatically receives a 'bad press'.)

17. See M. B. Wallace, 'Herodotus and Euboea', *Phoenix* 28 (1974) 27.

18. The Persian nobility had great privileges and local powers, but faced correspondingly drastic penalties when out of line; Intaphernes (3.119f.), Oroites

(3.127f.) and Aryandes (4.166) all suffered at the hands of Dareios, supposedly the mildest of the Persian kings.

19. See H. C. Avery, 'Herodotus' Picture of Cyrus', *AJPh* 93 (1972) 529.

20. The historian provides the evidence to refute the judgement in the case of the Lydians. Before their defeat by Kyros they were the most valiant and warlike of peoples, though they lived in a favourable clime and were wealthy (1.79). The Persian situation, too, is at least ambiguous; did the Persians continue to live in the harsh uplands of Iran after gaining their empire?

21. Amestris' only other appearance is at 7.114 where she is cited as affording an instance of a Persian *nomos* of human sacrifice.

22. The statement that the Seven (or rather Six) Persians were allowed free entry to Dareios' presence 'unless he was in bed with a woman' may equally be translated 'with a wife' and is not evidence for undue sexual activity (3.118).

23. Giving way to feminine entreaties may be thought a sign of weakness. Dareios succumbed partially to the rationalising of Intaphernes' wife and made what would appear to be a generous gesture (3.119).

24. But it is the Pythia, not the historian, who is the authority for this statement.

25. The real commander was the polemarch, Kallimachos, who fell in action; during the immediate post-war period Miltiades' son Kimon was a very popular and influential figure, and as a commander largely responsible for the extension of Athenian power. But Herodotos did not draw solely on such sources.

26. On which see Luitgard Camerer, *Die praktische Klugheit bei Herodot* (1965). For Herodotos' sources for the Ionian revolt and his use of them, see D. Lateiner, 'The Failure of the Ionian Revolt', *Historia* 31 (1982) 129. Also useful are G. A. H. Chapman, 'Herodotus and Histiaeus' Role in the Ionian Revolt', *Historia* 21 (1972) 546 and P. B. Manville, 'Aristagoras and Histiaios; the Leadership Struggle in the Ionian Revolt', *CQ* 27 (1977) 80.

11 STRENGTHS AND WEAKNESSES

From the viewpoint of contemporary historiography — and perhaps still more from that of fashionable sociological history — Herodotos is afflicted by serious shortcomings. Maybe he will receive due honour from the practitioners of the latest fashion, oral history, as their founder. A number of his weaknesses have been touched on during this study and we have seen that often there is a valid explanation, sometimes a complete justification in the conditions under which he wrote.

Amongst charges of deliberate falsehood or prevarication, inconsistency, errors of fact and judgement, weaknesses in chronology, geography and military and political history — a lengthy indictment! — the most common accusation is that of undue credulity, and easy acceptance of unreliable sources of information.[1] Much of the older criticism on this ground, dating back to Cicero at least, falls to the ground when we observe how careful is Herodotos to classify his information, especially as 'what is said', and not to guarantee it as true or even as plausible. It is however too simple-minded to put all of Herodotos' errors, inconsistencies and incredibilia down to his sources. But although some of what the historian does appear to accept as veritable seems to us far-fetched, improbable or even impossible, he disbelieves a great deal. For example he refused to accept that Skyllias[2] swam ten miles under water (8.8); he does not believe that an Egyptian Pharoah would prostitute his daughter (2.121ε) nor that in North Russia humans hibernate for six months (4.25) nor that lycanthropy is current among the Neuroi (4.105). It seems implausible to him that bees render travel impossible north of the Danube (5.10); let the pious believe, if they will, that statues fell to their knees (5.86).

On the other hand, the enormous number of Xerxes' forces as reported by Herodotos have led many critics to accuse him, if not of deliberate exaggeration, then of irresponsible reporting. He does seem to have believed in the traditional figures, if his arithmetical labours are any indication. That these numbers are a sheer physical impossibility does not seem to have occurred to him. However, one should not overlook the evident irony of his final inclusion of 'women, eunuchs, camels and Indian dogs' to double the total.

Most incredible of all in this connection perhaps is the 'numbering' at Doriskos (7.59) — but the ordinary Greek would have been hard put to it to suggest a better way, given the fictitious total! The figures for the fleet present a notorious problem, complicated not by later authorities so much as by the similar figure, evidently traditional, offered by Aischylos in the *Persians*. The 1,200 total seems to have two bases; one is the figure of 600 occurring on other occasions (6.9, 95) which appears to have been a conventional number;[3] since the invasion of Xerxes was held to have been more massive in scale than any other such operation, the 'standard' figure was doubled in popular tradition. Secondly, Agamemnon's fleet against Troy comprised 1,000 ships; surely Xerxes had a yet more considerable force? Twelve hundred gave Xerxes a nice margin of superiority; Herodotos not only accepted it, which is somewhat surprising,[4] but by various calculations actually increased the total slightly. At the disastrous Battle of Lade, the Ionian contingents (some of them clearly round numbers) add up to 353; the Persian fleet, allegedly of 600 ships, mostly Phoenician, would not tackle the insurgents without first making all efforts to subvert the loyalty of the various detachments, successfully as it turned out; this procedure would hardly have been necessary if the Persians outnumbered the rebels by nearly two to one. But having accepted the fleet totals for the Ionian revolt and the campaign of 490, Herodotos was bound to set the figures for Xerxes' fleet much higher, and no doubt did it in accordance with popular belief.

In the previous chapter it was pointed out that the stories of Themistokles' messages to Xerxes were probably fictional, and we may say that Herodotos failed to exercise his critical judgement upon them. The reason for this lack of scepticism was most likely that the source appeared authoritative enough, and the generally accepted version of events incorporated these incidents, though with variations, in the accounts of Thukydides, Diodoros and Plutarch; no alternative tradition denying them was available.[5]

Despite such blemishes. throughout the *History* we find constant evidence of Herodotos' estimating probability in the light of reason, and judging between alternative versions; proving his honesty also by admitting where he cannot decide. Reason prevails in the not altogether incredible case of Kroisos crossing the River Halys by the engineering expedients of Thales; the historian prefers to believe that he crossed by the existing bridges (1.75). He rejects the Chaldaean priests' claim of a god's nocturnal visit to a selected woman (1.182), but prefers the authority of priests at Memphis to the 'silly Greek tales' (2.2), though the former is still not vouched for as gospel. The 'air full of feathers' in Skythia he interprets as snow. He is not however surprised that rivers were drunk dry by Xerxes' host, nor would the statement astonish anyone who accepted the traditional magnitude of that army.[6]

Deliberate falsification would be a more serious charge even than credulity against a historian. The first requirement however for the prosecuting counsel would be a motive. The discussions in earlier chapters have disclosed a quite remarkable lack of axes to be ground; indeed Herodotos has unhesitatingly reported much that is unfavourable to his supposed favourites, and vice versa. An informative case is that of the dichotomous attitude towards Pausanias (see Chapter 10). The 'victims' here are Thebans and consequently the bias of the critical 'Plutarch' can readily be inferred. Of the Medising Thebans some received no penalty, for example the innocent children of Attaginos (contrary to regrettably established custom) but Pausanias took the rest to Korinth and 'destroyed' them (9.88). The fact that they were not 'destroyed' on the spot but taken to Korinth, headquarters of the Hellenic league, suggests a formal execution with the authority of the Council. Herodotos does not attach blame to Pausanias. Plutarch, as we have seen, can detect malice, but in most cases it can be sheeted home to the prejudices of informants. Herodotos' deficiency consists in failing invariably to detect the slant of certain 'information'; or, if he did detect it, in his practice of including it as 'newsworthy', with or without a qualification.

A few errors of fact are due to faulty observation, but their paucity serves perhaps to emphasise the value of Herodotean personal investigation; geographical data are amongst the most prominent in the category and will be discussed below. Others depend on a lack of knowledge for which our prodigious researcher can hardly be blamed. His notorious comment that all Persian proper names end in -s (1.139) is due to an inevitably amateurish[7] interest in etymological peculiarities, like the fact that the names of all Greek festivals end in -ia (1.148) (easily explained by any student of grammar), and the meanings attributed to the names of Persian kings (6.98). His observation of the hind legs of the camel is not anatomically correct, but he is right about the animal's genitals (3.103). He has heard, and repeats without other qualification, that lionesses breed but once in a life-time, and a pseudo-scientific explanation is offered (3.108). Horns, he is told, fail to grow on animals in cold climates (4.29), and the converse is illustrated from a Homeric statement (Od. 4.85) that horns grow quickly in Libya; elsewhere, Homer's authority is not so readily accepted. Similar misinformation, accepted or merely passed on through lack of knowledge, is that only the Indus and the Nile are inhabited by crocodiles (4.44) or that the men of some Indian tribes emit black semen (3.101). These were matters that Herodotos had no means of verifying; 'winged snakes' in Egypt elicited an attempt at verification by means of their alleged remains (2.75) but gold-bearing ants as large as small dogs (3.102) lay far beyond the ambit of his travels. According to modern standards, if the historian did not simply discard such fanciful stories, he should have provided a strong caveat.

A different category comprises erroneous assertions about ethnology. The Colchians (2.104) are said to be descended from Egyptians left by Sesostris on his expedition to the north, and strenuous efforts by the historian to document the statement seem to indicate that he was aware of the implausibility. The nomadic Geloni are said to have been 'originally Hellenic' (4.108) and even the Spartan royal house (along with certain customs) originated from Egypt — this last a curious exemplar of Herodotos' belief in the primacy of all things Egyptian (6.53).

A famous example of the rejection of a story by perfectly legitimate reasoning, based on erroneous 'fact', is that of the reported cirumnavigation of Africa by Phoenicians, who claimed the sun was 'on the right', i.e. north of them, as they sailed westward (4.42). This to Herodotos was simply impossible, since for Mediterranean peoples the sun can never be to the north. (We shall come shortly to the historian's view of the shape of the world.) Similarly he dismisses the 'melting snow' explanation of the Nile flood as ridiculous (2.22ff.); the river flows from very hot regions, as is evident from the hot winds blowing from the south. Next, the whole area is rainless (an unjustifiable extrapolation from Upper Egypt) and 'it must always rain within five days after a snowfall'. Thirdly, the men of Nubia are black, which is due to the heat of the region. This whole passage on the Nile is a striking mixture of intelligent reasoning and baseless hypotheses; the final judgement, though seemingly preposterous, is based on the (apparently) more southerly course of the sun in winter and a fair understanding of evaporation. (I am doubtful whether the 'old wives' weather wisdom about snow and rain bears investigation!) More creditable, since based on personal observation, is the geological discussion of the Nile and its Delta.[8]

Inconsistency, already identified to some extent in the depiction of character, is certainly not entirely absent from factual statements. A prime example is the statement at Book 5.48 that Kleomenes 'did not reign very long' in Sparta, which does not accord with all that is elsewhere recorded of him; as we have seen there were diverse traditions regarding this most independent of Spartan kings. A less important case is the Persian action in Kyrene (4.203) which does not tally with the previous account of Dareios' intentions. At 7.144 we are told, correctly, that Athens was not a great naval power before Themistokles' intervention; yet at 7.161 her envoys claim the naval command — seemingly on the basis of the number of ships available, though neither they nor the crews were battle-tested. (Later, they abandoned the claim under pressure from the allies.) The numbers of Greek dead at Plataia are far too small in view of the fierce and lengthy fighting narrated (9.70 with 9.61 and 63).[9] At 7.61 the genealogy of Perses is incompatible with that given at 1.7. But such blemishes are, on the whole, minor, and might have been removed had the work been subjected to a full revision before publication in written form.

Three areas of considerable contention remain; chronological, geographical and military information. Some discussion of the background to the two former was undertaken in Chapters 2 and 3; all three lead into rather complex technical questions and some-times minute historical problems — areas lying outside the terms of reference of this book.

The major chronological problems to be faced by Herodotos were, first, the lack of any coherent and accepted chronology for Greek history, and second, the difficulty of obtaining correctly and reconciling with Greek affairs the recorded chronology of Egypt and the Middle East generally. The prime datum for his view of early Greek history is the statement (2.53) that 'Homer and Hesiod' lived some 400 years before Herodotos' own time.[10] But within this timespan very few accurate placings are even attempted; indeed, for the earlier legendary generations recorded in traditional poetry Herodotos appears both more knowledgeable and confident. Some events can be roughly placed from the Spartan king-lists (but as these do not correspond too closely with generations no certainty is attainable). Reigns or their equivalents (priesthoods, annual magistracies) and family trees were in fact the only methods of dating open to a fifth-century Greek. Thukydides, taking great care with an accurate chronology of the contemporary events he recorded (a somewhat simpler task!), had recourse to three separate reference points in establishing the date of the starting-point of the Peloponnesian War, namely, the annual archon at Athens, the year of the priestess of Hera at Argos and the ephor at Sparta, thus providing most Greeks with a datum within their comprehension. Herodotos however has world history and a vast timespan to cover; within Greece for ancient days he can only offer local traditions, such as that the Phoenicians occupied Thera eight generations before its colonisation from Laconia. In time closer to his own he attempts synchronisms, such as between Gyges and Archilochos (1.12), between Thrasyboulos and Periandros (1.20), and Kroisos and the Spartan king Anaxandridas (1.67); or the statement that Periandros' tyrannical behaviour occurred 'in the generation before Polykrates' (3.48). With the last, we have reached the last quarter of the sixth century BC, a period when firm tradition enables him to establish broad relations throughout the Mediterranean and Middle East, for example between Polykrates of Samos, Amasis of Egypt and Kambyses of Persia. He can comment astringently upon mistaken Greek notions about the notorious courtesan Rhodopis, whose floruit in Egypt really belongs to the reign of Amasis. But much vagueness persists.[11]

In Eastern chronology some data appear firmly established. Early in his account we find an equation, twenty-two generations equalling 505 years, for the Heraklid predecessors of Kandaules in Lydia — but this appears legendary. A similar length of time is allotted to Assyrian domination of 'Upper Asia', namely 520 years (1.95) but without generation- or reign-count. The scale of the Egyptian history is very different; 10,000 or 20,000 years are estimated for the alluvial deposits — the first known approach to 'geological time'; the Delta has been built up comparatively 'recently', while L. Moeris has been present a mere 900 years (2.13 and 149) as against the 2,300 since the foundation of Tyre and the 16,000 years to Amasis' reign from the change from eight major gods to twelve (2.43f.). Here also correlation with some semi-legendary events of the Greek past is attempted by dating the Phoenician occupation of Thasos five generations before the birth of Herakles, son of Amphitryon.[12] Amphitryon himself, or 'his' inscription, is said to have been contemporary with Laios, father of

Oidipous (5.59). Reigns of kings in recent times enabled certain exact datings to be made; the thirty-six years of Dareios are mentioned at his death (7.4), and such data can now be confirmed or otherwise from Oriental sources. But that chronological exactitude was not one of Herodotos' prime concerns is shown by the frequent appearance of phrases such as 'about this time', 'a few years later', or even merely 'later'. Nor would his audience have been at all perturbed by the absence of precise dating.[13]

Upon reaching the fifth century Herodotos is on much firmer ground; the events all lay practically within living memory when he wrote, or introduced his researches, sixty or seventy years into the century. From Herodotean data chronology at least partially satisfactory to moderns can be established for the Ionian revolt. Events during the Persian invasions of Greece proper are dated fairly accurately, but not to months and days; indeed, as was long pointed out, the information is not systematically provided but 'rather accidental'.[14] Later sources have provided exact chronology, though not with complete certainty in all cases.[15]

Geography, as shown in Chapter 2, had acquired some status as an avenue of intellectual inquiry, both on the descriptive and theoretical sides. One of the main problems with Herodotean geographical statements is whether they are at first or second hand, or maybe fifth or tenth hand.[16] Notoriously, either he failed to visit Thermopylai, where he describes the 'pass' as running north and south, or his observation was less careful than usual; it does of course represent part of the main north-south route, even today, though its orientation is more nearly east and west. His measurements for distances in Egypt (2.5ff.) are suspect,[17] and those of the Black Sea are very difficult to justify. A shocking error is the statement that a man travelling light could cross the 'neck' of Asia Minor in five days (1.72, 2.34), a distance of between 300 and 350 miles or at least 500 km. The second description of Skythia is inconsistent with that given earlier (4.16ff.; 99ff.), and seems artificially schematic, a feature to be discussed shortly. On the other hand, the details of Xerxes' route, profuse as they are, leave little to be desired; yet the major battles of the invasion still leave certain topographical issues in dispute — perhaps through failure to correlate diverse sources.[18]

In terms of theory Herodotos deserves a better reputation. Greek geography, like art and philosophy, tended to be neat and tidy, to schematise; Aristotle would even apply this mode of thought to literary aesthetics. In Herodotos, not surprisingly, there are strong traces of this tendency; witness the ten-days-journey distances between oases in (unknown) Western Libya, and the schematic nature of the second description of Skythia, both already noticed. The Nile mouths lie 'opposite', i.e. on the same longitude as, the mouth of the Danube (2.33) because the Danube appears as a European counterpart of the Egyptian river; it is comparable in volume of water, and flows from west to east, as the upper course of the Nile was assumed to do, since a large river flowing east, with crocodiles in it, had been reported from south of the Sahara (2.32).[19] Again, if there are Hyperboreans, as the poets tell, 'beyond the North Wind', there should also be Hypernotians beyond the South Wind — but of them even legend shows no trace (4.36).

On the credit side, Herodotos rejects legendary beliefs about distant, unknown areas, as well as undue schematisation. The 'River Ocean' which according to the symmetrists circumscribes a round disc of lands (4.37), he cannot accept — though he believes, correctly, that there is one continuous sea which surrounds the unknown lands. Similarly, though Ionian geographers counted three separate continents, Europe, Asia, Africa, he declares that they all form part of one landmass.[20] Arabia is said to be the most southerly of lands; Herodotos might well have qualified this statement by his common formula 'of those we know'; for of India his information extends only, and vaguely, to the Indus, and of Africa south of the Nile cataracts and the Sahara there were only vague ideas and uncorroborated hearsay (3.107). Even the not-too-distant Ammon (Siwah) oasis shows the weakness of oral information, and also once more the difficulty of harmonising variant versions.[21] We noted above his scepticism regarding tales of the unknown North of Europe (3.115 *et al.*). Limited knowledge is also responsible for the erroneous estimate of the relative areas of the conjoined continents (4.42 and 5.3).

The observations on Egyptian land-forms are particularly perceptive.[22] Extrapolation from the land-form changes wrought by the comparatively small rivers of his homeland was intelligently applied to the Nile and its delta, and other geological evidence brought to bear (2.10ff.). (It is interesting that he quotes the case of Ephesos; once a port, it appealed to the Roman Emperor Hadrian six centuries later to get its harbour dredged, and now lies several kilometres from the coastline.) In geography, then, we should grant Herodotos at least a pass.

There is not much point in discussing Herodotos' understanding of the military strategy and tactics of semi-legendary campaigns, like that of Kyros against the Massagetai. The narrative of the historically recent and vitally important battles of the Persian invasions, however, the climax of the *History*, should make sound military sense. That this is not always the case is sometimes blamed on the historian's lack of military experience of lengthy campaigns — the frustrations felt by the troops at the ten-day battle of Plataia are only too evident in Book 9 — as most Greek inter-city warfare was decided in a single brief pitched battle; on this practice the Persian general Mardonios is allowed some scathing remarks (7.9). It looks as if the outsider had indeed a good view of the game. Certainly the average Greek could have had no experience of warfare on anything like the scale of that produced by Xerxes' invasion. It is true that at Mykale in 494 the Ionians had assembled a fleet of 350 ships, but this fleet was not kept in being for very long. At least a similar number had to be maintained in action during the invasion of 480, whether or not one pays credence to the enormous number of enemy vessels reported by Herodotos — and the eye-witness Aischylos! Land forces too would pose logistic problems well beyond the range of anything previously encountered (those on the Persian side were of course greater still). But general tradition largely ignored such problems, being of course concerned to magnify the sheer size of the Persian forces in order to glorify the Greek achievement.[23] However it is noticeable that Herodotos does pay great attention, comparatively speaking, to supply matters; on the Persian side, the preliminary engineering works, the bridges and canal get detailed treatment (7.22, 25, 33ff.) and there is frequent reference to the collection of supplies and formation of depots (e.g. 7.186). The lack of these last during the retreat is noticed (8.115).

The problem of supplying Pausanias' large force (over 100,000 according to Herodotos (9.30), but perhaps half that number of effective fighting men) for the decisive campaign of Plataia is also thrice mentioned, especially in regard to water (9.25, 39, 50); the necessity for ample supplies of drinking-water during the Greek summer would hardly escape even the most unmilitary informant. This particular aspect of grand strategy then appears to have been pretty well understood by Herodotos, and the general application of it is put in the mouth of Artabanos, in discouraging advice to

Xerxes (7.49).

Reasons for selection of invasion routes and of defence positions may not have been so fully comprehended. From what Herodotos records we can easily see, though it is never explicit, that the massive invasion strategy of Xerxes demanded the northern land-route, with supporting naval force and supply-ships. It was intended to steamroller the Greek defence by sheer weight of numbers; the previous use of the Thracian route by Mardonios had been foiled by communicational and navigational problems, on the later occasion dealt with by the engineering works. The only alternative, a direct naval invasion across the Aegean, had failed twice, at Naxos before the Ionian revolt and after initial success at Marathon (5.33ff., 6.112f.). On reaching northern Greece, however, the routes available to the invading army are discussed (7.128f.), while the Greek defence force sent to block Xerxes' entry found that both the multiplicity of routes and the unreliability of the local rulers made the position untenable.

Nor is the basic premise of the joint land and sea defence of Thermopylai and Artemision made explicit. It is hinted at in the fact that the land and sea fighting was simultaneous, though Herodotos' precise expression seems to imply that this was a coincidence; this is followed, however, by the statement that the aim of both forces was to stop the invasion at that point. He also provides the information that means of reciprocal communication had been established, and that once the land pass was lost, the fleet no longer saw any purpose in remaining. As for Thermopylai (discussed in Chapter 6 above), we have the information that Leonidas' force was only an advance guard, so that the intended strategy was neither a mere delaying action nor the sacrifice of a Spartan king to comply with an oracle (7.220). But Herodotos' fondness for the oracular led him to attribute to Leonidas the ambition of saving his homeland through his own death, rather than that of holding out by all means in his power till the arrival of the main body.[24] Thus legend has triumphed over strategic insight.

Herodotos also saw the impracticability of the 'isolationist' strategy of Fortress Peloponnese. Walls across the Isthmus were useless as long as the Persian fleet was in being (7.139). He allowed Demaratos to suggest to the Persians an alternative strategy (7.235) which would take advantage of the strong Greek tendency to separatism. The historian was only too well aware of the isolationist feelings among the city-states; he is chastised therefore by 'Plutarch', and may be thought to lend too much weight to them in his accounts of the Salamis and Plataia campaigns.[25] What is really remarkable, but not explicitly stressed by Herodotos, was the fact that Spartan commanders (with strong Athenian backing) were able to hold together contingents of considerable diversity of interest long enough to defeat and expel from Greece both the naval and land invasion forces.[26] Distance from the event perhaps makes this essential factor more striking to us; the historian's restraint is all the more remarkable since he has allowed his feelings about the succeeding internecine troubles to be glimpsed (above Chapter 9).

The historian's account of Salamis has been briefly examined in Chapter 7. Obviously Herodotos knew little of naval tactics; his description of the training ordered by the Phokaian admiral before the Battle of Lade in 494 (6.12) includes a manoeuvre proper to highly-trained, 'professional' fleets such as that of Athens in his own day[27] and unlikely to have been practised till after Salamis. The story of the 'supernatural' voice which ended the tactical retirement of the allied fleet (8.84) is also an expression of failure to comprehend naval tactics, not due originally to Herodotos but perpetuated by him and not invariably subject to sensible interpretation by moderns.

Inaccuracy or inadequacy on the topographical data of the Salamis encounter has led to constant reinterpretation by moderns. A complication is the need to harmonise Herodotos' description with that of Aischylos; poetic licence in the latter case must have been severely restricted by the familiarity of his audience with the area, practically in view from their seats in the theatre; the case is different with regard to the size of the forces, where patriotism abetted imagination.

Marathon, fought on a small plain beside the sea, ought to present a simple case (6.111ff.). But there exists uncertainty over the location of one of the main reference points, the Herakleion; another, the marsh (or marshes), is no longer to be seen, and changes in the course of the Charadra, the water-course bringing flood rains from the flanks of Mount Pendeli, have certainly occurred; thus the only certainty is the position of the Soros, the burial-mound of the 192 Athenian dead,[28] which tells us little about the exact area of the fighting. However the tactics are more important than the precise topography; these were made possible by the tenacity of the Athenian infantry and the remarkable battle-discipline they showed. Herodotos gives us the basic information that Miltiades (not, as we have seen, in command, but a divisional commander who had had experience of Persian methods of warfare) had the line lengthened to avoid being outflanked by the superior numbers;[29] this involved weakening the centre, which as expected gave way, while the stronger wings were able to turn in upon the advancing enemy centre. The initial charge, replacing the marching advance usually adopted by heavy Greek infantry, was intended to lessen the effect of Persian archery (compare the Plataia battle, 9.49 and 62). It is duly recorded as a 'first', along with the extraordinary statement that the Athenians were the first Greeks not to panic at the sight of Persian forces.[30] Here Herodotos in his enthusiasm for the brilliant victory has too readily accepted Athenian self-congratulation, and the real 'first', the astonishing feat of maintaining a preordered formation and plan of battle (unlike the mere 'rugby scrummage' of conventional Greek pitched battles) goes unstated. It is all the more surprising because Herodotos has earlier remarked (5.78) that only in the previous generation Athens had not been a battle-field force to reckon with.

The general strategy of the Plataia campaign presented no problem to Herodotos, who realised the necessity for Mardonios to fight with a secure base, and in country suitable for his superior cavalry. The Greek force on the other hand must give battle, for the threatening Persian army could not be left in occupation of Central Greece for another year, with the prospect of more defections. (Mardonios' attempt to procure the defection of Athens is fully documented, 8.136, 140ff.) The tactical movements, however, in which the Greeks tried both to retain the protection of the hills and to bring the main forces to battle, an impossible combination, completely bewildered all inexperienced witnesses, as we have seen in Chapter 7 in the case of Amompharetos; interchange of position or 'leapfrogging' while on the move is represented as due to intercity jealousies or insubordination. However the inability of the historian to reduce all the ill-informed tales to the form of an army-training manual is easily understood.[31]

A few weaknesses have thus appeared in geography and topography, with points of the compass (remembering that Herodotos had no compass) and distances. None of them are serious enough to reduce our general level of approbation of the achievement of Herodotos with the materials at his disposal. In military and naval strategy and tactics he was by no means expert, and consequently did not perceive certain implications, but no fool either, and his sources evidently were in the main either inexpert or prejudiced — or both! Inconsistency and failure to harmonise varying accounts are perhaps frequent enough to suggest, not perhaps carelessness, but the lack of any final revision and possibly even of time to complete the work.[32] As to general credulity, enough evidence has been put forward to show that though Herodotos did not invariably use research and reason to discredit tall tales or biased accounts, he successfully did so in the majority of cases. In dealing with all these problems he was the first to operate on such a scale, and indeed often the first to tackle them at all.

Notes

1. Useful (recent) discussions, apart from those in general works, are the following: R. Crahay, 'La critique de l'incroyable', *RUB* 14 (1961/2) 17; B. Baldwin, 'How credulous was Herodotos?', *Greece and Rome* 11 (1964) 167; J. A. S. Evans, 'Father of History or Father of Lies', *CJ* 64 (1968) 11 and (hostile) O. K. Armayor, 'Sesostris and Herodotus' autopsy of Thrace Colchis Inland Asia Minor and the Levant', *HSCPh* 84 (1980) 52 (see also note 9 to Chapter 3).

2. On the possibility of his feat see F. J. Frost, 'Skyllias: Diving in Antiquity', *G & R* 15 (1968) 180.

3. Possibly based on a Babylonian sexagesimal figure; there were five squadrons, perhaps each of sixty ships, doubled for the campaign to 120, therefore totalling 600.

4. He knew the size of the fleets of his own day, but it would hardly have done to point out to an Athenian audience that very possibly the Greeks had numerical superiority at the battle of Salamis!

5. Themistokles' eventual 'Medism' would tend to produce 'evidence' that he had always shown pro-Persian inclinations. The 'Letters of Themistokles' are in themselves not evidence, save for what was in the tradition or could plausibly be inferred.

6. F. D. Maurice, 'The Size of the Army of Xerxes', *JHS* 50 (1930) 210, examined the route of Xerxes from a military logistic angle and found that the 'defile' of the bridge crossing, the topography of the Gallipoli peninsula and in particular the paucity of water supplies would have very severely limited the number of troops that could be marched by that route, to, say, one-tenth of the Herodotean figure.

7. The sophists were only just beginning to lay the foundations of etymology and formal grammar. See the examples of Herodotos' interest at 2.52 (names of gods) and 7.61 (Persian/Perses).

8. See the discussions in A. B. Lloyd, *Herodotos Book II: Introduction* (1975), and *Commentary*, pt. 1 (1976).

9. The highly disparate numbers of Athenian and Persian dead at Marathon may suggest inflation of the enemy figure, but not, evidently, any tampering with the Athenian number. However the same imparity in personal protection between the opposing infantry as Herodotos makes responsible in part for the Plataia victory, and the fact that any wounded would most likely be overtaken and despatched while trying to escape to the ships, make a figure of loss of a third of the probable total

of 20,000 not at all incredible. See n. 29 below.

10. That orthodox opinion now places Hesiod a good deal later than the Homeric poems does not affect the situation. However this view is opposed by M. L. West, *Hesiod, Theogony* (Oxford, Clarendon Press, 1966) 40–8.

11. For example, a reasonably well-documented period in Athenian history of the second half of the sixth century is still debated: see J. G. F. Hind, 'The Tyrannies and the Exiles of Peisistratos', *CQ* 24 (1974) 1–18, and P. J. Rhodes, 'Pisistratid Chronology Again', *Phoenix* 30 (1976) 219. E. Levy, 'Notes sur la chronologie athénienne au VIe siècle', *Historia* 27 (1978) 513.

12. The term semi-legendary is used since Herakles' descendants were 'known' down to the early kings of Sparta, some of whom at least were real.

13. Of the large quantity of writing on this topic I mention the important study of H. Strasburger, 'Herodots Zeitrechnung', *Historia* 5 (1956) 129 (= Marg 688); W. den Boer, 'Herodot und das Systeme der Chronologie', *Mnemosyne* 20 (1967) 30; R. Ball, 'Generation Dating in Herodotos', *CQ* 29 (1979) 270.

14. How and Wells, *Commentary on Herodotus*, Vol. I (1928), 442 (App: XV).

15. See for instance J. F. Lazenby, 'The Strategy of the Greeks in the Opening Campaign of the Persian War', *Hermes* 92 (1964) 264; K. N. Sachs, 'Herodotos and the Dating of the Battle of Thermopylai', *CQ* 26 (1976) 232.

16. The article of Armayor cited in note 1 above represents the extreme of scepticism.

17. F. Oertel. 'Herodots ägyptischer Logos u.d. Glaubwirdigkeit Herodots', *Antiquitas* 18 (1970); and Lloyd, *Herodotus Book II*.

18. See especially the studies of W. Kendrick Pritchett, *Studies in Ancient Greek Topography*, Pt 1 (1965) 71–121; Pt 2 (1969) 1–36.

19. R. Dion, 'Le Danube d'Hérodote', *Rev. Phil.* 42 (1968) 7.

20. See. S. Mazzarino, 'L'image des parties du monde', *A. Ant. Hung.* 7 (1959) 85.

21. F. J. Groten, 'Herodotus' use of variant versions', *Phoenix* 17 (1963) 79.

22. It has been thought that much of this material was drawn from Hekataios, but this cannot be established in detail; the argument largely rests on certain descriptive material which is known to correspond closely with the fragments of the earlier writer. See now Lloyd, *Herodotus Book II*.

23. It may be objected that during the years Herodotos was preparing and writing his *History* Athens was constantly conducting large-scale combined operations with fleets of up to 200 ships in and beyond the Aegaean as far as Egypt. Hence discussions with Athenian commanders of the period could have been helpful; the historian's friend Sophokles was one such.

24. Amongst much discussion, see for example J. A. S. Evans, 'The Final Problem of Thermopylai', *GRBS* 5 (1964) 231.

25. As shown in Chapter 7, the rivalries and sometimes open hostility between states are reflected in accusations of dereliction by various contingents.

26. Although in the preliminary stages Herodotos makes clear that there was a great lack of unanimity in face of the Persian threat, and speaks of 'those who adopted the better policy', later he simply refers to 'the Greeks' and despite rather exaggerated claims on the part of Athens, the general impression seems to have been that 'the Greeks' defeated 'the Persians' — the latter an equal inaccuracy, for many Greeks fought on the side of the Persians at both Salamis and Plataia. The thirty-odd *poleis* who 'adopted the better course' were in fact a minority. The view that Herodotos displayed malice (or favour) in this regard therefore seems perverse; see e.g. S. Spyridakis, 'Salamis and the Cretans', *P.d.P.* 31 (1976) 35.

27. It is true, however, that the Ionian fleet some few years before had displayed enough expertise to defeat the Phoenicians off Cyprus (no report on size of fleets); and Artemisia's dubious feat in disabling a ship of her own side in order to effect her

escape suggests that such a specialist crew was capable of the elaborate manoeuvre. It may be that Dionysios actually intended to bring the whole fleet up to such a standard, and the toil involved provided a grievance strong enough for the Ionians to 'withdraw their labour'.

28. It would seem plausible that the corpses would be interred at or near the site where the majority fell; but there was a deal of movement during the battle, and the parallel of the Tomb of the Plataians (if that is its true designation) shows from its position some distance away at the foot of the hills that the dead must have been specifically conveyed thither. (The literature on the battles of the Persian invasions is too extensive to list, but see note 31 below.)

29. Herodotos does not give a figure for the Persian troops engaged, and educated guesses vary. The Persians used numerical superiority whenever possible, but the number they could bring in a direct sea-borne invasion was clearly limited. The number of their dead is given at 6,400, not necessarily a greatly inflated figure since their protective armament was greatly inferior to that of the Athenians, and in the flight to the ships any wounded would have been cut down. Thus the casualty figure might represent one-third of a force of some 20,000.

30. There are two compelling reasons for rejecting this claim: (a) the Ionian Greeks had fought, with mixed success, against Persians; (b) a Greek hoplite with metal body-armour to protect him would feel a personal superiority over the less well-protected Persians; 'outlandish' dress would not be likely to affect his morale. Compare Herodotos' own remarks on Thermopylai (7.221) and Plataia (9.62).

31. A very restricted bibliography on some of the points mentioned must include J. Schreiner, 'The Battles of 490 BC', *PCPS* 196 [NS16] (1970) 97; A. Ferrill, 'Herodotus and the Strategy and Tactics of the Invasion of Xerxes', *AHR* 72 (1966) 102; J.-F. Lazenby, 'The Strategy of the Greeks in the Opening Campaign of the Persian War', *Hermes* 92 (1964) 264; G. Roux, 'Hérodotë raconte la bataille de Salamis', *BCH* 98 (1974) 51; G. Shrimpton, 'The Persian Dead at Marathon', *Phoenix* 34 (1980) 20. Also N. Whatley, 'On the Possibility of Reconstructing Marathon and Some Other Ancient Battles', *JHS* 84 (1964) 19.

32. See the chapter on structure. But it should be noted that the ends of numerous ancient works and the beginnings of others were lost owing to the ravages of time and predators with six, four or two feet. The text of Thukydides as we have it ends in mid-sentence, while we also know from Xenophon's continuation that it was never completed.

THE WRITER AND THE HISTORIAN

The previous chapters have largely been occupied, on the one hand, with showing what resources, literary, intellectual and informative, were available to Herodotos for his ambitious task of composing a rational history of the Perso-Hellenic conflict; and on the other, showing what constraints, both internal and external, affected the methods used for compiling the material and the manner of presentation. But a major factor in the immediate success and age-long popularity of Herodotos' *History* would appear to have been largely ignored, namely his literary skill. Passing reference only has been made, for the present work is not an essay in literary criticism, a field in which the author claims little competence, and one which at once makes almost inevitable a more subjective approach than I have tried to maintain throughout.[1]

Furthermore, readers of Herodotos will not have failed to observe for themselves, even through the veil of a translation,[2] his outstanding qualities as a literary artist. Some of these were set out by Lucian, the late Greek critic, some 1,800 years ago (see Chapter 2). However it will do no harm to list some of the special merits which make Herodotos (to quote the publisher's blurb for a recent book on him) such 'a good read'. One does not have to be a student of history, an archaeologist, ethnologist or any other kind of specialist; his appeal is to the human race.

The first and perhaps the greatest of his merits is the apparent simplicity of his style, even bordering on seeming naïveté at times. Despite occasional reminiscences of epic language, mainly in the speeches, what is conspicuous is the total lack of 'fine writing' or obvious striving after effect. Such artlessness can in general only be achieved by deliberate artistry of a high order, as the Roman poet Horace pointed out in his verse essay, 'Don't let your technique show'. Herodotos believed in letting the facts speak for themselves;[3] there is a conspicuous absence of highly-coloured and emotive language in the narrative. One may not even notice this — a tribute to the historian, and to his translator! But it is to be found, naturally, in some of the speeches; political or patriotic oratory is not usually content with the plain statement of fact and logical argument; thus it would have been too deliberate underplaying of the role of dramatist-historian (see Chapter 6) merely to allow the protagonists of various views to summarise their arguments in low key. Occasionally, indeed, this is the case, as with the final speech of Themistokles before the Battle of Salamis (8.83), or Artabazos' warning to Mardonios (9.41). As had been shown earlier, one of Herodotos' technical devices was variety in manner of presentation. But much splendid oratory is forthcoming in the numerous set speeches, of which it would be superfluous to quote examples here. It is not confined to political and military matters, of course, but since individuals are of so much interest to the historian, as much artistry is expended upon the dramatisation of their stories as upon the historically important orations of captains and kings. A piece of some elaboration is the story of Adrastos the fugitive fratricide and Atys the doomed son of Kroisos (1.34ff.). A brilliantly written scene, this has even led some critics to suppose that Herodotos is here following an actual play. Wrongly, for sure; what is certain is that if we were lucky enough to come upon a drama from the hand of Herodotos we would not be disappointed.

But he does not need a grand tragic stage, as it were, to exercise his skill; the tale of the dealings between the overadmiring Kandaules, his wife and the opportunist Gyges is most economically and tersely sketched, with some detail and an ingredient of sardonic humour (1.8–12). But there is not the slightest reason to suppose, despite the existence of a play on the Gyges story, that Herodotos' versions of both these episodes, as to the dress and wording of the traditional tales, are not his own; they happen to be outstanding examples of the skill with which he has dramatised many minor and major incidents.

Homeric epic narrative is also, in a sense, simple. There is ornamentation of language, true, and at times of description, with elaboration of detail especially in the long similes. But Herodotos eschews both elaborate epithets and almost all obvious literary devices; as we have seen in regard to his dispassionate reporting, he prefers to let facts speak for themselves. Take the case of Pythios' plea for the release of one of his five sons from military service; as we know this was contrary to the *nomos* of the Persians, and it produced an angry tirade from Xerxes, who as Herodotos evidently thought, supposed that Pythios was trading on the good reciprocal relations established earlier (7.27ff.). Herodotos concludes his account thus: 'He ordered those whose duty it was to find the eldest of Pythios' sons, cut him in half and place the two halves one on the right hand, the other on the left of the road, and the army to march between. The officers did so, and the army marched out between them' (7.35f.). Immediately follows the catalogue of the splendid array which accompanied the king from Sardis towards the Hellespont.[4] The dramatic effect of such bare narrative of distasteful events is amplified by the contrast. Similar economy is shown at the end of the equally violent tale of Hermotimos' revenge (8.106). The restraint with which the fatal struggle at Thermopylai is recounted stands as a supreme example of such artistry (7.223f.). An example of similar restraint in a totally different and more pleasant context is offered by the account of the Spartan queen bathing her twin sons, full of gentle irony (6.52).

A certain quality in the events narrated, perhaps that of the inevitability of dread changes of fortune, may lead to a mental comparison with the tone of the Authorised Version of the Old Testament. Translators have therefore sometimes ventured to put Herodotos' Greek into a rather archaic type of English. The epic mannerism, sometimes termed ring-composition, by which at the end of a paragraph the story is summed up in a phrase (e.g. 8.66, 'That is what Dikaios said') with the defining particles mentioned in Chapter 6, n. 6, also sounds archaic in the ear of contemporary readers. A further influence to such a tendency has been the older view that Herodotos represented an archaic period of thought, that of Pindar and Sophokles, while his successor Thukydides belonged to a more 'modern', sophisticated world. Although there is no certainty about the date of publication, it is likely that the two historians were more nearly contemporary than such a view suggests,[5] and this notion no longer prevails. Any translations should render Herodotos into completely contemporary language. At the time of composition, Herodotos was certainly no less 'modern' than the majority of his countrymen. In literary language and in philosophical and religious thought there was of course an *avant garde* (see Chapter 2) of which he was not a member; his subject-matter was hardly congenial to the new style, while as seen earlier it is difficult to identify the precise contributions of the progressives to his conception of history.

Exception however must again be made in regard to certain of the speeches. In these perhaps the tradition of epic was reinforced by the current popularity of the tragic drama; but nowhere do we find the prose equivalent of the elevated style, abundant and even abstruse metaphorical language, and specialised vocabulary of the stage. As pointed out in another connection, Herodotos knew he was not writing plays; but he also knew the value, especially for oral delivery, of an effective speech or dialogue. Present-day authors of historical novels evidently believe that the reading public enjoys speeches and dialogue, which in many cases appear the work of unfettered imagination. My personal distaste for such inflation does not extend to Herodotean speeches, for they serve a serious purpose (or several purposes).

But it is not only in narrating such dramatic events as great battles or personal tragedies that Herodotos' skill is revealed. Light-hearted or even comic narrative makes part of the 'great tapestry', as it has been called, of the *History*. In the anthropological and ethnological excursuses the humorous element must often have been supplied for his audience by the bizarre customs described, despite his 'dead-pan' presentation; the ancient Greeks will not have been less ready to be amused by the droll ways of foreigners than are present-day Anglo-Saxons. In the case of zoology and botany too, certain extravagances are reported, not as gospel but probably aimed to draw a smile from the less credulous among his hearers.

We have already noted the satirical tone of his introductory rejection of mythical 'causes' for the great conflict. Another shaft aimed at the epic is the comment 'Priam's sons were dying by twos and threes all the time', in a passage strongly criticising the plausibility of Homer's *Tale of Troy* (2.120). The Kandaules story again has its ironic side: the king 'conceived a passion for his own wife', obviously a foolish thing to do[6] and not common with the arranged marriages of Greek society; Eros had little connection with matrimony! And Gyges, faced with a dilemma by the insulted queen, 'chose survival' (1.11). Somewhat black is the irony of the conclusion of the story (8.116), in which the king of the Bisalti blinded his sons for joining Xerxes 'and that was their pay'.[7] Similarly 'Oiobazos' three sons were left behind [dead]' (4.84). The brother of the clever thief, told to cut off the trapped man's head to avoid recognition, 'thought it a good idea' and did so (2.121ß).

Political shafts include the famous *mot* attributed to Aristagoras, to the effect that you can fool people *en masse*; the Egyptians, 'though freed, could not get along without a king' (2.147), while Maiandrios knew that it was no use his abdicating, as the Samians evidently didn't want freedom (3.143).

More gentle irony appears in the consent of Herakles to have intercourse with the snake-woman provided he got the agreed fee (4.9): whereas 'history doesn't relate' what fee Pharaoh's daughter charged for her favours (2.126). The royal judges, to please Kambyses, 'discovered a law which assisted anyone wanting to marry his sister' (3.31). The shepherds of Arabia have sufficient skill in carpentry to make little carts for the fat tails of their sheep (3.116).

Even Herodotos' almost undiluted approbation of all things Egyptian admits some irony; in the context of the priest's report on previous Nile flood heights, we hear that 'Moeris hadn't been dead for even nine hundred years' (2.13) while 'the Egyptians call all who do not speak their language barbaric' — though this last is rather a hit at his own countrymen, other examples of which may be found both in Book 2 and elsewhere. The notice of the reversal of general practice in Egyptian manners and customs is in Herodotos' best dead-pan style, but certainly was intended to raise a smile.[8] Similarly, the comparison of Greek and Persian dining habits is surely tongue-in-cheek (1.133). However, in dealing with foreign religious beliefs, rites and customs Herodotos is careful to avoid any suggestions of irreverence or disrespect.

Ironical statements or suggestions of incredulity have been noticed in Chapter 7; here we may note the comment on wolves leading a blindfold priest to the sanctuary and back, 'Let him believe who can swallow that sort of tale' (2.122). A similar phrase is used of the statues that were reported to have fallen to their knees (5.86). In dealing with the gales that wrecked many Persian ships on the coast of Magnesia, he is extremely cautious about the Athenian view that their 'connection by marriage', Boreas the North Wind,[9] had come to their aid at this time (7.189). 'A story is told that . . .' and 'as the common talk would have it' are phrases showing some deference to the religious sensibilities of an Athenian audience, used in preference to an outright expression of disbelief. However a little later, when the Magi perform sacrifices not only to the supranational wind itself but also to Greek marine deities, they continue for three days, and on the fourth 'they succeeded in stopping it — or it abated of its own accord'. The Magi perhaps provide an exception to the statement made earlier that Herodotos showed invariable respect in religious matters; the Magi, apart from being the clerics of the enemy, nowhere appear in a favourable light partly owing to the affair of the False Smerdis and

pro-Dareian accounts thereof; in Book 7, before the supplication to
the wind, they appear in a highly equivocal light (7.19, 37) and in
Book 1 their advice to Astyages is always that of the self-regarding
courtier (e.g. 1.120).

Avowedly comic pieces are part of the narrative technique too,
though they are not nearly as common as the ironical phrase. They
include of course the Clever Thief story, often referred to in earlier
chapters, but perhaps exceptional in being both totally fictional
and lacking relevance to any historical fact; more apposite are the
anecdotes of how the Alkmaionids attained their wealth and
eminence in Athens. One can imagine a mischievous gleam in the
historian's eye as he sketched the caricature figure of Alkmaion
staggering from Kroisos' treasury with gold stuffed in every
possible repository of clothing or person; and at the no more
edifying spectacle of Hippokleides (probably a member of the rival
Philaid clan) 'dancing away his marriage'.[10]

The discursive nature of Herodotos' narrative is a matter for
more subjective judgement. While some persons, of whom the
present writer is one, constantly digress in their thoughts, without
perhaps possessing the same facility as Herodotos of returning not
at all out of breath to their main theme, there are other possibly
more precise intellects that prefer to keep the principal line of
argument firmly in front of themselves and their audiences. All
irrelevancies they dismiss as frivolous, and permit essential background information only to enter, and then in the form of footnotes. But the greater part of mankind are not endowed with
particularly orderly habits of mind, and the general approval of the
History by generations of readers must gain a verdict in favour of
Herodotean discursiveness. For with the rambling narrative comes
that liveliness which distinguishes the 'Father of History' from
many of his successors. To take but one example from ancient
historiography; the later Greek writer Polybios gave the world a
reasonable account of the rise of the power of Rome, a subject of
no less universal import than the repulse of Persia by the Greeks.
He is conscientious, intelligent, rational — and dull! No one reads
him but specialist historians. It is not the case that Herodotos was
distracted from serious historical analysis by his omnivorous
appetite for 'facts', however implausible, and by a general lightness
of approach. And to issue a *Reader's Digest* version of Herodotos
would seem not only a ridiculous but an impossible task.

It has been an inestimable advantage to later generations that the history of a central and critical period of Ancient Greece was presented in such an attractive manner. The main purpose of Herodotos' writing, as set out in his Proem (see Chapter 1) has been admirably fulfilled. The deeds or 'works' of both Greek and barbarian have certainly not fallen into oblivion, and anyone who wishes to study the history of the period must start with Herodotos. But it is not the case that his aim was merely 'to glamorise the Persian Wars' as has recently been claimed.[11] As a result of the current fashion for 'oral history', some of his problems with sources may be better understood, and his reputation as a historian is not likely to suffer thereby.[12] Any study of the major subject area, the wars of Greeks and Persians, can add to his account only small items, gathered from archaeological study, a few epigraphic items and references in non-historical literature, together with a few statements of later history writers who certainly did not have access to more authentic sources than those utilised by Herodotos himself. Otherwise, cautions may be expressed, interpretations and judgements offered other than those made explicit in the *History*.

Herodotos was not omniscient, and there was inevitably a certain hit-and-miss element in his gathering of oral information. Thus a vital clue for the comprehension of the Battle of Salamis is found in the later historian Diodoros,[13] namely that the Egyptian squadron of the Persian navy was despatched to the western exit from the Channel[14] and it would have been these ships against which the Korinthians fought. But such supplements are comparatively few; any written documents to which later historians had access were themselves much later than the *History*. That Herodotos undoubtedly erred at times in both fact and judgement has been shown in the preceding chapter and needs no further examination here.

The non-historical sections of the work are perhaps of less indisputable value. We may discard much of the zoological information; Aristotle a century later, and following him Theophrastos, were the real founders of scientific study in zoology and botany, but the sciences made little progress in the West, partly owing to the repressive nature of the medieval and indeed the renaissance and even post-reformation church; they became firmly established only in the late eighteenth century. In anthropology and ethnology Herodotos' information is on the whole to be accepted as reasonably correct, exception being made for occasional rather perverse interpretations such as the Egyptian origin of the

Colchians (2.104ff.), based on evidently misconstrued oral information and unscientific reasoning. Modern students may well draw with profit on his wide-ranging observations of manners and customs, diet and dwellings. The most elaborate of his descriptions is of course that of ancient Egypt. Scientific Egyptology is also a comparatively late development, now approaching a century and a half; it was incapable of full study before the decipherment of the Egyptian scripts.[15] So Herodotos provided, with a fair degree of accuracy but some rather strange blunders, most of the knowledge of Ancient Egypt available before the nineteenth century.

Geographical information, as we have seen in Chapter 11, is at times quite seriously in error; the reasons are intelligible enough for the most part, and the mistakes and miscalculations, save for certain crude blemishes, need not cause concern. The foundation for accurate cartography was laid by the late Greek scholar Claudius Ptolemaios (Ptolemy) of Alexandria in the second century AD, but knowledge of world geography did not advance rapidly till the great voyages of discovery of the fifteenth century.

Thus on the whole criticism of the veracity and of the usefulness of Herodotos' non-historical material should be kept in check; deficiencies and inaccuracies are mostly venial. Reproof is perhaps justified where gross exaggeration or fantasies have passed quite undetected or without sceptical comment. Two factors have to be borne in mind; one is the researcher's desire for fullness of information (perhaps even in preference to authenticity), and the other, the aim of providing entertaining rather than encyclopaedia-style reports. Furthermore, the enormous scope of the work is such that it would have been a superhuman achievement to present it free of all blemishes. Herodotos was indeed human; he gives us the impression of a genial, indeed a congenial character, and we should regard his attempt to establish at one blow both the art and the science of history in as genial and detached a frame of mind as the author himself has displayed.

There are more positive qualities to be considered in assessing his standing as a historian. First of these perhaps is his sense of time, a historical perspective not previously evident in any writer. Most previous literature showed a remarkable indifference to a time-scale and to chronological relations. Herodotos not only realised the childhood of Greek society and culture in relation to the age-old civilisations of the Orient, but strove to bring historical events into a reasoned relationship with one another.[16] Sometimes of course his information was inadequate for his purpose.

His predecessors, if the 'logographers' (see Chapter 2) may properly be so termed, had compiled chronicles usually limited strictly to one *polis* or area, or extending at best to the Hellenic world. It was Herodotos who passed beyond chronicle to both reasoned historical narrative and to a 'universal' history,[17] extending outside Hellas to the known world. He gave himself freedom, in every respect and with full justification, to garner, to winnow or to pass on information at his own discretion. His form of *historiē* differs also from that of the early philosophical inquirers, though its method was largely derived from or inspired by theirs. His interests are more concrete, and more everyday, suited to the broader audience he wished to reach. But like the monists, he proceeds from an objective standpoint; indeed the fact that he has no axe to grind can even lead to the complaint that his is a negativist philosophy of history.[18] But note that while the writer with the best claim to be Herodotos' precursor, Hekataios, opened his work with the statement 'Hekataios of Miletos recounts the following', and Herodotos' successor in the same manner begins 'Thukydides son of Oloros, an Athenian, compiled the narrative . . .', in our historian's case we read 'Here is the exposition of the *research* of Herodotos'.[19]

As here, the name of Thukydides constantly crops up in discussion of Herodotos' merits and shortcomings. I do not intend to add further to the innumerable comparisons and contrasts that have been drawn, except for one point: the later historian's claim of the unrivalled greatness of his own subject, the Peloponnesian War. While this is certainly not indisputable on other grounds, an observation may be made which helps to clarify our view of Herodotos' work. Both great conflicts had, from one point of view, negative consequences. The Persian dream of a world-empire extending to Europe was destroyed, and in the long run of course even their Asiatic Greek subjects were lost to them, to say nothing of Alexander's 'revenge'. Now as a result of the Peloponnesian War, no comparatively great power amongst the *poleis* was able to dominate Greece from within; thus she eventually fell prey to external powers, first Macedon and then Rome.

The Persian Wars, however, also had a positive result, the great surge of confidence leading to the manifold achievements of the fifth century BC. Thus it is natural that the Herodotean narrative, despite the gloomy utterances of some of its personages, gives off an aura of optimism, contrasting with the tragic gloom of Thukydides. It thus illustrates the brighter side of the classical Greek spirit, and for that alone has deserved its long popularity.

Notes

1. Scholarly critics will no doubt find plenty of ammunition with which to demolish this claim, but the effort to justify it has been made.
2. No criticism is intended of any particular English translation, but the problem is a universal one and style almost impossible to render adequately.
3. So J. L. Myres, *Herodotus, Father of History* (Clarendon Press, Oxford, 1953).
4. An important element in Herodotean structure is contrast; see Chapters 5 and 6.
5. On his showing Thukydides began to write in 431 BC, at the outbreak of the Peloponnesian War, while as shown earlier the latest datable events mentioned by Herodotos belong to the first couple of years of that war.
6. But despots were notoriously subject to such ill-advised emotional involvements, as the case of Xerxes illustrates.
7. The Greek word here, *misthos*, is used of the pay of mercenary soldiers, and in general a fee for services rendered, as in the case of Herakles and the snake-woman just below.
8. On the whole question see Lloyd, *Herodotus Book II* (1975).
9. The prevalent north or north-east wind of summer in the Aegaean, now called the meltemi. A northerly gale in winter, though of different meteorological origin, would of course have been attributed to the same deity.
10. The fact that the original source of this fable is an Indian folk-tale has little importance. That frequently Greeks (and eminent Greeks) are the butt of Herodotos' wit is perhaps the best argument for 'Plutarch's' accusation of malice.
11. S. Spyridakis, 'Salamis and the Cretans' (Herodotos 7.169ff.) *P. d. P.* 31 (1976) 35. This critic even finds (unmotivated) distortion in the account of why the Cretans were not present at Salamis.
12. A rather slighting definition of him as 'our only half-way respectable source' (for the Ionian revolt), while damning with faint praise admits his prime importance for historical study.
13. Bk. 11, 17.2, probably from the fourth-century historian Ephoros.
14. See Chapter 7 above. Herodotos was largely following Athenian versions of Salamis, for obvious reasons, whereas Ephoros could have drawn on a Korinthian source.
15. On the general question see Lloyd, *Herodotus Book II* (1975).
16. See H. Frankel, *Wege und Formen Frugriechische Denkens* (1955).
17. S. Mazzarino, *Il pensiero storico clasico* (1966), 1.130.
18. The phrase is that of G. J. Gruman in *History and Theory* 1 (1961) 75.
19. See Carla Schick in *Rend. Acc. Lincei* 8 (1956) 7.7.349.

SELECT BIBLIOGRAPHY

The list is divided into two parts: Part A, a selection of introductory and general writings in English only, as well as translations, on Herodotos and the history of the period, especially the Persian Wars; and Part B, more specialised works on particular aspects mainly of the last thirty years.

Part A

Truesdell S. Brown, *The Greek Historians* (Heath, Lexington, 1973).

Hermann Bengston, *The Greeks and the Persians: The Defence of the West* (Weidenfeld and Nicholson, London, 1969).

Charles W. Fornara, *Herodotus; an Interpretative Essay* (Clarendon Press, Oxford, 1971).

T. R. Glover, *Herodotus*, Sather Lectures 3 (Berkeley, University of California Press, 1924).

A. W. Gomme, *The Greek Attitude to Poetry and History*, Sather Lectures 27 (Berkeley, University of California Press, 1954).

A. Hignett, *Xerxes' Invasion of Greece* (Oxford University Press, London, 1963).

W. How and J. Wells, *A Commentary on Herodotus*, 2 vols (new impression: Clarendon Press, Oxford, 1928).

J. L. Myres, *Herodotus, Father of History* (Clarendon Press, Oxford, 1953).

G. E. M. de Ste. Croix, 'Herodotus', *Greece & Rome* 24 (1977) 130.

A. de Selincourt, *The World of Herodotus* (Secker & Warburg, London, 1962).

C. G. Starr, 'The Awakening of the Greek Historical Spirit', *NC* 6 (1966) 1 (also separately: Knopf, New York, 1968).

Translations

H. Carter, *Herodotus; the Histories* (Oxford University Press, London, 1962).

A. D. Godley, *Herodotus, with an English translation* (Loeb

178 *Select Bibliography*

Classical Library, Harvard, 1946–   ).
G. Rawlinson *et al.*, *Herodotus* (Murray, London, 1856–60;
Everyman edition, Dent, London, 1910).
A. de Selincourt, *Herodotus; the Histories* (Allen Lane,
Harmondsworth, 1954; Penguin, reprints 1966 on).

Part B

Texts

C. Hude, 3rd edn (Clarendon Press, Oxford, 1927).
Ph. E. Legrand (Budé, Paris, 1946–56).

Lexicon

J. E. Powell, *A Lexicon to Herodotus* (Cambridge University
Press, London, 1939; rep. Olms, Hildesheim, 1969).

Bibliographies

L. Bergson, 'Herodotus 1937–60', in *Lustrum* 11 (1966) 71–138.
G. T. Griffith, in *Fifty Years (and Twelve) of Classical Scholarship*
(Oxford, 1968).
E. Hampl, 'Herodot. Ein kritische Forschungsbericht nach metho-
dischen Geschichtspunkten' in *Grazer Beitrage* 4 (1975) 97–136.
P. Mackendrick, 'Herodotus 1954–1963', *CW* 56 (1962) 269.
——,'Herodotus 1963–1969', *CW* 63 (1969) 37.
W. Marg and W. Nicolai, 'Literaturverzeichnis' in W. Marg (ed.),
Herodot, eine Auswahl aus der neueren Forschung, 2nd edn
(Darmstadt Wissenschaftliche Buchgesellschaft, 1965), 757–81.

General Surveys

H. F. Bornitz, *Herodot-Studien* (de Gruyter, Berlin, 1967).
H. Drexler, *Herodot-Studien* (Olms, Hildesheim, 1972).
K. von Fritz, *Die griechische Geschichtsschreibung*, vol. I (de
Gruyter, Berlin, 1967), 104.
Ph. E. Legrand, *Hérodote: Introduction*, 2nd edn (Budé, Paris,
1955).
R. W. Macan, *Herodotus, the Fourth, Fifth and Sixth Books*, 2
vols (Macmillan, London, 1895).
——, *Herodotus, the Seventh, Eighth and Ninth Books*, 2 vols
(Macmillan, London, 1908).
Anne Mantel, *Herodot historien*, in Dutch with an English
summary (Hakkert, Amsterdam, 1975 (1976)).

W. Marg (ed.), see above, Bibliographies.

M. Pohlenz, *Herodot, erste Geschichtsschrieber des Abendlandes* (Neue Wege zur Antike 7/8, Leipzig, 1933; 2nd edn Teubner, Stuttgart, 1961).

Special Aspects

1. Sources, sources criticism, reliability

W. Aly, *Volksmärchen Sage und Novelle bei Herodot und seinen Zeitsgenossen*, 2nd edn (Vanderhoeck & Ruprecht, Göttingen, 1969).

B. Baldwin, 'How Credulous was Herodotus?', *Greece and Rome* 11 (1964) 167.

H. Barth, 'Zur Bewertung und Auswahl des Stoffes durch Herodot', *Klio* 50 (1968) 33.

E. J. Bickerman and H. Tadmor, 'Darius I, pseudo-Smerdis and the Magi', *Athenaeum* 66 (1978) 239.

P. Bicknell, 'Herodotos Kallimachos and the Bean', *Acta Class* 14 (1971 (1972)) 147.

R. Crahay, 'La critique de l'incroyable', *RUB* 14 (1961/2) 17.

R. Drews, *The Greek Accounts of Eastern History* (Harvard University Press, 1973).

J. A. S. Evans, 'Father of History or Father of Lies; the Reputation of Herodotus', *CJ* 64 (1968) 11.

——, 'Herodotus and the Ionian Revolt', *Historia* 25 (1976) 31.

D. Fehling, *Die Quellenangaben bei Herodot: Studien zur Erzahlkunst Herodots* (de Gruyter, Berlin, 1971).

W. G. Forrest, 'The Tradition about Hippias' Expulsion from Athens', *GRBS* 10 (1969) 277.

F. J. Groten, 'Herodotus' Use of Variant Versions', *Phoenix* 17 (1963) 79.

D. Hegyi, 'The Historical Authenticity of Herodotus in the Persian Logoi', *A. Ant. Hung.* 21 (1973) 73.

——, 'The Historical Background of the Ionian Revolt', *A. Ant. Hung.* 14 (1966) 285.

B. M. Mitchell, 'Herodotus and Samos', *JHS* 95 (1975) 75.

A. Momigliano, 'Historiography on Written Tradition and Historiography on Oral Tradition' in *Studies in Historiography* (Weidenfeld and Nicholson, London, 1966), 211.

J. W. Neville, 'Was there an Ionian Revolt?', *CQ* 29 (1979) 268.

——, 'Herodotus on the Trojan War', *G & R* 24 (1977) 3.

F. Oertel, 'Herodots ägyptischer logos und die Glaubwirdigkeit

Herodots', *Antiquitas 18* (Bonn, 1970).

G. Schepers, 'Source Theory in Greek Historiography', *Anc. Soc.* 6 (1975) 259.

B. Shimron, 'πρῶτος τῶν ἡμεῖς ἴδμεν', *Eranos* 71 (1973) 45.

G. G. Starr, 'The Credibility of Early Spartan History', *Historia* 14 (1965) 257.

H. Verdin, *De historische-kritische methode van Herodotus* (Paleis der Academie, Brussels, 1971).

——, 'Notes sur l'attitude des historiens grecs à l'égard de la tradition locale', *Anc. Soc.* 1 (1970) 183.

——, 'Les remarques critiques d'Hérodote et de Thucydide sur la poèsie en tant que source historique' in *Historiographia Antiqua*, Festschrift Peremans (Louvain University Press, 1977).

A. E. Wardman, 'Myth in Greek Historiography', *Historia* 9 (1960) 403.

H. D. Westlake, 'λέγεται in Thucydides', *Mnemosyne* 30 (1977) 345.

J. Wikarjak, 'Qua ratione Herodotus in historia scribenda rerum delectum egerit', *Eos* 51 (1961) 237.

2. *Methods of research, including travel* (see also above)

O. Kimball Armayor, 'Sesostris and Herodotus' Autopsy of Thrace Colchis Inland Asia Minor and the Levant', *HSCPh* 84 (1980) 52.

——, 'Did Herodotus ever go to the Black Sea?', *HSCPh* 82 (1978) 45.

A. Cook, 'Herodotus; the Act of Inquiry as a Liberation from Myth', *Helios* 3 (1976) 23.

J. A. S. Evans, 'Oral Tradition in Herodotus', *Canadian Oral History Assoc. Journal* 4 (1980) 8.

J. R. Grant, "Εκ του παρατυχόντος πυνθανόμενος', *Phoenix* 23 (1969) 264.

A. J. Podlecki, 'Herodotus in Athens?' in *Greece and the Eastern Mediterranean*, Stud. Schachermeyr (de Gruyter, Berlin, 1977), 246.

3. *Literary and philosophical influences*

A. Dihle, 'Herodot und die Sophistik', *Philologus* 106 (1962) 207.

H. Erbse, 'Tradition und Form im Werke Herodots', *Gymnasium* 65 (1961) 239.

D. Grene, 'Herodotus; the Historian as Dramatist', *JPh* 58 (1961)

477.

R. Kassel, 'Herodot und der Gyges-drama', *ZPE* 14 (1974) 226.

F. Lassere, 'Hérodote et Protagoras; le débat sur les constitutions', *MH* 33 (1976) 65.

——, 'L'historiographie grecque à l'époque archaique', *QS* 4 (1976) 113.

K. Latte, 'Die Anfänge der griechischen Geschichtsschreibung' in *Entretiens Hardt* 4 (Geneva) 1956 (1958) 1.

A. Lesky, 'Tragödien bei Herodot' in *Greece and the Eastern Mediterranean* (Festschrift Schachermeyr) (de Gruyter, Berlin, 1977).

A. Momigliano, 'The Place of Herodotus in the History of Historiography', *History* 43 (1958) 1 [= *Secondo contributo . . .*, Ed. di storia e lett, Rome, 1960, 29].

——, 'Greek Historiography', *History and Theory* 17 (1978) 1.

L. Pearson, *Early Ionian Historians* (Clarendon Press, Oxford, 1939).

A. Roveri, 'La nascita delle forme storiche da Ecateo ad Erodoto', *BUIFCS* 13 (1963) 3.

B. Snell, 'Gyges und Kroisos als Tragödien-figuren', *ZPE* 12 (1973) 197.

H.-P. Stahl, 'Herodots Gyges-Tragödie', *Hermes* 96 (1968) 385.

——, 'Learning Through Suffering? Croesus' Conversation in the History of Herodotos', *YCS* 24 (1975) 1.

H. Verdin (1977): see Bibliography section B1 above.

M. Vilchez, 'Tradición e innovación en Herodotus', *Habis* 3 (1972) 29.

F. W. Walbank, 'History and Tragedy', *Historia* 9 (1960) 28.

4. The supernatural element; religious and moral notions

R. Crahay, *La littérature oraculaire chez Hérodote* (Les Belles Lettres, Paris, 1956).

J. Elayi, 'Le rôle de l'oracle de Delphes dans le conflit greco-perse d'après les histoires d'Hérodote', *Iranica Antiqua* 13 (1978) 93; 14 (1979) 67.

——, 'Deux oracles à Delphes', *REG* 92 (1979) 224.

J. A. S. Evans, 'The Oracle of the "Wooden Wall" ', *CJ* 78 (1982) 24.

J. Fontenrose, *The Delphic Oracle* (University of California Press, Berkeley & London, 1978).

P. Frisch, *Die Träume bei Herodot*, Beitrage zur klass. Philol. 27

(Hain, Meisenheim, 1968).

J. Herrmann, 'Nomos bei Herodot und Thukydides' in *Gedacht-nisschrift H. Peters* (Springer, Berlin, 1967), 16.

J. Kirchberg, *Die Fonktion der Orakel im Werke Herodots*, Hypomnemata 11 (Vandenhoeck & Ruprecht, Göttingen, 1965).

T. Krischer, 'Solon und Kroisos', *WS* 77 (1963/64) 174.

R. G. A. van Lieshout, 'A Dream on a καιρός of History', *Mnemosyne* 23 (1970) 235.

I. M. Linforth, 'Named and Unnamed Gods in Herodotos', *UCPCPh* 9 (1928) 201.

W. Marg, 'Selbstsicherheit bei Herodot', *Studies Robinson II* (1953), 1103 [= Marg (1965), 290].

P. G. Maxwell-Stuart, 'Pain, Mutilation and Death in Herodotus, Bk 7', *P. d. P.* 31 (1976) 356.

A. Piatowski, 'Le sourire ironique d'Hérodote', *Studii Clasice* 10 (1968) 51.

J. De Romilly, *The Rise and Fall of States according to Greek Authors*, Jerome Lectures (University of Michigan Press, Ann Arbor, 1977).

O. Regenbogen, 'Die Geschichte von Solon und Kroisos' in *Kleine Schriften* (Beck, Munich, 1961), 101 [= Marg (1965) 57].

G. Schneeweiss, 'Kroisos und Solon; die Frage nach dem Gluck' in *Apophoreta U. Holscher* (Habelt, Bonn, 1975).

P. Walcot, 'Herodotus on Rape', *Arethusa* 11 (1978) 137.

E. Wolff, 'Das Weib von Masistes', *Hermes* 92 (1964) 51.

D. E. W. Wormell, 'Croesus and the Delphic Oracles' Omniscience', *Hermathena* 93 (1959) 20.

5. *Political and social attitudes*

J. Annequin, 'Remarques sur la femme et le pouvoir chez Hérodote', *DHA* 2 (1976) 387.

J. Bleicken, 'Zur Entstehung der Verfassungstypologie in fünfte Jahrhundert', *Historia* 28 (1979) 148.

J. W. Boake, 'Plutarch's Historical Judgment with Special Reference to the *de Herodoti Malignitate*' (Diss., Toronto, 1975).

P. T. Brannan, 'Herodotus and History: the Constitutional Debate', *Traditio* 19 (1963) 427.

K. Bringmann, 'Die Verfassungsdebatte ... und Dareios Aufstieg', *Hermes* 104 (1976) 266.

L. Camerer, *Die Praktische Klugheit bei Herodot: Untersuchungen zur den Begriffen Techne Mechane Sophia* (Koln (Diss., Tübingen) 1965).

K. M. Cragg, 'Herodotus' presentation of Sparta' (Diss., University of Michigan, 1976).

R. Develin, 'Herodotos and the Alkmeonids' (forthcoming).

H. J. Diesner, 'Die griechische Tyrannis bei Herodot', *Forschungen und Fortschritte* 34, 9 (1960) 260.

J. A. S. Evans, 'Despotes Nomos', *Athenaeum* 43 (1965) 142.

——, 'The Dream of Xerxes and the Nomoi of the Persians', *CJ* 57 (1961) 109.

——, 'Herodotus and Athens; the Evidence of the Encomium', *AC* 48 (1979) 112.

A. Ferrill, 'Herodotus on Tyranny', *Historia* 27 (1978) 385.

C. W. Fornara, 'Hellanicus and the Alcmaeonid Tradition', *Historia* 17 (1968) 381.

——, 'The Cult of Harmodius and Aristogeiton', *Philologus* 114 (1970) 155.

K. von Fritz, 'Die griechische ἐλενϑερία bei Herodot', *WS* 78 (1965) 5.

P. Gauthier, 'Les tyrans dans le monde grec antique', *REG* 81 (1968) 553.

D. Gillis, 'Marathon and the Alcmaeonids', *GRBS* 10 (1969) 133.

F. D. Harvey, 'The Political Sympathies of Herodotus', *Historia* 15 (1966) 254.

H. Homeyer, 'Zu Plutarchs *de Malignitate Herodoti*', *Klio* 49 (1967) 81.

L. Hubert, 'Herodot und die politische Propaganda seiner Zeit', *Rostock Univ. Wiss. Zeitschr.* 18 (1969) 317.

G. Maddoli, 'Erodoto e gli Ioni: per l'interpretazione di 1.141.2', *P.d.P.* 34 (1979) 256.

G. Nenci, 'Encomie et societé chez Hérodote' in *Actes du IXe Cong. de l'assoc. G. Budé*, 1973 (Les Belles Lettres, Paris, 1975).

S. I. Oost, 'The tyrant kings of Syracuse', *CPh* 72 (1976) 224.

J. de Romilly, 'Le classement des constitutions d'Hérodote à Aristote', *REG* 72 (1959) 81.

——, 'L'objectivité dans l'historiographie grecque' in *Proc. 3rd Int. Hum. Symposium* (Athens, 1975), 107.

J. Schwarz, 'Hérodote et Périclès', *Historia* 18 (1969) 367.

F. Stoessl, 'Herodots Humanität', *Gymnasium* 66 (1959) 477.

H. Strasburger, 'Herodot und die perikleische Athen', *Historia* 4 (1955) 1 [= Marg (1965) 574].

V. M. Strogecki 'Herodotus and the Alcmaeonids' (English resumé) *VDI* 41 (1977) 145.

C. Talano, 'Isteio ed Erodoto per la storia della tirannide', *Rend. Acad. Arch. Napoli* 44 (1969) 173.

R. Tölle-Kastenbein, *Herodot und Samos* (Duris-Verlag, Bochum, 1976).

K. H. Waters, *Herodotos on Tyrants and Despots: a Study in Objectivity*, Historia Einzelschriften 15 (Steiner, Weisbaden, 1971).

——, 'Herodotos and Politics', *G & R* 19 (1972) 38.

J. Wikarjak, 'Elementy Polemiczne w Dziele Herodota', *Eos* 53 (1963) 41 (Latin summary).

6. *Individuals: importance and characteristics*

H. C. Avery, 'Herodotus' Picture of Cyprus', *AJPh*, 93 (1972) 529.

G. A. H. Chapman, 'Herodotus and Histiaeus' Role in the Ionian Revolt', *Historia* 21 (1972) 546.

J. A. S. Evans, 'Histiaeus and Aristagoras', *AJPh* 84 (1963) 115.

——, 'What Happened to Croesus?', *CJ* 74 (1978) 34.

F. J. Frost, 'Themistocles' Place in Athenian Politics', *CSCA* 1 (1968) 114.

——, 'Themistocles and Mnesiphilus', *Historia* 20 (1971) 20.

C. Guratsch, 'Der Sieger von Salamis', *Klio* 39 (1961) 48.

H. Homeyer, 'Zu den Anfangen der griechische Biographie', *Philologus* 106 (1962) 75.

P. B. Manville, 'Aristagoras and Histiaios: the Leadership Struggle in the Ionian Revolt', *CQ* 27 (1977) 80.

M. Miller, 'The Herodotean Croesus', *Klio* 41 (1963) 58.

E. H. Schulte, *Herodots Darstellung der grossen griechische Feldherrn* (Diss., Marburg, 1966).

A. C. Sheffield, *Herodotus' portrayal of Croesus: a study in historical artistry* (Diss., Stanford, 1973).

7. *Causation and motivation* (see also 6)

P. Hohti, 'Über die Notwendigkeit bei Herodot', *Arctos* 9 (1975) 31.

——, 'Die Schuldfrage der Perserkriege in Herodots Geschichtswerke', *Arctos* 10 (1976) 37.

H. R. Immerwahr, 'Historical Action in Herodotus', *TAPhA* 85 (1954) 16.

——, 'Aspects of Historical Causation in Herodotus', *TAPhA* 87 (1956) 241.

A. Momigliano, 'Some Observations on Causes of War in Ancient Historiography' in *Studies in Historiography* (Weidenfeld & Nicholson, London, 1966), 112.

H. Rawlings, *Prophasis in pre-Thucydidean Literature* (Hermes Einzelschr. 33, 1975 = Diss., Princeton, 1970).

J. de Romilly, 'La Vengeance comme explication dans l'oeuvre historique d'Hérodote', *REG* 74 (1971) 314.

R. Sealey, 'Herodotus, Thucydides, and the Causes of War', *CQ* 51 (1957) 1.

P. Tozzi, 'Erodoto e la responsibilità dell'inizio della rivolta ionica', *Athenaeum* 55 (1977) 127.

A. E. Wardman, 'Herodotus on the Cause of the Greco-Persian Wars', *AJPh* 82 (1961) 133.

J. Wikarjak, 'Podania Aitiologiczne u Herodota', *Eos* 54 (1964) 20 (Latin summary 32).

8. *Structure and narrative method*

I. Beck, *Die Ring-Composition bei Herodot und ihre Bedeutung für die Beweistechnik*, Spudasmata 25 (Olms, Hildesheim, 1971).

Laura Boffo, 'Il logos di Orete in Erodots', *Rend. Acc. Lincei* s. VIII, 34 (1979) 85.

H. R. Breitenbach, 'Herodotus Pater Historiae', *Schweiz. Zeitsch. für Geschichte* 16 (1966) 465.

Silvana Cagnazzi, 'Tavola dei 28 logoi di Erodoto', *Hermes* 103 (1975) 385.

J. Cobet, *Herodots Exkurse und die Frage der Einheit seines Werkes*, Historia Einzelsch. 17 (Steiner, Wiesbaden, 1971).

R. Drews, 'Herodotus' Other Logoi', *AJPh* 91 (1970) 181.

H. Erbse, 'Der erste Satz im Werke Herodots' in *Festschrift Snell* (Beck, Munich, 1956), 209.

A. Heuss, 'Motiven von Herodots lydischem logos', *Hermes* 101 (1973) 385.

P. Hohti, *The Interrelation of Speech and Action in the Histories of Herodotus*, Comm. Litt. Hum. 57 (Helsinki, 1967).

V. Hunter, *Past and Process in Herodotus and Thucydides* (Princeton University Pres, 1982).

H. J. Immerwahr, *Form and Thought in Herodotus*, APA Monograph 23 (Western Reserve University Press, 1966).

T. Krischer, 'Herodots Prooimion', *Hermes* 93 (1965) 159.

――, 'Herodots Schluss-Kapitel, seine Topik und seine Quellen', *Eranos* 72 (1974) 95.

D. Lateiner, 'No Laughing Matter: a Literary Tactic in Herodotos', *TAPhA* 107 (1977) 173.

R. Lattimore, 'The Composition of the History of Herodotus', *CPh* 53 (1958) 9.

J. G. Macqueen, 'The 'Ασσύριοι λόγοι of Herodotus and their Position in the Histories', *CQ* 38 (1978) 284.

R. Merkelbach, 'Inhalt und Form in symbolischen Erzahlungen der Antike' in *Eranos Jahrb.* 35 (1966) 146.

H. Schwabl, 'Herodot als Historiker und Erzahler', *Gymnasium* 76 (1969) 253.

H. Strasburger, 'Komik und Satire in der Griechische Geschichts-schreibung' in *Festgabe P. Kirn* (Schmidt, Berlin, 1961).

K. H. Waters, 'The Purpose of Dramatisation in Herodotos', *Historia* 15 (1966) 167.

――, 'The Structure of Herodotos' Narrative', *Antichthon* 8 (1974) 1.

M. White, 'Herodotus' Starting-Point', *Phoenix* 23 (1969) 39.

9. *Chronology, geography, topography, military history*

O. K. Armayor, 'Did Herodotus ever go to the Black Sea?', *HSCPh* 82 (1978) 45.

R. Ball, 'Generation Dating in Herodotus', *CQ* 29 (1979) 270.

W. den Boer, 'Herodot und das Systeme der Chronologie', *Mnemosyne* 20 (1967) 30.

R. Dion, 'Le Danube d'Hérodote', *Rev. Phil.* 42 (1968) 7.

A. Ferrill, 'Herodotus and the Strategy and Tactics of the Invasion of Xerxes', *AHR* 72 (1966) 102.

A. R. Hands, 'On Strategy and Oracles 480–479', *JHS* 85 (1965) 56.

K. Kraft, 'Bemerkungen zu den Perserkriegen', *Hermes* 92 (1964) 144.

D. Lateiner, 'The Failure of the Ionian Revolt', *Historia* 31 (1982) 129.

J. F. Lazenby, 'The Strategy of the Greeks in the Opening Campaign of the Persian War', *Hermes* 92 (1964) 264.

S. Markianos, 'The Chronology of the Herodotean Solon', *Historia* 23 (1974) 1.

――, 'Herodotus' Trustworthiness regarding the Dating of Solon's Nomothesia and Apodemia' (in Greek, English summary), *Hellenica* 28 (1975) 5.

A. Masarrachia, 'La battaglia di Salamine in Erodoto', *Helikon* 9/10 (1969/70) 68.

F. D. Maurice, 'The Size of the Army of Xerxes', *JHS* 50 (1930) 210.

S. Mazzarino, 'L'image des parties du monde', *A. Ant. Hung.* 7 (1959) 85.

M. Miller, 'Herodotus as Chronographer', *Klio* 46 (1965) 104.

——, 'The Accepted Date for Solon; Precise, but Wrong', *Arethusa* 2 (1969) 62.

F. Mitchel, 'Herodotus' Use of Genealogical Chronology', *Phoenix* 10 (1956) 48.

G. B. Phillip, 'Wie das Gesetz es befehl: Bemerkungen zu einer neuen Leonidas-legende', *Gymnasium* 75 (1968) 1.

W. K. Pritchett, *Studies in Ancient Greek Topography*, Pt 1, 71 Pt 2, 1 (University of California Press, Berkeley, 1965, 1969).

G. Roux, 'Hérodote . . . raconte la bataille de Salamis', *BCH* 98 (1974) 51.

K. N. Sachs, 'Herodotus and the Dating of the Battle of Thermopylai', *CQ* 26 (1976) 232.

J. Schreiner, 'The Battles of 490 BC', *PCPS* 196 [NS 16] (1970) 97.

C. G. Starr, 'Why did the Greeks Defeat the Persians?', *P.d.P.* 86 (1962) 321.

H. Strasburger, 'Herodots Zeitrechnung', *Historia* 5 (1956) 129.

M. B. Wallace, 'Herodotus and Euboea', *Phoenix* 28 (1974) 27.

K. H. Waters, 'Herodotos and the Ionian Revolt', *Historia* 19 (1970) 504.

J. Wikarjak, 'De terris inter septentriones et orientem solem spectantibus quid tradiderit Herodotus', *SPhP* 3 (1977) 3.

10. *Greeks and barbarians*

M. M. Austin, *Greece and Egypt in the Archaic Age* (*PCPhS* Suppl. 2, Cambridge Phil. Soc., 1970).

T. S. Brown, 'The Greek Sense of Time in History as Suggested by their Accounts of Egypt', *Historia* 11 (1962) 259.

——, 'Herodotus Speculates about Egypt', *AJPh* 86 (1965) 60.

H. Diller, 'Die Hellenen-Barbaren Antithese im Zeitalter der Perserkriege' in *Entretiens Hardt* 8, 1961 (Geneva, 1962).

D. Hegyi, 'Die Begriff βάρβαρος bei Herodot', *AUB* v–vi (1977/8) 33.

188   *Select Bibliography*

R. Lamacchia, 'Erodoto nazionalista?', *Atene e Roma* 4 (1954) 87.
A. B. Lloyd, *Herodotus Book II: Introduction*, EPRO 43 (Brill, Leiden, 1975).
——, *Herodotus Book II: Commentary* (1976).
R. Rtskhiladze, 'La specificité de l'Orient dans les histoires d'Hérodote', *A. Ant. Hung.* 22 (1974) 487.
K. S. Rubinson, 'Herodotus and the Skythians', *Expedition* 17 (1975) 438.
H. Schwabl, 'Grecs et barbares' in *Entretiens Hardt* 8 (Geneva, 1969).
Ingomar Weiler, 'The Greek and non-Greek World in the Archaic Period', *GRBS* 9 (1968) 21.

11. *Publication; date and method*

J. Cobet, 'Wann wurde Herodots Darstellung der Perserkriege publiziert?', *Hermes* 105 (1977) 2.
J. A. S. Evans, 'Herodotus' Publication Date', *Athenaeum* 57 (1979) 145.
S. Flory, 'Who Read Herodotus' Histories?', *AJPh* 101 (1980) 12.
C. W. Fornara, 'Evidence for the Date of Herodotus' Publication', *JHS* 91 (1971) 32.
——, 'Herodotus' Knowledge of the Archidamian War', *Hermes* 109 (1981) 149.
A. French, 'Topical Influences on Herodotus' Narrative', *Mnemosyne* 25 (1972) 9.
F. D. Harvey, 'Literacy in the Athenian Democracy', *REG* 79 (1966) 585.
F. G. Kenyon, *Books and Readers in Ancient Greece and Rome* (Clarendon Press, Oxford, 1932).
H. W. Parke, 'Citation and Recitation: a Convention in early Greek Historians', *Hermathena* 67 (1966) 80.
J. Schwartz, 'Le séjour athènien et les redactions des histoires d'Hérodote', *BFS* 36 (1957/58) 335.
E. G. Turner, *Athenian Books in the Fifth and Fourth Centuries BC*, Inaugural lecture (Lewis, London, 1952).

12. *Aims and philosophy of history*
(Most of the general works mentioned above have relevant passages)
H. R. Immerwahr, 'Ergon: History as a Monument in Herodotus

and Thucydides', *AJPh* 81 (1960) 261.

S. Mazzarino, *Il pensiero storico classico*, 2nd edn (Laterza, Bari, 1966).

D. M. Pippidi, 'Sur la philosophie d'histoire d'Hérodote', *Eirene* 1 (1960) 75.

T. Sinko, 'L'historiosophie dans le prologue et l'epilogue de l'oeuvre d'Hérodote d'Halicarnassos', *Eos* 50 (1959/60) 3.

INDEX

Adeimantos 84, 140
advisers 64, 105, 138–9
Agariste 110, 123
agnosticism 18
  agnostics and atheists 97
Aigina 122, 134n9
aims of *History* 1–3, 39, 136, 173
Aischylos 31, 82, 160
  Persians 21, 146–7, 153
akoē *see* hearsay
Alkmaionid(s) 50
  H's defence 67, 91, 124–5, 172
Amasis 71, 105–6, 157
Amestris 110, 129, 146
Amompharetos 85, 163
Anaximander 6, 15–16
anecdotes 7, 34, 142, 145, 172
anthropology and ethnology 6–7, 39, 170
anthropomorphism 18, 96
Arabia 159
Archias 81
Argos 128
  Argives 139
Arion 29, 76
Aristagoras 65, 124, 126–7, 132, 148
Aristotle 8, 21
Artabanos 66, 71, 109, 138
Artacheēs 41, 62
Artaphernes 69
Artaÿktes 98, 114–15
Artembares 114
Artemisia 19, 129, 138, 146
artistry 8, 21, Ch 12 *passim*
Asia as Persian 66, 72
Assyrian empire 159
Assyrian logoi 53, 55
Astyages 51, 109, 111, 144
Athenian(s)
  empire 5
  H's attitude to 121, 163, 171
Athens, encomium on 67
  Herodotos in 25, 74
  political history 48–50
Atossa 64, 74n, 135
Atys and Adrastos 21, 107, 109, 147, 168
audience 97, 107, 123, 158, 175

aimed at Ch 4 *passim*
  Athenian 53, 121
autocracy 137
  see also despotism, tyranny
autopsy 24–5, 90–1, 158

Babylon 51, 53
  Babylonians 129
  Herodotos' knowledge 27, 52
Bakis 31, 106–7
barbarian(s) 3, 42, 78, 120
bias 35, 76, 83, Ch 9 *passim*
  see also philobarbarism
biography 136
Black Sea 5, 26, 158
Boiotian(s) 83, 88, 123
  see also Thebans
books and writing 14, 26
  as divisions of *History* 56, 70
botany 40, 170, 173

catalogues 44, 61, 87
  see also epic
causation 1, 4, 100–1, 136, 139
  see also explanation
chance (Tychē) 103–4
characterisation 65, 68, Ch 10 *passim*
Charon (historian) 17
chronology 156–8
  chronological data 17
  chronological limits 5
  chronological order 72
  oriental 86
'Clever Thief' 43, 57, 69, 172
composition, methods, Chs 1, 3, 4 *passim*
  order of 23
  ring-composition 62, 71, 169
  unfinished 55
  unity of 55
constitutional debate 36–7, 78–9
continents 159
credulity 17, 87, 106, 152–3, 164
  disproved 35–6
  qualified 108
cycle of fortune 105
  see also Fate
Cyprus 30, 71, 127

Dareios 64, 86, 106, 138–9, 144–5, 158
Datis 84, 110
Deiokes 51, 131, 140–1
Delphi 25, 80, 124
  Delphic oracle 25, 73, 97, 106–7, 112
Demaratos 41, 67, 81, 138
Demokedes 42, 64, 89
despot(ism) 133, 145
  see also autocracy, tyranny
diffusionist theory 119
digression(s) 5, 41, 43, 45, 50–1, 55–6, 70–1, 172
Dikaios 80–1, 93n14
Dionysios of Miletos 16
Dionysios of Phokaia 127, 162
documents, Greek 17, 25, 31, 86–8, 157
  non-Greek 27, 86
Dodona 25, 80
dramatisation 9–10, 63–9, 136, 138, 148
  see also speeches
dreams 108–110

Egypt 26–7, 52–3
  Egyptian informants 79
  logoi 52–3
  marvels 53
  superiority 42, 52, 89, 119, 155
entertainment 7, 40–3, 50, 70
environmental factors 19, 114, 151n20
Ephesos 19, 159
epic influence 1, 9, 13, 51, 62, 64–5, 136, 169
  criticised 170
  rejected 67
Eratosthenes 6, 17
errors 49, 154–5
ethnology 111
  see also anthropology
Euripides 29, 130
Eurybiades 9–10, 84, 143
explanation 2, 64, 144
  see also causation

Fate 1, 103–5, 147
  see also chance, cycle
festivals 1, 11n1, 13, 25, 41, 70
folk-lore 43
folktale 105, 113, 141

Gelon 132, 140–1

genealogy 17, 49, 61–2
geography 6, 88, 158–60, 174
geology 156–7, 159
gnome *see* reasoning
god(s) 1, Ch 8 *passim*
  jealous 105
  providence 103
  responsibility 1, 102
Gorgias 20–1, 70
Greece, *passim*
  Greek(s), *passim*
Gyges 21, 29, 47, 114, 168

Halikarnassos viii, 18–19, 81, 85
Harpagos 51, 111
hearsay (akoē) 27, 32, 34–5, 77, 90
  see also logos
Hekataios 6, 16, 61, 79, 126, 175
Hellanikos 17, 94–5n27
Hermotimos 106
Hesiod 13, 22n1, 156
Hippias of Athens 91
Hippias of Elis 17, 80
Hippokrates 19
Histiaios 62, 132, 148–9
historical insight 6
  perspective 5, 24, 157, 175
historiē 2, 25, 55, 85, 89, 175
Homer, Homeric: *see* epic
humanity 39, 149, 174
humour 50, 144, 168, 170–2
  see also irony

impartiality 39, 42, 110–11 (Ch 10 *passim*), 154
  see also bias
inconsistency 120, 143, 145, 148, 156, 164
  see also variant versions
individual(s)
  importance 126 Ch 10 *passim*
  informants 77, 80–1
  multiple introduction 72–3
Intaphernes 37, 43
Ionian(s) 145
  attitude to 125
  dialect 18
  fleet 153, 160
  Lydian domination 47
  mercenaries 26–7
  philosophers 15–16, 18
  revolt 5, 125–7, 148–9
  see also logographers
irony 29, 41, 49, 112, 140, 152, 162,

170-1
    see also humour

'journalistic' features 40, 43

Kambyses 98, 133, 138, 143, 171
Kandaules 103, 113, 170
Karia(n) viii, 18
Kleisthenes of Athens 49
Kleisthenes of Sikyon 49-50, 108
Kleomenes 65, 106, 156
Korinth(ian) 53, 84, 172
Kroisos 4, 47, 100, 138, 147-8
Kroisos and Solon 56-7, 111-12,
    147
Kypselos 77, 141
Kyrene 26, 108, 156
Kyros 4, 51, 57, 115-16, 138, 144

Lade, battle 84-5, 127, 153, 162
legend(s) 4, 47, 101
    criticised 4, 29, 36, 140
    rejected 159
    see also myth
Leonides 42, 62, 72, 82-3, 141-2,
    161
Libya 54, 88-9, 159
    see also North Africa
literary influences *see* Epic, Tragedy
literary sources 29-31
logographers 16-17, 21, 175
logos (and logoi) 29, 32, 55, 70
Lucian (critic) 22n14
Lydia(n) 4, 47, 121, 157
Lygdamis, revolt against viii, 19,
    94n16 (133-4)
lyric poets 29

Magi 109, 171-2
Marathon, battle 10, 44, 91-2
    sources 82
    tactics 162-3
Mardonios 37, 66, 81, 139, 160, 163
marvels, mirabilia 7, 38, 53, 70-1
    see also records
Masistios 62
Maskames 77
Medes 4, 51
    medism 67, 128, 154
    see also Deiokes
Megabates 126
Megakles 50, 125
memory, Herodotos' 28, 71, 92, 114
Miletos 15-16, 18, 30, 127, 148

military experience 94n16
    reporting 160-4
    see also strategy
Miltiades 82, 148, 163
Mnesiphilos 9, 12n, 68
morality 98, 110-15
Mykale 121, 160
myth as evidence 63, 87
    in recent history 24, 72

nemesis 147
    see also revenge
Nile 26, 120, 155, 159
Nomos 20, 34, 39, Ch 8 *passim*,
    119-20, 133, 143-5
North Africa 26, 91
    see also Libya

objectivity 119
    see also impartiality
Ocean 'River' 30, 88, 159
official version(s) 30, 35-6, 82-3
Olympia 25, 70, 80
Olympus, Mt 25
Omens 84, 97, 110
omissions 81-2
    see also subject-matter
Onomakritos 30, 107
optimism 175-6
oracles 147
    form of 33n17
    frequency in *History* 1, 31,
        99-100, 106-8
    Herodotos' credence 106
    importance in society 107-8
oral history Ch 7 *passim*, 140, 152,
    172
    tradition 29, 66, 69, 157
    see also sources
Oroites 37-8, 100
Otanes 37, 78

patterns, historical 49, 57, 73, 147
Pausanias 73, 85, 142, 154
Peisistratos 120, 124-5, 132
Peloponnese 122, 128
    Peloponnesian war 6, 175
Periandros 73, 132-3, 141
Perikles 57, 110
    Periklean Athens 110
Persian(s) *passim*
    armed forces 139
        see also Xerxes
    couriers 56

customs and religion 104–5, 110,
    114, 129, 171
  fleet 153, 173
  government 37–8, 78, 133, 145
  imperialism 51, 72, 101, 106,
    114–5n7, 139, 144, 175
  informants 77
Pheidon 80
Pheretime 100, 129
Philaid(s) 82, 148
Philippos 41, 57
philobarbarism 3, 42, 119–21
  see also bias
philosophers
  Ionian 15–16
  Pythagoras 20
  Sophists 20–21
Phoenicians 49, 121, 153, 157
Phokians 83
Phrynichos, tragedian 30
physis and nomos 20, 39, 120
picturesque details 107, 145
Pindar 30, 169
Pixodaros 81
Plataia, battle 84–5, 156, 160
'Plutarch' 3, 119, 154, 162
poiētēs 8, 111–12
political views of Herodotos 37,
    123–4, 130–4
  theories 78, 133
Polykrates 37–8, 73, 132
polytheism 101
pragmatism 125, 133, 138
Proem 2–3, 24, 173
  see also aims
prose literature, early 1, 14
Protagoras 78
publication, date of 11–12n10, 23,
    32n1
  method 7, 14, 55–6, Ch 6 *passim*
  see also recitation
Pythia *see* Delphic oracle
Pythios 168–9

reasoning 31–2, 35, 49, 63, 88,
    90–1, 153–5, 159
recitation 7, 70
records 40–2, 130
  athletic 41, 80
relevance, dubious 38–9, 70, 131
religious views 44, 96–110, 171
revenge 100–1, 105–6, 113, 120
Russia, S. 20, 39, 88, 91

Salamis, battle 9, 30, 44, 82, 121,
    173
Samian(s) 19–20
  informants 127
Samos 19
  Herodotos on 90
  strategic importance 37–8
Sardis 29, 38, 126, 148–9
scope of *History* 2–4
  see also subject-matter
Sestos (Ch. 5) 47, 115, 121
Sicilian tyrants 30, 110
  see also Gelon
Sicily, knowledge of 20
Skythia 88, 111, 159
  Skythian campaign 145
  see also Russia
Soklees 68, 132–3
Solon as historical 116n14
  source 29
  'wise man' 99, 104, 112–13
Sophokles 20–1, 169
sources Ch 7 *passim*, 24, 173
  epigraphic 87–8
  evaluation 31–2
  foreign language 79
  oral 27
  uncorrelated 91
  written 86–7
  see also oral, documents
Sparta, Herodotos at 25
  attitude to 130–1
Spartan(s) 5
  courage 122, 131
  history 48–9
  kinglists 156
  kings 16, 40
speeches 9–10, 64–9, 170
  indirect speech 65, 69
  see also dramatisation
strategy 126, 160–4
  defence 122
  Plataia 163
  Salamis 162
  Thermopylai 82–3
structure Ch 1, Ch 5 *passim*
subject-matter 2–3, Ch 4 *passim*
  reasons for exclusion 3, 44
  reasons for inclusion 3, 35–7
supernatural Ch 8 *passim*
  see also gods
Susa 45, 100, 146, 149
Syloson 141

Tempe 25, 102
Thales 15, 152
Thasos 26, 157
Thebans 83, 154
    see also Boiotians
Themistokles 9–10 (*see also* Salamis)
    character 10, 72–3, 142–3
Thermopylai battle 72, 82–4
    topography 158
Thespians 83
Thukydides 1–2, 104, 142, 157,
    175–6
Thurioi viii, 26, 125
tolerance moral 110–13
    religious 102
    see also impartiality
tradition 85
    see also oral history
tragedy, Attic 21, 68–9, 72

travels of Herodotos 24–7, 158
tyranny 19, 48, 110, 131–2

variant versions 35, 77, 83–4, 128,
    159
variety 69, 73
vengeance *see* revenge, gods

women, attitude to 128–30

Xanthos, 'historian' 17
Xenophanes 18, 96
Xneophon 97, 131
Xerxes 66, 71–2, 138, 146–7
    forces of 5, 46n, 152–3, 160–1
    see also Persian

zoology 40, 70, 173
Zopyros 53, 77–8